Lifestyle

English for work, socializing & travel

Upper Intermediate Coursebook

Irene Barrall & John Rogers

Contents

1

A Tense overview
B Question forms
C Emails
D **Communication strategies** Developing conversations
E **Interaction** Making a good impression

Connections

Tense overview

Reading: First impressions

1 Discuss these questions.

1 Some psychologists say that it takes people 20 seconds to form a first impression. Do you agree? How long does it take *you*?

2 People who have to speak in front of an audience generally try to make a good first impression. How do they do it?

2 Read the magazine article below. Do you agree with what the author says about presentations? Why?/Why not?

3 Find an example of each of the following in the article.

1 the present simple

2 the past simple

3 the present perfect

4 the past perfect

5 a future form

Looking for maximum impact

As the saying goes, you never get a second chance to make a first impression.

Have you ever wondered why first impressions are so important? According to communication experts, their importance can be explained by the fact that people not only hold on to them, but also seek to reinforce them. In other words, when you make a great first impression, people keep looking for the good points in you. On the other hand, if you mess up, you have to work really hard afterwards to project a positive image.

A few years ago, I attended an international conference and was struck by how most presenters started their talk. All of them had already been introduced; most of them had a slide behind them with the title of their talk, their name and affiliation. Everyone in the audience had received a programme with the same information and an abstract of the talk. Yet, how did the talk start? 'Good afternoon. My name is John Smith and I work for Waits Academy. My presentation today is about ...' How could you be more uninspiring?

No wonder that the workshop I remember best is the one where the presenter adopted a radically different approach. Her very first words were: 'Where do people learn languages?' Complete silence in the audience. After a few seconds, she then replied: 'Between their ears.' She had us. We all thought it was a brilliant opener, we all expected the talk to get even better, and it did.

So, next time you're going to give a presentation, make an important phone call or write an email, ask yourself these two questions: 'How am I going to command attention? How am I going to enter the other person's world?'

Listening: Getting it right

4 Read these quotes. How do they relate to first impressions?

> **A** *'Luck is what happens when preparation meets opportunity.'*
> *(Seneca)*

> **B** 'It's always the badly dressed people who are the most interesting.'
> (Jean-Paul Gaultier)

> **C** 'I don't like that man. I must get to know him better.'
> (Abraham Lincoln)

5 🔊 1.1 Listen to three people talking about first impressions. Match the quotes in exercise 4 to the conversations.

1 Vladimir   Quote _____
2 Rick   Quote _____
3 Liliana   Quote _____

6 🔊 Listen again and complete the sentences.

Conversation 1

1 When _____ you first _____ her?

2 She _____ _____ biochemistry.

3 I _____ already _____ her once without being aware of it.

Conversation 2

4 _____ you _____ what it _____ to really know someone?

5 I _____ always _____ in that idea.

Conversation 3

6 But competition _____ _____ fierce, no doubt about that.

7 I _____ _____ *How To Make A Positive First Impression.*

Grammar: Tense overview

7 Look at the tenses used in the sentences in exercise 6. Then write 1–7 in the appropriate spaces in the table below.

	Present	Past	*will* future
Simple			
Continuous			
Perfect			
Perfect continuous			

>> **For more information on the English tense system, see pages 156–162.**

8 Match these sentence halves. Then complete the table in exercise 7 by writing a–e in the appropriate spaces.

a By the end of this year,   well before the deadline.

b I was exhausted on Tuesday   because I'd been entertaining guests till 2 a.m.

c I've been working all morning,   but I still have a lot to do.

d This time next week, I'll be   we'll have been going out for three years.

e We'll have finished everything   heading for Singapore.

9 Explain the use of the different tenses in these pairs of sentences.

1 a We work for a Canadian NGO.

   b We are working on an educational exchange programme.

2 a What did you do when the head nurse came in?

   b What were you doing when the head nurse came in?

3 a When the visitors arrived, they were redecorating the office.

   b When the visitors arrived, they had redecorated the office.

4 a She's given some lectures on Brazilian culture.

   b She gave some lectures on Brazilian culture.

5 a I've been filling in forms all day.

   b I've filled in my visa application form.

Speaking: What makes you tick?

10 What is most important for you about someone you meet for the first time? Add your own ideas to the list. Then work in pairs and agree on the three most important points.

- They have a firm handshake.
- They tell you a lot about themselves.
- …

TALKING POINT

How can companies make a good impression when emailing a potential customer?

And when phoning a business contact for the first time?

Listening: Speed is the word

1 Discuss these questions.

1 How can people make new business contacts?

2 What questions would you ask when meeting a potential business contact for the first time?

2 What do you understand by 'speed business networking'? Look at the text and see if you are right. Do you think it can work?

Looking extremely graceful in her smart two-piece suit, Louise Delville is casually holding a drink in one hand and a list of names in the other. She is listening intently to a man who is talking to her with genuine enthusiasm. They frequently exchange warm smiles.

You'd be forgiven for believing that these two are at an ordinary party. But after a few minutes, a gong sounds and each moves to a different partner. 'Ah,' you think, 'speed-dating!'

You are not far from the truth, although Louise is not looking for someone romantically compatible. She has just received an MBA from a prestigious business school, and her ambition is to become a business development manager.

This evening, together with dozens of other graduates and as many executives, she is attending a speed-networking event. The aim of this particular event is to enable young graduates and business executives alike to establish valuable connections.

3 Look at the text again and make questions for these answers.

1 A smart two-piece suit.

2 A list of names.

3 Just a few minutes.

4 No, it isn't.

5 She'd like to become a business development manager.

6 Because they hope to make useful professional connections.

4 Write three questions about speed networking – things you'd really like to know about it. Then work in pairs and compare your questions.

5 🔊 1.2 Listen to a radio programme about speed networking. Which of your questions, if any, does it address?

6 🔊 Listen again and complete the interviewer's questions.

1 _____ _____ ask you a couple of questions?

2 How _____ _____ work?

3 _____ you _____ job seekers and employers, for instance?

4 _____ _____ people attend such events, by the way?

5 _____ people _____ to walk around and mingle in any way they like?

6 How long _____ they _____ to one another?

7 _____ _____ during those six minutes?

8 _____ _____ effective?

7 Do you agree with the woman's assessment of how effective speed-networking events are? Why/Why not?

Grammar: Question forms

8 Put the questions in exercise 6 into two groups and complete the sentence below.

yes / no questions	wh- questions
Questions number ¹_____, _____, _____ and _____	Questions number ²_____, _____, _____ and _____
The usual word order in yes / no questions is: auxiliary before subject. The auxiliary can be any form of be, have or do, or a modal like can, will, should, etc.	The usual word order in wh- questions is: question word + auxiliary + subject. Question words are how, why, when, who, whose, which, what and where.

> **!** When a question word is the subject of a question, we do not use do does did: see for example questions 4 and 7 in exercise 6.

>> **For more information on question forms, see pages 162–163.**

9 Make questions from the groups of words in the box. Then match the questions to B's answers in the conversation below.

> a yourself five time see do years' where you in
> b hope what achieve you do to
> c this you career influenced choose what to
> d with up going anyone to you are follow
> e from you graduate did where
> f in are business of what you line
> g changed a college how person you has as
> h been Bonn how you in working have long

1 A: _____?

   B: I'm in property investment.

2 A: _____?

   B: Well, my favourite aunt was an estate agent. I used to help her in the summer.

3 A: _____?

   B: Since I graduated in 2004.

4 A: _____?

   B: The Munich Business College.

5 A: _____?

   B: It's showed me the value of teamwork, and it's made me more goal-driven.

6 A: _____?

   B: I'd like to set up my own international real estate agency.

7 A: _____?

   B: Well, I want to make valuable business connections.

8 A: _____?

   B: Sure! I'm having lunch with a realtor from California on Thursday.

Speaking: Question time

10 Work in pairs. Your task is to ask your partner questions until their reply consists <u>exactly</u> of the short sentence on your card.

> Sentence on A's card: (No, never.)
>
> A: Are you sometimes late for work?
> B: Well, yes, but not very often.
> A: Do you ever have breakfast in bed?
> B: Only when I'm ill.
> A: Have you ever been to Korea?
> B: No, never.

Student A: Turn to File 1, page 114.
Student B: Turn to File 63, page 126.

11 Work in pairs. Take turns to ask (and answer) as many questions as you can to get to know each other better. You have three minutes altogether.

Find out which pair has asked the most questions.

Writing: An evaluation questionnaire

12 Work in pairs. You have just organized a speed-networking event for young graduates and employers. In order to continue to ensure quality, you want some written feedback from the participants on specific aspects of the event. Agree together on six key questions.

TALKING POINT Some big companies, such as Deloitte, organize speed-networking events for their own members of staff from different departments. What do you think of the idea?

Reading: Emailing dos and don'ts

1 Discuss these questions.

1 How many emails do you receive every day? How many do you send?

2 What kind of emails do you find difficult to deal with? Why?

3 What can sometimes be difficult about writing emails in English?

2 Complete the emailing guidelines with the words in the box.

asterisks attachments copy in details locate paragraphs
personal proofread relationship subject line

TOP 10 EMAILING TIPS

1 Think carefully and creatively about your _____. It should capture the reader's attention and state the purpose of the email clearly.

2 Focus on one subject per email, so that the reader can _____ the message easily and deal with it appropriately.

3 Always double-check that you are sending the message to the right person, and _____ any relevant individuals.

4 Remember that emails, just like letters, can be formal or informal: the style used depends on the writer/reader _____.

5 Use fancy fonts, colours and emoticons ('smileys') in _____ emails only.

6 Do not use CAPITAL LETTERS – it is like shouting; you can use _____ to make a point *stronger* if bold, italics and underlining don't come out clearly in your emails.

7 Use relatively short sentences, use _____ and, whenever appropriate, use headings and bullet points.

8 You can include a 'signature' (i.e. your contact _____ , like on a business card), but keep it short and up-to-date.

9 Be careful with _____: if you have to send a large one, you might want to tell the recipient in advance.

10 Always _____ your emails and use spell-check and grammar check before sending them off.

3 Work in pairs. Discuss these questions.

1 Are the guidelines in exercise 2 valid in your country and in your company?

2 Which guideline would you say is the most useful? Why?

3 What other guidelines can you add to the list?

4 Read the email. Decide which three guidelines the writer did not follow. Then suggest improvements.

To: Edina Haver
From: Julian Peresti
Subject: Warm greetings

Dear Edina

It was great to meet you at the Debrecen Trade Fair earlier this month, and we are delighted that you have accepted our invitation to attend our annual conference in March.

Please note that WE HAVE HAD TO RESCHEDULE THIS EVENT FOR TUESDAY, 23 MARCH, INSTEAD OF WEDNESDAY 24.

Could you please confirm that you will be able to attend?

Sorry for any inconvenience.

We look forward to seeing you again.

With bets wishes,

Julian

Julian Peresti,
PR Manager,
Stedex International

5 Test your knowledge of formal and informal email opening and closing expressions.
Student A: Turn to File 2, page 114. Student B: Turn to File 70, page 128.

6 Read Edina's reply to Julian's email in exercise 4. Underline the most appropriate option each time.

¹ Dear Sir, / Hiya buddy! / Dear Julian,

² Thank you for your email of the 12th inst. / Thank you for your email. / Thanks for dropping me a line.

³ I'm sorry to hear that the conference has been rescheduled. / What a shame you've changed the date of the conference. / It is with profound regret that I hear your conference has been brought forward to 23rd March.

⁴ Because of previous arrangements between 9 and 11 a.m. on the 23rd, I'm afraid I won't be able to come. / Owing to prior engagements between 9 and 11 a.m. on the 23rd, I am afraid I will not be in a position to participate. / I've got zillions of things to do in the morning, so there's no way I could be there.

⁵ Nevertheless, being free after 11 o'clock, I might be able to be there early afternoon. / But I've got nothing to do after 11, so I could just make a dash for it. / However, I'm free after 11, so I could be there for the afternoon.

⁶ By the way, OK if I'm there just for the afternoon? / Please let me know if it's all right to attend only the afternoon sessions. / I would be grateful if you could inform me whether it is convenient to attend only the afternoon sessions.

⁷ Looking forward to hearing from you soon. / Write soon. / I look forward to receiving your reply in due course.

⁸ Bye bye, / Best wishes, / Sincerely,

Edina

Word focus: Making and changing arrangements

7 Complete these extracts from emails with the words and phrases in the box.

available   come up   do   good   got something on   instead   postpone   suits   tied up   work

1 We've got an appointment for 9:30, Monday 25th, but I'm afraid something's _____. Could we fix another time?

2 Sorry, I can't make Thursday or Friday. How about earlier in the week? Does Tuesday _____ for you?

3 I suggest we meet next week. What's a _____ day for you?

4 Would it be possible to _____ our meeting?

5 Wednesday is fine for me. What time _____ you?

6 I'm afraid I can't _____ 10:30 on Monday. I've _____ that morning.

7 I'm _____ all day on Friday, I'm afraid. How about next Monday _____?

8 Could you please let me know if you'd be _____ for a conference call next Tuesday from 10:00 to 11:30?

Speaking: Style in emails

8 Consider the three different registers in exercise 6 and discuss these questions.

1 If you used the most formal expressions in an email to someone you know well, what would they think?

2 If you used the most informal expressions in an email to someone you hardly know at all, what would they think?

9 Work in pairs. You both have half the sentences of an email, but all jumbled up. Your task is to reconstruct the email. You mustn't write anything or show each other your sentences.

Student A: Turn to File 3, page 114. Student B: Turn to File 68, page 127.

10 Work in pairs or in small groups. Think of three ways in which you could use email to improve your writing skills and further develop your English.

Compare with another group and come to a decision on the best four ways.

TALKING POINT Which emailing tips do people most often fail to follow? How does that make you feel?

Listening: It's good to talk

1 Discuss these questions.

1 What are the most usual small talk topics in your culture and which ones are best avoided?

2 Think about people you enjoy chatting with. What personal qualities do they have?

3 What makes a conversation successful and enjoyable?

2))) **1.3** Listen to six conversation extracts. How does the second speaker sound each time?

3))) **1.4** Listen to the questions from the same conversations (1–6) and match them to responses (a–f).

a Yes, of course. Ben and I go back at least ten years.

b They're really nice. I just feel as if we've been working together for years.

c Not very. About 20 minutes in the morning. A bit longer in the evening, but it depends on the traffic.

d No. I really want to see a bit more of my family.

e Great idea. So we can catch up with all our news!

f Fine, thank you. Our new project is really interesting, I find.

> **i** In normal conversation, minimal answers are often taken as a sign of indifference, lack of interest, or even rudeness. Adding a simple comment would help the conversation to develop.

4 Work in pairs. Ask each other the questions from the conversations (use the audio script on page 137 to help you). Give your own answers, adding a comment each time.

5 Sometimes, a person can feel excluded from a conversation. Why does this happen? What can be done about it?

6))) **1.5** Listen to three extracts from conversations. Which strategy from the table below does the third person use in each case?

Conversation 1: _____ Conversation 2: _____ Conversation 3: _____

If nobody asks you a question directly and you would like to be included in a conversation, it is often enough for you to do one of the following:		
a express an opinion	b make a comment	c ask a follow-up question

7 Work in pairs. A is having different conversations with B. What could C say to join the conversation? Use one of the strategies in exercise 6.

1 **A:** Ponte Vecchio is one of the best Italian restaurants in town.
  B: Yeah. We had dinner there last Saturday. Fabulous!
  C: _____

2 **A:** I thought the match was terrific.
  B: Kerad's second goal was a thing of beauty.
  C: _____

3 **A:** Simon's been on sick leave for more than a month.
  B: And no one knows when he'll be back.
  C: _____

4 **A:** I'm a tax inspector.
  B: Mm. That can't be an easy job.
  C: _____

5 **A:** This weather seems to be driving everyone mad.
  B: It does, doesn't it. Absolutely dreadful.
  C: _____

6 **A:** The guys in Accounts are looking exhausted.
  B: They're all overworked, that's the problem.
  C: _____

8 🔊 **1.6** Listen and compare C's responses to the ones you thought of in exercise 7.

9 How can an active participant in a conversation encourage a quieter one to take part? What exactly could they say?

10 🔊 **1.7** Listen to these conversations. Complete the questions that are used to involve the quieter person.

Conversation 1

B: … I'd say they're just completely incompetent. … What _____ _____ _____, Connie?

C: Well, I think those guys are quite good, actually.

Conversation 2

B: … I doubt it will save us a lot of money. Have you got a _____ _____ _____, Carol?

C: Erm … I think you're right, Bill. Besides, it will have a bad effect on morale.

Conversation 3

B: Erm … You've been to Vietnam, haven't you, Stanley? What did you _____ _____ _____?

C: Well, I was there on holiday …

Speaking: Count me in!

11 Work in pairs. Student A chooses a conversation starter; B answers; A comments and/or asks a follow-up question.

Change roles: B chooses another conversation starter, etc.
A: What line of business are you in?
B: I'm in the pharmaceutical industry.
A: Oh, really. What's your company called?

Conversation starters
What line of business are you in?
Thank goodness it's Friday!
Have you seen the headlines today?
So your company headquarters are now in Zurich.
How many people does your company employ?
I hope we can make it to the quarter finals.
Business travel is such a pain.
Pamela has changed her hairdo again.

---

12 Write four statements / questions that you could use as conversation starters. Then work in new pairs and have more mini-conversations like the ones in exercise 11.

13 Work in groups of three (A, B and C). Roleplay three conversations on these topics:

- Topic 1: The retirement age should be lowered, not raised.
- Topic 2: It's the individual's job – not the State's – to put money aside in case they fall ill.
- Topic 3: Working from home has more disadvantages than advantages.

Student A: Turn to File 4, page 114.
Student B: Turn to File 69, page 127.
Student C: Turn to File 76, page 129.

Reminder

Tense overview page 5 + Grammar reference pages 156–162
Question forms page 7 + Grammar reference pages 162–163
Developing conversations page 10

Reading: It's not just what you say

1 Discuss these questions.

1 Think of a presentation, a talk, a lecture or a workshop that you really enjoyed. Apart from the content, what exactly was it that you liked about it?

2 What are the keys to a successful presentation? Make a list of useful tips.

2 Read the article. Are any of your tips mentioned?

According to Albert Mehrabian (Professor Emeritus of Psychology, UCLA), when we communicate feelings and attitudes, what makes people believe we're telling the truth depends mostly on our body language (55%) and our tone of voice (38%), while our words account for only 7%.

Although business and academic presentations are not just about feelings and attitudes, Mehrabian's findings are well worth bearing in mind. A key idea is that the verbal (the words we use; the content) and the non-verbal (our tone of voice and body language) need to be in harmony, to support each other.

Good presenters, of course, know their subject matter and are well prepared, but they are also aware of how their non-verbal communication affects their audience. For example, they know their voice is an instrument, so they turn the volume up or down, raise or lower the pitch, speed up or slow down as appropriate.

As regards body language, good presenters generally have four or five items on their checklist: appearance, posture, gestures, facial expressions and eye contact. They know that appearance matters, so they dress up or down depending on the context; they stand their full height and avoid moving from side to side or swaying; they control their gestures and facial expressions, using them to emphasize a point. They are also aware of the importance of eye contact. When talking to large groups, they often choose about ten friendly-looking people in different sections of the room and regularly make eye contact with them.

3 Work in groups of four. Ask and answer questions about the article.

Students A1 and A2: Turn to File 5, page 114.
Students B1 and B2: Read the information below.

Part 1

Work together. Put these words and phrases in the correct order to make questions.

You both need to write down all three questions.

1 Mehrabian's the is of key idea what theory ?

2 consist does communication what non-verbal of ?

3 do can contact what eye about presenters ?

Part 2

Use the article to work out the answers to questions 1–3 together. Make sure you remember the answers as you need them for Part 3.

Part 3

Each one of you now works with a partner from the other pair. Answer the questions your partner asks you.

Then ask your questions. Help or correct your partner whenever necessary.

Word focus: Structuring presentations

4 🔊 **1.8** Listen to the openings of four different presentations. How positive a first impression do they create? Rate them from 1 (= least positive) to 5 (= most positive). Compare your answers and tell each other which criteria you used.

1 |———1———2———3———4———5|

2 |———1———2———3———4———5|

3 |———1———2———3———4———5|

4 |———1———2———3———4———5|

5 Complete the opening expressions in the table.

Openings:	
Telling an anecdote	A funny thing [1]_____ _____ _____ a few weeks ago. I was …
Using a quote	[2]_____ _____ _____ was Jim Rohn, the great American entrepreneur, who said: 'Effective communication is 20% what you know and 80% how you feel about what you know.'
Asking a question / Mentioning a surprising fact	[3]_____ _____ _____ that one of the most frequent employee complaints in large organizations is: 'We're kept in the dark'?

6 🔊 **1.9** Listen to the fourth presenter for a little bit longer this time and complete the table.

| Introducing the topic: | This morning, I'd [4]_____ _____ _____ a programme which … |
	As you know, I'm here today to talk about …
Outlining your talk:	I have divided my talk into three main parts.
	I'll begin with a brief overview of … / Firstly, I'll give you …
	Then I'll [5]_____ _____ _____ the consequences of … / Secondly, I'll discuss …
	And [6]_____ _____, we'll look at ways in which … / And, finally, I'll tell you about …
Concluding:	Let me sum up. / To sum up then, …
	To summarize the main points of my talk, …
	I'd like to conclude by reminding you of …

7 🔊 **1.10** Listen to parts of a talk on Tai Chi and complete the script.

Student A: Turn to File 7, page 115. Student B: Turn to File 75, page 129.

Speaking: Planning a presentation

8 Work in pairs. Choose one topic each and help each other prepare a presentation outline.

- My city
- Smoking
- Why we all need a pet
- How to make friends and be popular
- How to prepare for an exam
- My company
- Commuting made easy
- Working abroad: some advice
- How to be a great colleague
- How to achieve a work–life balance

1 Think of an opening that will make an impact.

2 Briefly introduce your topic.

3 Outline your talk (three parts). You do not need to provide the content.

4 Think of a strong conclusion.

5 Think about your tone of voice and body language as well as what you say!

9 Work in small groups. Take it in turns to present your outline to the group.

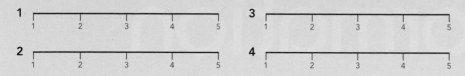

2

A Modal overview
B Future forms
C Effective speaking
D **Communication strategies** Persuasion techniques
E **Interaction** Pitching an idea

Transformation

Modal overview

Reading: Change for the better

1 What inspires people to make changes in their lives? Do you think people should encourage friends to make changes that would make them healthier, wealthier or happier?

2 Can you think of ways to encourage people to do these things?

1 save for retirement

2 use stairs rather than take the escalator or elevator

Read the newspaper article and see if it mentions your ideas.

3 The article mentions two ways of helping people to make better choices. How are they similar and how are they different? Which do you think is more effective, and why?

4 What do you think the expressions in *italics* in the text mean?

5 Work in pairs. Discuss these questions.

1 Do you think that it's reasonable to have laws to make people recycle and save for their retirement? What should the rules and penalties be?

2 Why is it difficult to break habits? If a friend asked your help to do the following, what would you advise?

stop smoking   lose weight   save money for a holiday

Nudge theory

Getting people to look after themselves and do the right thing isn't always easy. We all know that it's healthier to take the stairs rather than the elevator and that we really should recycle, save for our retirement, and so on. The trouble is we don't always do what's best. And, often, people don't want lots of rules to tell them that they have to do the right thing. Sometimes we need [1]*a nudge in the right direction* to help us make the better choice.

One solution is to highlight the best alternative, so it's easier to select. For example, some organizations in the US think that their staff ought to save more money for when they retire. They have altered their pension schemes so employees are now enrolled automatically. A percentage of staff salary is put aside for retirement, and when they get a pay increase, their contributions get adjusted accordingly. Employees don't have to take part in the scheme – they can opt out if they choose not to save – but the default option is 'in'.

Another approach is to make the better choice more fun. At the Odenplan metro station in Stockholm, they've converted steps into a giant piano keyboard that plays musical notes when anyone treads on it. It's an unusual way to get people to take more exercise, but 66% more people now climb the station stairs instead of taking the escalator.

It's a clever idea, but it can be [2]*hard to break bad habits*. Once [3]*the novelty wears off*, will people [4]*revert to their old ways* and take the escalator?

Grammar: Modal overview – obligation, permission and prohibition

6 Look at the examples in the table below. Which verb in bold expresses the following?

a strong obligation   1 _____   2 _____

b obligation   3 _____   4 _____

c no obligation/necessity   5 _____   6 _____

d permission to do something   7 _____   8 _____   9 _____

e prohibition   10 _____   11 _____   12 _____

Obligation

Some organizations think that staff **ought to** *save more money.*

Employees **don't have to** *take part in the scheme.*

We really **should** *recycle.*

They **have to** *do the right thing.*

We **must** *remember to renew our visa.*

Passengers **don't need to** *buy a ticket because they can pay on the train.*

Permission / Prohibition

The media **are allowed to** *take photographs during the press conference.*

Staff **aren't allowed to** *use the telephone to make personal calls.*

They **can** *opt out if they choose not to save.*

You **can't** *park outside this building without a permit.*

You **mustn't** *talk during the presentation.*

You **may** *turn over your exam papers now.*

>> For more information on obligation, permission and prohibition, see pages 165–166.

7 Choose the best option to complete the sentences.

1 As soon as the training course is finished, you *must / can / should* all go home early.

2 Do we *have / should / ought* to put the cardboard and paper in separate recycling bins?

3 Students *don't need to / aren't allowed to / don't have to* look at the questions before the exam begins.

4 I really *don't need to / can't / must* finish the financial report today or the directors will be furious.

5 She *mustn't / doesn't need to / isn't allowed to* buy a computer because she can use a company laptop.

6 Before opening a Premier savings account, customers *should / can / may* provide three separate proofs of identity.

8 Complete the draft guidelines using verbs of obligation, permission or prohibition. More than one answer may be possible.

☐ ☐ ☐

Janis

What do you think of these ideas for our facility guidelines? We can discuss tomorrow.

Regards

Ian

- Visitors don't [1]_____ to wear protective clothing in the reception area, but they [2]_____ wear a safety suit in the main plant.

- Chemical monitors are available; they are not essential, but visitors [3]_____ wear one if they intend to stay in the plant for longer than two hours.

- Visitors [4]_____ to eat in the canteen if accompanied by a member of staff, and they [5]_____ also use the coin-operated drinks machines.

- For safety reasons, visitors are [6]_____ to smoke anywhere in the facility, including outside areas. They also [7]_____ to refrain from bringing food into the facility.

- Some doors in the plant are marked with a red cross. Visitors [8]_____ enter these areas without the director's permission.

- All identity badges [9]_____ be handed in to reception before visitors leave the building.

9 Prepare a set of guidelines for your place of work or study, or another building that you know well.

Speaking: Making improvements

10 Work in pairs or small groups. Look at the scenarios in File 12, page 116. Choose three of the scenarios and discuss improvements that might help the situations.

11 Choose one of the scenarios you discussed and present your ideas to the class.

TALKING POINT   What habits annoy you? What could you do to encourage people to give them up? What good habits would you like to have?

Reading: Motivators

1 You have a friend who has taken the same professional examination three times and failed. Read the two quotes. Which do you think would be most suitable for your friend?

1 *'If at first you don't succeed, try, try, again.'*

2 *'If at first you don't succeed, try, try again. Then quit. There's no point in being a damn fool about it.'*

2 Think of something you need to do next week at home or at work. How will you motivate yourself to get it done? How will you feel after you have achieved your goal? How will you feel if you do not achieve it?

3 Complete the quiz below about motivators. What are you more likely to do in each situation, a or b?

Motivators

1 You are offered an important new project. What is your first reaction?
  a Worry what will happen if it goes wrong.
  b Wonder what recognition you'll get when you succeed.

2 You're taking part in a race. While you train, you …
  a feel guilty about the dessert you had at lunch, and spend extra time in the gym.
  b imagine how great it will feel to be the first to cross the winning line.

3 You're halfway through a building project at home. What are you going to do this weekend?
  a Keep working. You might not meet your deadline if you don't continue.
  b Go out and celebrate progress. You deserve to relax and enjoy yourself.

4 When a task becomes difficult, what is more likely to make you carry on?
  a Thinking about what people will say if you don't meet the objective.
  b Planning a reward for yourself when the work is finished.

4 Check the analysis in File 16, page 117. Do you agree with the ideas? What other factors can motivate people?

Listening: Motivation techniques

5 1.11 Listen to Doug Lambert speaking to his mentor about a new project and answer the questions.

1 What usually motivates Doug – the challenge or the reward?
2 Does Doug's mentor suggest that he shouldn't take on the new project?
3 What does Doug intend to ask his manager?

6 Listen again and complete the table.

Types of motivation:	1 _____ – motivation comes from inside the person and may involve setting goals or personal targets
	2 _____ – motivation comes from outside the person and may involve a reward or penalty
Motivation techniques:	3
	4
	5
	6
What can have a negative impact on motivation?	7

7 Which of the motivation techniques in exercise 6 would be most effective for you? Which do you think is most effective in general?

8)) **1.12** Listen to five people speaking about unusual motivation methods. Answer the questions.

1 Which motivation techniques from exercise 6 do they use?

2 Do you think that the technique each speaker chooses will work for them?

Grammar: Future forms

9)) Listen to the five conversations again and complete the sentences.

Future form	Example
1 Present simple	*The race _____ place this _____.*
2 *will*	*He reckons _____ _____ more than ten kilos.*
3 *going to*	*My parents _____ _____ _____ _____ around China.*
4 Present continuous	*We _____ _____ to Stavanger in ten days' time.*
5 Future perfect	*I _____ _____ _____ it by July.*

>> **For more information on future forms, see pages 161–162.**

10 Match the sentences in the table above to these functions.

a plans and intentions

b predictions

c arrangements

d actions completed at a point in the future

e scheduled or timetabled events in the near future

11 Complete the sentences with the most appropriate future form.

1 According to the timetable, the last train _____ (leave) at midnight.

2 By next March I _____ (work) here for eight years.

3 He's always late. I bet he _____ (not be) on time for the meeting this afternoon.

4 You want it by Friday? I'm afraid we _____ (not have) a delivery by then.

5 They _____ (not meet) the president until Thursday morning.

6 Some experts believe that the price of gas and electricity _____ (rise) in the autumn.

7 Is the designer confident that she _____ (complete) the brochure before the launch date?

8 Have you had any thoughts about next year and what shares you _____ (invest) in?

Speaking: Comparing solutions

12 Work in pairs. What could these companies do to improve staff motivation?

Problem 1

Dynamo Software

The software designers are unhappy. They have interesting ideas for new software but are unable to develop them because they spend all their time working on routine projects. Many of the employees are bored and frustrated by the situation and key staff are talking about leaving.

Problem 2

Kingsmead Broadband

There has been a very high turnover of staff in the call centre. Employees work an eight-hour shift with a half-hour break. Call centre workers use a script (a written list of what to say) to deal with customers' internet problems. Customer satisfaction with the call centre is low and as a result callers are often unhappy and can become aggressive.

---

13 Imagine that you are the managing director of one of these companies. Present your ideas to staff to say what you intend to do to improve the situation.

14 Read about ways in which some companies tackled similar problems. Discuss the advantages and disadvantages of each solution. Turn to File 14 on page 116.

TALKING POINT Is there a particular day of the week or time of day when you find it hard to get motivated? What do you do to help you stay focused during these times?

Word focus: Body language

1 Look at the photos and describe what each person is doing. Which poses make you think the person is confident or unconfident? Why?

2 Body language generally consists of facial expressions and physical gestures. Put the words in the box in the correct category below. Can you find examples of these in the pictures? Add two more words or phrases to each column.

> bite nails   cross arms / legs   fidget   frown
> give thumbs up   grin   nod   raise eyebrows
> shake head   shrug   stand / sit upright   yawn

Facial expressions	Physical gestures

3 Work in pairs. Discuss these questions.

1 Which of the facial expressions and physical gestures in exercise 2 would you associate with the following emotions?

boredom   amusement   surprise   anxiety
displeasure   agreement

2 Do you know of any cultures where they might be associated with a different emotion?

3 What cross-cultural problems can occur with non-verbal communication?

Listening: Power poses

4 🔊 **1.13** You are going to hear life coach Jill Murray give a talk about body language. Which two photos A–F does she describe?

5 🔊 Listen to the first part of Jill Murray's talk again. Notice how she pauses / emphasizes particular words (underlined).

It may surprise some of you to hear this,/ but how we sit and stand has a direct effect on how we feel./ In tests,/ people who use power poses report feeling more confident./ So,/ what is a power pose?/ Well,/ for instance,/ sitting with your hands behind your head and your feet on the table,/ that's a power pose./ Another example is standing upright with your hands resting on a table or desk./ Remarkably,/ people who sit,/ or stand,/ in these poses for just a few minutes/ report feeling more powerful than they felt before adopting that position./ They not only think they look more impressive, they actually feel more impressive, too.

6 🔊 **1.14** Listen to the rest of her talk and mark it in a similar way. Add slashes (/) where she pauses (note that there are no commas to help you) and underline the words she emphasizes.

In contrast low power poses make people feel less confident. One example includes sitting with your arms close to your sides and hands folded. Another example is standing with your arms or legs crossed. People who hold these poses for a few minutes report feeling less powerful. This might be because when we feel threatened or under attack we adopt a defensive pose to become less visible and to protect our body. However when we take up more space our body sends the brain signals that help it to reduce stress and increase confidence.

So how can we put this information to use? Well the main message we can take away from this research is that if we sit or stand in a power pose even for a short time it could give us a vital confidence boost when we most need it. Try it next time you're preparing for an interview before you give a talk or before an important meeting. You might be surprised at the difference it makes!

7 Work in pairs. Take turns delivering part of the talk. Try to use pauses, emphasis and appropriate body language. Your partner should listen and provide constructive feedback on your performance.

Student A: Use exercise 5. Student B: Use exercise 6.

Speaking: A short talk

8 You are working on an international team. Each member of the team is asked to prepare a short talk (1–2 minutes) on one aspect of non-verbal communication in their culture. Prepare your talk. You can include some of the topics below or use your own ideas.

- Dress codes • Physical gestures • Facial expressions • Distance you stand from another person

9 Look at your talk again and use slashes to mark where you will pause, and underline words that you want to emphasize. Give your talk to the team.

TALKING POINT
- Are there any gestures or expressions that you find irritating?
- What other aspects of cross-cultural awareness are most important when working or travelling in another country?

Reading: Getting what you want

1 Calvin is trying to persuade his mother to let him have a cookie. Describe the persuasion technique he is using. Why does he say 'she's on to me'? (You can check your answer in File 32 on page 119.)

2 Psychologist Robert Cialdini has identified the following six persuasion techniques. Match each one to its description (1–6) below.

Authority   Consistency   Likability   Reciprocity   Scarcity   Social proof

We use persuasion in many different situations both at work and at home, and we are more successful on some occasions than others. Next time you need to **win** someone **over**, here are six techniques that could help

1 _____ Do something good for someone and they usually **return the favour**. That's why free gifts work as a sales strategy even if the gift is only a pen.

2 _____ Once people make a decision, they like to **stick to it**. So if a car salesperson **ups their price** at the last moment, the buyer is quite likely to agree to **hand over** more money.

3 _____ How do companies persuade us to buy their brand of toothpaste? Simple: they make sure that the person selling the idea looks like a dentist in a white coat.

4 _____ People are more easily persuaded if they think someone is nice. That's why a business where someone sells products to friends and acquaintances can do well.

5 _____ We have more confidence in something if lots of other people are doing the same thing. You would probably prefer to eat in a restaurant that's full than one that is almost empty.

6 _____ You're more likely to buy something if you're told it's the last one in the shop, or if there's a special offer for a limited time. That's why signs like 'Sale – final day' get shoppers reaching for their wallets.

3 Complete these sentences with the correct verb phrase in **bold italics** from the text.

1 The staff don't like the new work hours but I'm sure we could _____ them _____ if we explain why they're necessary.

2 You helped me with my presentation last week; now I'll _____ and help with yours.

3 If my phone provider _____ of calls again, I'm going to cancel the contract.

4 Place your order today and you won't need to _____ any money until the goods are delivered.

5 That's a good suggestion, but it'll be less costly to _____ the original plan.

4 Work in pairs. Discuss these questions.

1 How do salespeople and advertisers use these techniques to persuade us to buy?

2 Have you ever been influenced by these techniques? Give examples.

3 Which techniques do you find easy to resist? Why?

Listening: A persuasive travel agent

5 🔊 **1.15** Listen to a conversation in a travel agent's. What does the customer want – and what does he agree to buy?

6 🔊 Listen again and complete the examples with phrases that the speakers use.

Persuasion technique	Example
1 Social proof	*And _____ that it's the most romantic city in the world.*
2 Authority	*_____, the head of our company went there only last weekend.*
3 Likability	*It's your _____ because we have a very special offer on at the moment.*
4 Reciprocity	*Look I _____, I'll give you an additional five per cent discount. I shouldn't really, but it's such a romantic present.*
5 Scarcity	*I don't want to _____ on you, but the offer does end at midnight tonight.*
6 Consistency	*Now, as I'm _____, there are transfer fees on top of that price.*

7 Look at these strategies for resisting someone who is trying to persuade you. Do you use any of them? Which do you agree or disagree with?

1 Don't agree to anything before you know the request.

2 Don't apologize when you don't want to do something.

3 Keep it simple – you don't need to give a detailed reason.

4 Don't use phrases like 'I'd like to help' or 'I'd love to but …' – unless you mean it.

5 Remain polite, but firm.

8 Look at part of a conversation below. How would you respond?

A: Hi Dev, I haven't seen you for ages. Actually, I'm really pleased that I ran into you. I wonder, could you do me a favour?

B: 1 _____

A: You see, my cousin's in town this weekend but I'm working. Could you show him around on Saturday evening? Maybe take him to dinner?

B: 2 _____

A: Oh, really? That's such a shame. You'd really like my cousin. Well, what about Sunday?

B: 3 _____

A: Really? Well, maybe he could come with you, er?

B: 4 _____

A: Look, I'd really appreciate it if you could help me out with this. I'm worried he'll be lonely. You must have some free time over the weekend.

B: 5 _____

9 🔊 **1.16** Now listen to the dialogue. Does speaker B use any of the phrases that you used? Which strategies in exercise 7 does he use?

Speaking: Winning people over

10 Work in pairs. Look at the scenarios in File 15, page 116 and discuss these questions.

1 What persuasion techniques might work in each situation?

2 What strategies could you use to resist being persuaded?

11 Roleplay two of the scenarios. Use some of the strategies that you discussed in exercise 7. Take it in turns to be the person doing the persuading.

12 Was it more difficult being the persuader or the person being persuaded?

Reminder

Modal overview page 15 + Grammar reference pages 165–166
Future forms page 17 + Grammar reference pages 161–162
Persuasion techniques page 21

Reading: Great ideas

1 Read the pitches for business ideas. Work in pairs or small groups and discuss the following.

1 Which business idea do you think is most and least useful? Why?
2 Choose two ideas to invest in. Explain why you chose them.
3 What resources would the people need to set up these two businesses?
4 How much should they charge for the services?
5 Suggest ways to market the two ideas.

PERFECT PITCH?

Got a fantastic idea? Don't know who to pitch it to? Send it in and we will feature the seven best ideas every day on our website. Here are the ideas that we selected today. Think you can do better? Then send us a pitch in no more than three sentences. Remember – short is sweet!

A How much time do you waste waiting in queues each day? We offer a service where someone will stand and wait for you while you're free to go and do something more interesting.

B Packing your suitcase before you go on a business trip is a boring and time-consuming job. Just give your clothes measurements to our service. We'll deliver a ready packed suitcase to your door two hours before you leave, including clothes, toiletries and an interesting book to read on the plane.

C Want a very special party outfit to make your special event go with a bang? This service will design a costume and make it to your measurements, all made from balloons. We can include company logos or any other message you want.

D Do you need to find a way to escape from someone who won't stop talking? We'll call your phone anytime you want and you can pretend that you need to leave urgently. Just one press of a button and you're free!

E Does your garden look like a jungle? Do you have better things to do than cut the grass? Then why not rent some goats to eat your problems away?

F Is your son or daughter an only child? This company will match them to another only child in the neighbourhood so they have someone they can play with and climb trees with.

G Do you love to watch horror movies but feel too scared to watch them on your own? This escort service will provide someone to accompany you to the cinema and say calm and soothing things when you get frightened.

2 Which of these services do you think already exist? Turn to File 9, page 115 and find out.

Word focus: Structure a pitch

3 A pitch should be short and contain clear information about your idea. Complete the flowchart with the words in the box.

anticipate   competition   focus   hook   introduce   name   request   rhetorical   summarize   target   unique

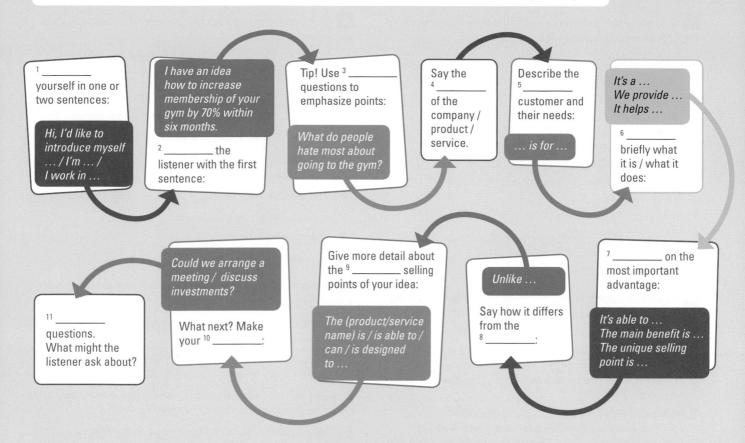

1 _____ yourself in one or two sentences:

Hi, I'd like to introduce myself … / I'm … / I work in …

I have an idea how to increase membership of your gym by 70% within six months.

2 _____ the listener with the first sentence:

Tip! Use **3 _____** questions to emphasize points:

What do people hate most about going to the gym?

Say the **4 _____** of the company / product / service.

Describe the **5 _____** customer and their needs:

… is for …

*It's a …
We provide …
It helps …*

6 _____ briefly what it is / what it does:

Could we arrange a meeting / discuss investments?

What next? Make your **10 _____**:

11 _____ questions. What might the listener ask about?

Give more detail about the **9 _____** selling points of your idea:

The (product/service name) is / is able to / can / is designed to …

Unlike …
Say how it differs from the **8 _____**:

7 _____ on the most important advantage:

*It's able to …
The main benefit is …
The unique selling point is …*

4 Work in pairs and answer the questions.

1 A pitch which takes two minutes or less is called 'an elevator pitch'. Why do you think this is?

2 Which points from the flowchart in exercise 3 would be useful to include in a …

a ten-second elevator pitch?
(one or two sentences summarizing the idea)

b one-minute elevator pitch?
(an introduction and brief summary of the idea)

c two-minute elevator pitch?
(an introduction and brief summary, with some detail and information about what you need)

5 🔊 **1.17** Listen to a pitch and answer the questions.

1 What rhetorical question does the speaker ask?

2 What is the name of the product?

3 What makes it safe to use?

6 🔊 Listen again and make notes. Summarize the information into a ten-second pitch (one or two sentences). Compare your ideas with a partner.

Speaking: Make a pitch

7 Work in pairs. Choose one of the bullet points in File 84, page 131 or a topic of your own and discuss ideas for a product or service that could be developed.

8 Use your ideas to prepare two pitches: one of you will make a ten-second pitch for your product and the other will make a one-minute pitch. Practise your pitch with your partner. Remember to use pauses, emphasis and appropriate body language.

9 Work with another pair and present the two pitches. When you are listening to a pitch, do the following.

Make notes about:

● something that worked well

● the speaker's body language – is it appropriate?

● the speaker's use of pauses and emphasis

● which was more effective – the ten-second or the one-minute pitch? Why?

At the end of the pitch, ask a question about the product or service.

Would you invest in the other pair's idea?

Writing: Pitch an idea

10 Choose another topic from exercise 7, or a new topic of your own, and write a short pitch for your idea for the blog in exercise 1. Note that language for blogs is usually informal.

Interaction

1 Complete these sentences with the time expressions in the box. Use each expression once.

> tomorrow afternoon   since 2009   recently   by Friday
> in the late 1980s   in ten years' time   every month
> during the meeting

1 Heinrich started working for Gamma Engineering _____ .

2 Ralph has been working on his thesis _____ .

3 She'll have finished her report _____ .

4 Paolo probably won't be working for the same company _____ .

5 Kaori is giving a business presentation _____ .

6 She gives a presentation _____ .

7 I almost fell asleep _____ .

8 I've been drinking too much coffee _____ .

2 Read this conversation between two colleagues, Lucy (L) and Tom (T). Then put the verbs in brackets in the correct tense.

T: *Lucy! Hi! Good to see you. I ¹_____ (not see) you for ages. Where have you been?*

L: *Hi, Tom. Didn't you know that I ²_____ (spend) the last six months in Brazil?*

T: *In Brazil? Really? I wish I ³_____ (know). I ⁴_____ (go) to a conference in Salvador at the beginning of October. Who ⁵_____ (know), maybe we could've met up somewhere?*

L: *I ⁶_____ (doubt) it. I was on safari ⁷_____ (observe) wildlife) in the Pantanal then.*

T: *Mm. That ⁸_____ (sound) very exciting indeed. So while you ⁹_____ (enjoy) yourself on safari, the rest of us ¹⁰_____ (do) all the hard work.*

L: *Oh, Tom! It was only five days. That's the only holiday I ¹¹_____ (have) in those six months. Anyway, what ¹²_____ (be) all the hard work about in Salvador? Networking, I suppose?*

T: *Well, yeah, you could say that. Actually, it was a really good conference and I ¹³_____ (make) some very useful contacts.*

L: *Um, that's interesting. Tell me more.*

T: *First, we ¹⁴_____ (open) an office in Salvador. It's just a matter of weeks now, not months. And we ¹⁵_____ (invest) heavily in a huge development project, and …*

L: *Look, what ¹⁶_____ (you / do) after work today? We could go somewhere nice for a drink and continue our little chat. What do you say?*

3 Look at the conversation again and make questions for these answers.

1 Nearly six months.

2 To Salvador.

3 Because he wanted to attend a conference there.

4 No. She had only one in six months.

5 In a couple of weeks.

4 Make questions to elicit the missing information in these sentences.

> *I watched _____ on TV.* → *What did you watch?*

1 I talked to _____ this morning.

2 _____ told me about your new project.

3 Exactly _____ people attended the conference.

4 I left early because _____.

5 _____ invited me to the party.

6 Jamie owes me _____ euros.

7 This iPad belongs to _____.

8 Enrica used to live in _____.

9 I borrowed $50 from _____.

10 _____ lives in Trieste.

5 Cross out the option which doesn't make sense in each sentence.

1 You *don't have to / ought to / shouldn't* go to Jim's talk if you aren't interested in the topic.

2 She can get a visa at the border. She *needn't / doesn't have to / mustn't* apply for one in advance.

3 In my opinion, Klara *shouldn't / isn't allowed to / ought not to* do so much overtime. She's ruining her health.

4 You *don't need to / should / must* go to the nearest emergency exit as soon as the alarm goes off.

5 I really don't think that smoking *should / ought to / must* be allowed on any of our premises.

6 Why haven't you put your helmet on? You know you *can't / don't have to / mustn't* enter this warehouse without it.

6 Complete these sentences with *must / mustn't* or with *have to* in the correct form and tense.

1 These documents are strictly confidential. You _____ let anyone else have access to them.

2 Jane's new neighbours are terrible. She _____ complain about the noise at least five times since they moved in.

3 _____ Peter _____ work overtime last week?

4 I haven't been in touch with Eduardo for ages. I _____ remember to give him a ring tonight.

5 If Yolanda moves to Brussels, she _____ drive to work anymore, because the bus service is so good there.

6 I _____ eat too much tomorrow, otherwise I'll feel sick on the plane.

7 Dave's disappointed because he can't be with his family on Saturday. He _____ work.

8 No one _____ disturb the boss while she is in a video conference.

9 Tell Michel not to worry, he's got plenty of time. He _____ hurry.

10 We were inundated with enquiries yesterday. I'm glad I _____ deal with them myself.

7 Choose the forms that can complete these sentences. Sometimes more than one form may be possible.

1 I'll discuss the matter with the manager as soon as she _____ back.

   a will come **b** comes **c** is coming

2 They _____ production to Slovakia in May.

   a will be relocating **b** are relocated
   c will have relocated

3 They _____ production to Slovakia by May.

   a will be relocating **b** have relocated
   c will have relocated

4 I _____ why they had modified the contract, but then I forgot.

   a will be asking **b** will have asked
   c was going to ask

5 Have you heard the news? Jamie _____ Vladi as team leader.

   a will replace **b** is going to replace
   c is replacing

6 The timetable says the first bus _____ at 06:15.

   a leaves **b** leaving **c** has left

7 Where _____ in two years' time?

   a are you working **b** will you be working
   c will you have worked

8 In my presentation, I _____ at three ways of improving sales.

   a 'll look **b** 'm going to look **c** 'll be looking

8 Put each word in the box into the correct group according to its stress pattern.

> agreement approach business career
> colleague company confidence deliver
> department event favour industry message
> novelty percentage persuade postpone
> relevant suggestion target

O o	o O	O o o	o O o
image	request	manager	impression

9 Complete this crossword puzzle.

Across

3 'Send your email messages to Jane Hogben, but please remember to _____ me in every time.'

6 _____ networking events helps people to establish valuable contacts in a very short time.

7 In your culture, do people _____ their head to express agreement or disagreement?

8 'Thursday morning is no good, I'm afraid. I've _____ something on.'

10 'I can't see you tomorrow – I'll be _____ up all day.'

14 'I can't make Wednesday morning. I'm afraid something's _____ up.'

15 People sometimes need to be given a _____ in the right direction to help them make the better choice.

16 Many people _____ their head when they want to show disbelief, disapproval or sadness.

18 Before you click on 'Send', _____ sure your message is addressed to the right person.

19 Habits that people have had for years are really hard to _____.

20 'OK. I'm free all day tomorrow. What time _____ you?'

Down

1 Experienced salespeople can generally make good _____ of a range of persuasion techniques.

2 Which _____ or expressions do you find irritating when someone is talking to you?

4 Opposite of bring forward (e.g. a meeting, a match, etc).

5 If you can't use _____ or italics in your emails, you can always put an important word or phrase between asterisks.

9 Good presenters are aware of how their non-_____ communication affects their audience.

11 If you _____ a question, an issue or a topic, you avoid talking about it or dealing with it.

12 'We look _____ to hearing from you soon.'

13 Job _____ are people who are trying to find employment.

17 'I had to take my _____ to the garage to have it fixed.'

25

3

A Present perfect and past simple
B Through the grapevine
C Problems and solutions
D Communication strategies Reacting to news
E Interaction Crisis management

What's up?

Present perfect and past simple

Reading: Have you heard?

1 Discuss these questions.

1 What forms of communication does your workplace or school use (e.g. a newsletter, or a traditional or electronic noticeboard)? Do you find them interesting?

2 In what other ways can people be informed of upcoming events and changes within the school or workplace? Which way is the most effective?

2 Imagine this is your company noticeboard. Only look at the headings first.
Which announcements would you read in full? Which ones would you skip? Work in pairs and discuss.

NEWS, EVENTS AND INFORMATION

NEW STARTER IN ADMIN
Steve Evans has joined us as Contract Support Administrator to help the Admin team keep on top of a heavy workload. Please introduce yourself and make Steve feel welcome.

Office Cleaning
Please note that all the offices on the first and second floors will be cleaned over the weekend. If you haven't done so yet, tidy your desk area before leaving, and make sure nothing is left on the floor.

Interim Results Available
Our Interim Results for the six months ended 31 July have now been released.

Our company has performed remarkably well. Despite the severe recession in most of our markets, there was only a temporary downturn in orders, which means we have remained profitable and generated cash.

Although our market share declined in the first quarter, it has been rising gradually since May owing to the multiple contracts we have won.

With markets now recovering, demand for our services has been picking up and we are very well positioned for the upturn. Well done everyone!

The full Interim Results Report can be downloaded from our Intranet.

CHARITY RUN
After last year's success, we've decided to organize another charity run for cancer research.

Last year you raised an amazing €12,500. How much will you raise this time?

Register today with Nelly (ext. 608 or nelly.dobson@cablex.com).

Congratulations to Liz
You'll all be delighted to know that Liz Steinbach has had a baby girl. Both mother and daughter are doing well. We're having a collection for flowers and a gift, so if you'd like to contribute, please see Nelly.

---

3 Look at the 'Interim Results Available' announcement. Find ten words and phrases which can be used to talk about favourable or unfavourable economic activity.

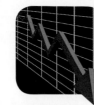

Grammar: Present perfect and past simple

4 Read the notes and complete the examples with verbs from the announcements in exercise 2.

Present perfect and past simple

1 We use the past simple to talk about finished actions and situations in the past.

Last year you [1]_____ *an amazing €12,500.*

Our market share [2]_____ *slightly in the first quarter.*

2 The present perfect is a present tense which we use to build a bridge between the past and the present. We use it to talk about actions or situations which happened or started in the past, but which are in some way connected with the present.

Main uses

a) Recent news / New information:

Steve Evans [3]_____ _____ *us as Contract Support Administrator.* (… so <u>now</u> he works for us)

Our company [4]_____ _____ *remarkably well.* (… so <u>now</u> we are in a good position)

b) Experience:

Suzana has travelled a lot, but she has never visited Egypt.

c) Duration from the past until now:

She has been office manager since 2009. (… and she is still office manager <u>now</u>)

3 If we want to emphasize that the action or situation is still continuing, we use the present perfect continuous.

Our market share has [5]_____ _____ *gradually since May.* (… and it is still going up)

>> For more information on the present perfect (simple and continuous) and the past simple, see pages 157–159.

---

5 Find all the other examples of the present perfect and the past simple in the announcements. Why did the writer use one or the other tense in each case?

6 Which of the following time expressions are used with the past simple and which are used with the present perfect? Which one can be used with both?

1 yesterday
2 since two o'clock
3 for years
4 last night
5 just after you left
6 It's / This is the first time …
7 in 2008
8 before the meeting
9 so far
10 four months ago
11 earlier this morning
12 yet
13 already
14 recently
15 just

7 Complete the sentences with the past simple or present perfect simple of the verbs in brackets.

1 Today _____ really hectic – and it's not even lunchtime yet! (be)

2 Julian _____ as a firefighter and paramedic since 1998. (work)

3 I _____ the whole article yet, but the introduction is fascinating. (not / read)

4 Who _____ you your first part- or full-time job? (give)

5 Hey guys, you know what? Our hospital _____ an award for outstanding achievement! (win)

6 It _____ such a long time ago. I don't remember the details. (happen)

7 What _____ you _____ for the past two years? (study)

8 How long _____ you _____ Mr Zhao? (know)

In which two sentences could the present perfect *continuous* be used?

Speaking: Updating

8 Work in pairs. Give each other true information about: your school / workplace; a friend / relative; yourself. Use different time expressions from exercise 6.

Four months ago, I redecorated my living-room.

I haven't been to the theatre for years.

9 Work in pairs. One of you is an office manager (OM), the other the manager's personal assistant (PA). Before going away for ten days, the OM drew up a list of things for the PA to do during his/her absence. Today the OM phones to get an update on the PA's progress. Roleplay the conversation.

Student A: Turn to File 17, page 117.
Student B: Turn to File 79, page 130.

TALKING POINT Which is worse, lack of information or information overload?

Listening: Water cooler talk

1 Where do you and your colleagues usually make small talk during the working day?

2 You are going to listen to a conversation which includes the words and phrases in the box. Before you listen, use them to complete the definitions.

> don't like the sound of   frantic   hush-hush   let down   let on   merger   redundancy   relocate

1 Something that is _____ is confidential and not to be discussed with other people.

2 If people or companies _____, they move to a different place.

3 A _____ is the joining together of two or more companies or organizations to form a larger one.

4 If you _____ something, you feel worried about something you have heard or read.

5 A _____ is a situation in which someone has to leave their job because they are no longer needed.

6 If you don't _____ to other people, you keep secret something that you know.

7 If you feel _____, you are disappointed because you feel someone has not done something that you trusted or expected them to do.

8 _____ activity is extremely hurried, uses a lot of energy, and is rather disorganized.

3))) **1.18** Listen to a conversation between two friends / colleagues and answer these questions.

1 How busy do you think Dan is? Why?

2 What's Vic's job?

3 How confidential is the news about the merger?

4 What's Dan worried about?

5 Does Dan let on to Bob?

4))) Listen to the conversation again and complete these sentences.

1 _____, anything new about the merger?

2 Well, the merger's still only a possibility, _____ _____.

3 _____, in fact, we aren't supposed to know. _____ _____, not all of us.

4 Well, I think Vic is, _____ … disappointed.

Word focus: Discourse markers

5 In spoken English, people often utter sounds or words like *erm, well, so,* etc. Do you agree with the statements below?

1 *Erm, like, you know, well, so* and *I mean* are just sounds and words that people use to fill gaps in conversations, and they don't mean anything.

2 Only uneducated or lazy people say things like this and it's a bad habit.

3 These sounds and words can help people to communicate.

6 Turn to File 13 on page 116. Does the information given there make you want to change any of your answers in exercise 5? Why?/Why not?

7 Look at the examples and complete the box.

1 She plays the violin, *I mean* the viola, really well.
2 You're more of an expert than me. *I mean*, you've got all that experience.
3 It's just not right. *I mean*, it's unfair, isn't it?
4 He was, *like*, disappointed.
5 I last talked to Paul, *like*, six weeks ago.

> **Discourse markers: *I mean, like, erm***
>
> **1** We often use *I mean* to …
> **a)** rephrase something we have just said (as in example _____)
> **b)** correct something we have just said (as in example _____)
> **c)** add new information (as in example _____)
>
> **2** *Like* can signal …
> **d)** an approximation (as in example _____)
> **e)** that what follows may not exactly express the speaker's ideas or feelings (as in example _____)
>
> **3** *Erm* is a sign of hesitation. It hardly ever signifies anything else.

8 Match these sentences to their meanings (a, b or c below).

1 1 The flight wasn't expensive. It was, like, a hundred euros.
 2 The flight wasn't expensive. It was … erm … a hundred euros.
 3 The flight wasn't expensive. It was, you know, a hundred euros.

 a It's going to take me a moment to remember how much it cost.
 b I think we both know how much it cost, so we share this understanding.
 c I want you to know that I'm speaking loosely and a hundred euros is an approximation.

2 1 Yes, the journey took six hours, but, well, we really enjoyed it.
 2 Yes, the journey took six hours, but we, like, really enjoyed it.
 3 Yes, the journey took six hours, but we didn't care. I mean, we really enjoyed it.

 a 'Really enjoyed' is the correct description of how we felt. What I said first wasn't quite right.
 b 'Really enjoyed' isn't precisely what I mean, but I mean something like that.
 c I think you may be surprised that we enjoyed it.

9 Work in pairs. Discuss which discourse markers from exercises 6 and 7 would best complete this conversation extract.

A: ¹_____, what was Isabel rattling on about at lunchtime?
B: ²_____, she just feels she's been passed over for the marketing job.
 And of course she isn't happy about it. ³_____, she's quite upset.
A: Shame. But frankly I think Nick is the right person for the job.
 He's got a wealth of experience, ⁴_____.
B: Yeah, that's right. He's been in the department for, ⁵_____, six years,
 hasn't he? And he's been playing golf with the boss for just as long. ⁶_____,
 according to Isabel, that is.

10))) **1.19** Listen to the conversation and complete the extract in exercise 9 with the discourse markers these particular speakers chose to use.

Speaking: Getting the message

11 Step 1: Work on your own. Choose one of the topics below and prepare to talk about it.
- A holiday I'll never forget
- My flat / house
- Someone I really admire
- How I met my partner
- A typical day at work / college
- My first business trip
- How my company has changed over the past two or three years

Step 2: Get into groups of three. Student A speaks, B and C listen without interrupting.

Step 3: When A finishes, B retells the story. Nobody interrupts.

Step 4: C gives feedback on the retelling (e.g. Did B omit or change anything important? etc).

A, B and C then change roles, following the same procedure as above.

12 Listen carefully to the story your teacher is going to read to you. Be prepared to retell it.

Teacher: Turn to File 102, page 135.

> **TALKING POINT**
> - Why do some people find it hard to keep a secret? Do you?
> - What kind of information do some companies sometimes hide from their employees?

Word focus: Talking about problems

1 Work in pairs. Here are things we can do with a problem. In what order do you usually proceed?

try to find a way around / solve / look into / identify / discuss / deal with / anticipate

2 In what situations, if any, might it be better to ignore a problem altogether?

3)) **1.20** Listen to five podcasts and match these headlines to the podcast number.

Never too old to learn _____

Don't blame young people _____

Travellers delayed _____

Switching from public to private _____

Bleak economic prospects _____

4)) Listen again and complete the sentences.

1 Passengers at Wilston Airport suffered severe disruption yesterday after it was _____ by a _____ glitch which left them unable to check in.

2 Germany's economic recovery prospects have _____ an _____ setback.

3 I don't want to be _____ _____, asking people to drive me around all the time.

4 An operation to transfer 800 government staff to private companies _____ _____ without a hitch yesterday.

5 According to recent research, teenagers _____ _____ _____ on lessons and homework because their brains are less developed than was previously thought.

5 Find the words and phrases in exercise 4 which match these definitions.

1 to find it hard (to do something)

2 a thing, person or situation that is annoying, or causes trouble or problems

3 a small and sudden problem, especially with technology

4 a problem that delays or prevents something, or makes a situation worse

5 to happen successfully, without any problems

6 Complete the sentences with the words in the box.

> agreeable dilemma hold key permanent political practical way out

1 The aim of the meeting was to discuss a number of _____ solutions to the problem of workplace hazards.

2 Their proposal is just a quick fix of limited value. What we need to do is develop a _____ solution.

3 Both parties worked hard to find a mutually _____ solution.

4 The opposition insisted they would not want to negotiate a _____ solution with the prime minister.

5 Adonis was in a _____, and could see no way out.

6 People are losing hope that there might actually be a _____ of the current stalemate.

7 Working well as a team is the _____ to success.

8 Professor Perkovic claims to have made a discovery that may _____ the key to our understanding of the universe.

7 Look at the sentences in exercise 6 and answer these questions.

1 Which four verbs are used to complete this phrase: to _____ a solution?

2 Which phrase means 'a fast, easy solution that's only temporary'?

3 Which two words refer to a kind of problem?

4 Which two words / phrases contain the idea of solution?

Listening: Problems will arise

8 Work in pairs. Think about some events you have attended (e.g. a talk, a trade fair, a conference, etc.).

1 Tell each other about the best event you've ever attended. What made it so successful?

2 What about the worst event you've ever attended? What were the problems?

9 Lina is telling Rose, a co-worker, about the problems she's been having with the organization of a forthcoming conference. Work in pairs and try to reconstruct Lina's side of the phone conversation.

R: Hi, Lina. How are you getting on with all the organizing?

L: _____

R: Sorry to hear that. What happened?

L: _____

R: Of course! He's our keynote speaker, isn't he?

L: _____

R: Oh, dear! Just one month before the event. Any particular reason why he withdrew?

L: _____

R: Really? It seemed such a successful company. What a shame! Erm ... And what about participant numbers, by the way?

L: _____

R: Why? How many have registered so far?

L: _____

R: Mm, right, but then this year we didn't start promoting the event till March, did we? Let's be patient, I'm sure numbers will grow.

10 🔊 1.21 Listen to the original conversation. Then answer the questions.

1 How close to the original was your reconstruction in exercise 9?

2 How do you think Lina can solve her two problems?

11 🔊 Listen again and / or look at the audio script on page 141 and answer the questions.

What does Lina say ...

1 in answer to Rose's first question?

2 to show she keeps having problems and she thinks they will never end?

3 to introduce an explanation of a problem?

4 that means: 'The company has experienced serious financial problems'?

5 that means 'worried'?

Speaking: Life's little ups and downs

12 Work in pairs or small groups. Tell each other about some of the following.

- something you organized that went off without a hitch
- an occasion when your career or studies suffered a temporary setback
- something you've never had difficulty doing
- a technical glitch that once made your life difficult for a while
- what neighbours can do in order not to make a nuisance of themselves
- the problems you think men can more easily solve than women (and vice versa)
- the kinds of dilemma that parents / teachers / doctors sometimes face

13 Work in pairs. One month before an annual get-together event for employees and families, your boss asks you and your partner to take over from the person who was organizing it.

Student A: Turn to File 19, page 117. Student B: Turn to File 74, page 128.

14 Tell the class about the solutions you came up with. Which pairs had the best ideas?

Writing: Email – everything's fine

15 Write an email to your boss about the event you discussed in exercise 13. Outline the problems you faced and how you overcame them, and reassure your boss that everything will go smoothly.

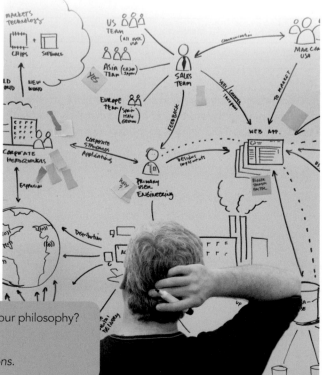

TALKING POINT Which of these sayings best reflects your philosophy?
Every cloud has a silver lining.
Trouble never comes alone.
There are no problems, only solutions.

Listening: What's going on?

1 What different ways of saying 'I don't know' do you know in English?

2 🔊 **1.22** Listen to five conversation extracts. Match each extract to the correct photo.

3 🔊 Listen to the conversations again and complete the sentences in the table.

Ways of saying 'I don't know'
In conversation, we're often asked questions we can't answer accurately or at all. We can signal when that is the case in many different ways.
1 I'm not _____ _____, but I think he's been downgraded.
2 I'm afraid I don't _____ a _____ what he's on about.
3 It's _____ to say, but I _____ it's the feeling of independence it gives you.
4 I haven't _____ faintest _____.
5 Your _____ is as _____ as _____.

4 Work in pairs. Use the audio script on page 141 to work out the meaning of the words and phrases in *italics*. Then turn to File 20 on page 118 to check your answers.

1 Dave seems *pretty low* these days, don't you find?

2 This is a rather *heavy-going* talk, isn't it?

3 *Mind you*, I still have to meet deadlines!

4 But whoever it is, he seems to be *winding* Karlo *up*.

5 *Fingers crossed* it's not a really awful one.

5 🔊 **1.23** Number the lines of this conversation in the correct order. Then listen and check.

_____ Oh, yes? Everything OK with him?

_____ **Are you serious?**

_____ Hi Rachel. I've just had Phil on the phone.

_____ Sure. When my research project comes to an end, things will be simpler.

_____ Well, it's not easy, I mean, not for either of us, but I simply can't go now.

_____ **Wonderful!** He's always wanted to go there. But … erm … how about you?

_____ Yeah. He's off to Berlin.

_____ **You poor thing!** What about later? Is there a possibility …?

_____ You'll never guess … He got the job. He's now regional director!

6 🔊 **1.24** Rachel gives the news about her brother to another friend, Elio. First, try to guess the missing expressions. Then listen and complete the text.

R: *D'you know what? My brother is moving to Berlin soon.*

E: *Philip?* **I can't** [1] _____ _____!

R: *It's true, I'm telling you. He's been promoted to regional director.*

E: **Wow! That's** [2] _____ _____. *And what does his wife say?*

R: *Well, she's happy for him, of course. But unfortunately, she won't be able to go right away.*

E: **That's** [3] _____ _____. *Is it because of the research she's doing?*

R: *That's right, yes. She's got another six months to do. So I guess she'll be in Berlin in December.*

E: [4] _____. *Just in time for the festive season, then.*

7 When we hear good, bad or surprising news, we can react with many different expressions. Complete the table with the expressions from the box. Then discuss your answers.

> Oh, that's awful.   You're joking.   No kidding?   Brilliant.   Splendid!
> Oh dear. I'm sorry.   That's terrible.   You're kidding me.   That's terrific!

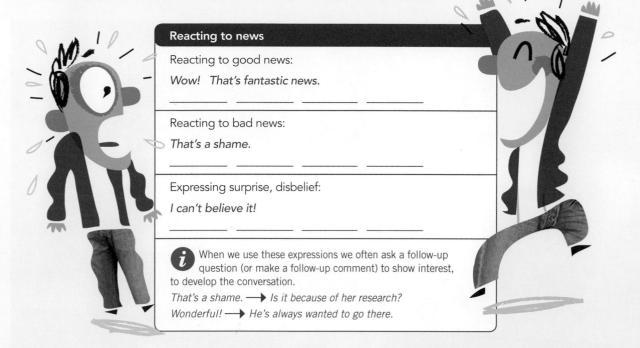

Reacting to news

Reacting to good news:

Wow!   That's fantastic news.

_____   _____   _____   _____

Reacting to bad news:

That's a shame.

_____   _____   _____   _____

Expressing surprise, disbelief:

I can't believe it!

_____   _____   _____   _____

i When we use these expressions we often ask a follow-up question (or make a follow-up comment) to show interest, to develop the conversation.

That's a shame. ⟶ *Is it because of her research?*
Wonderful! ⟶ *He's always wanted to go there.*

8 Add the other expressions in bold from exercise 5 to the table. Then add as any other expressions that you know.

9 Match each conversation starter (1–6) to two responses (a–l).

1 I've just failed my driving test for the fourth time.

2 My brother's getting married.

3 They've put up the price of petrol, too.

4 You know what? The car broke down again this morning.

5 Hey, we've got next Monday off!

6 I just got told off for being late.

a Brilliant! So maybe you'll start thinking about getting a new one at last.

b I can't believe it! Even my husband passed it first time.

c You're kidding me. I thought Ron was a confirmed bachelor.

d Oh, that's awful. Did you have to cancel your appointments, then?

e Seriously? What are you going to do with so much free time?

f Surely that can't be! It went up just a couple of days ago!

g Wonderful. A long weekend is just what I need.

h You poor thing. As if it happened every day.

i You're joking! And what do you get when you work unpaid overtime?

j That's great news. When's the big day, then?

k Terrible! What are they going to think of next?

l Oh, that's a pity. Did the instructor give you any advice?

Speaking: I'm with you

10 Work in pairs. Practise ways of saying 'I don't know' when answering questions you can't answer accurately or at all.

Student A: Turn to File 21, page 118. Student B: Turn to File 77, page 129.

11 Work in pairs. Student A uses the first conversation starter; Student B reacts and asks a follow-up question; A responds. Then A and B change roles, B uses the second conversation starter, etc.

Conversation starters

1 I've decided to quit smoking.

2 I learnt to speak Hungarian in one year.

3 We're not going anywhere this summer.

4 I've got a splitting headache.

5 I've just told the boss I don't like his style.

6 I'm going to Amsterdam for the weekend.

> A: *I've decided to quit smoking.*
> B: *That's terrific! From next year?*
> A: *Oh, give me a break. This time, I really am going to.*

12 Now think of *your own* conversation starters and have more mini-conversations with your partner.

Reminder

Present perfect and past simple page 27 + Grammar reference pages 157–159
Reacting to news page 33

Word focus: Euphemisms

1 Look at the information and discuss the questions.

> ℹ️ A euphemism is an indirect or positive expression used in place of a more direct one, e.g. *challenge* (instead of *problem*); *softness in the economy* (instead of *recession*).

1 What is the purpose of using euphemisms?
2 In what kind of situations is using euphemisms a good idea?
3 Are there particular groups of people who use euphemisms a lot?
4 Are there situations you can think of in which being direct is better?

2 Work in pairs. What do you think the euphemistic expressions in *italics* mean? Discuss with your partner.

1 My brother is *between jobs*.
2 *Low-income* families spend most of their money on food for their children.
3 My uncle's found a great *pre-owned* Mercedes.
4 '*We have to let you go*,' said the manager.
5 Our company is going to *downsize*.
6 The chief executive was *selective* in what he said about the cause of the oil spill.
7 Some public officials may expect *facilitation payments*.
8 Our parent company is currently *generating negative cash flow*.

3 Match the expressions in 2 with their 'plain English' equivalents.

a bribes
b dishonest
c losing money
d poor
e reduce the number of employees
f second-hand
g unemployed
h you're fired

Listening: Talking straight

4 ◢⟩) **1.25** Listen to six people breaking bad news in a way that some people find unclear, too indirect or misleading. Match their statements (1–6) to the responses (a–f).

a You mean, you won't be able to meet the deadline?
b Are you saying that you've failed?
c Does that mean a lot of production workers are going to be made redundant?
d Are you saying that almost half will lose their jobs?
e If I understand correctly, they threaten to go on strike?
f Does that mean some people think he's a liar?

5 ⟩) **1.26** Now listen to the six conversations and check your answers to exercise 4.

6 Work in pairs or small groups. Look at the audio script on page 142 and discuss these questions.

1 Which statements do *you* consider (a) unclear? (b) too indirect? (c) dishonest? Why?

2 What circumstances might motivate Speaker A to express themselves in the way they do?

3 What are your views on Speaker B's responses? What could be the relationship between A and B each time?

7 Work in pairs. Choose four sentences in exercise 2 as openers and have mini-conversations like the ones in the audio script on page 142.

A: We have to let you go.

B: Are you saying that
Does that mean ⎱ *I'm fired?*
You mean, ⎰

Reading: Breaking bad news

8 Discuss these questions.

1 What kind of bad news do employers sometimes have to break to their staff?

2 As an employee, how would you expect management to break unpleasant news to you and your colleagues? For example:

- trying to soften the blow … or talking straight
- via email … or in a staff meeting
- when the first signs of a problem appear … or when the crisis has erupted, etc.

9 Read the article on the right. How do your views compare with those of US employees?

10 Find the words and phrases in the article which mean the same as the following.

1 to make a special extra effort to achieve something

2 made stronger; intensified

3 dealt with

4 surprised by something unexpected

11 Are these statements true (T) or false (F)?

1 The economic downturn seems to have affected the need for open communication.

2 Forty-four per cent of the respondents say their company has downsized.

3 Employees expect to be informed before the problem is at its most acute.

4 The survey proves that it is better for management to soften the blow when breaking bad news to employees.

Speaking: Is that what it means?

12 Work in pairs. Practise asking probing questions when receiving bad news. Student A: Turn to File 23, page 118. Student B: Turn to File 80, page 130.

13 Act out the conversation you enjoyed most. Students listening should note and then comment on the euphemisms that were used, and the kind of challenging questions that were asked.

Openness pays off

According to a recent survey in the USA, employees are twice as likely to go the extra mile for their company and almost four times as likely to recommend it to others if they are satisfied with the ways in which it communicates difficult decisions.

The need for open and honest communication appears to have been heightened by the recession. According to the study, 44 per cent of workers say their company has taken some form of action in response to the current economic situation, such as downsizing or other types of cutbacks. Among these, almost half (49 per cent) say their employers handled the communication extremely well or very well.

Employees particularly welcome the following:

- thorough explanations of actions taken and the reasons behind them
- being kept informed of ongoing decisions and the reasons for them as the economy continues to be unstable
- being provided with early indications of future difficult decisions so employees are not caught off-guard
- open and honest communication: bad news should be given clearly and truthfully
- being regularly updated through frequent communication

4

A Countable and uncountable nouns
B The price of happiness
C Articles overview
D Communication strategies Handling meetings
E Interaction Making decisions

A better world

Countable and uncountable nouns

Reading: The power of kindness

1 Has anybody been kind to you recently? If so, was it someone you know or a stranger? How did you feel as a result?

2 Look at the logo for an organization called the Kindness Offensive. What do you think this organization does?

3 Read the article about the Kindness Offensive and answer the questions.

1 What did David and his friends do to grant the first two wishes?

2 What guidelines does the group have?

3 What medical term does David compare kindness to? Why?

4 What are the benefits for a person who helps others?

4 Complete these sentences with words from the article.

1 Hershey, Mars and Cadbury are all _____ manufacturers.

2 Some organizations have a _____ which sets out the aims and regulations that it will operate by.

3 If people were more thoughtful, the world would be a better _____.

4 Regular exercise can benefit your general _____ as well as your health.

5 Some people find that listening to relaxing music can lift their _____.

David Goodfellow and his friends wanted to make a positive impact on the world. As an experiment, they stopped passers-by and asked them, 'What can we do to help you?' At first **people** were suspicious, but when they realized that the offer was serious, they started making requests. One person asked for **chocolate** for their grandma and a little girl wanted a special birthday **treat**. The friends phoned companies and asked them to donate items to see how many of the wishes they could fulfil. A confectionery manufacturer agreed to send chocolates to the grandmother. The Russian State Circus gave the little girl tickets to see their show on her birthday.

It was such a success that David founded the Kindness Offensive. The organization's constitution states that its activities should be helpful, harmless and free. They regularly carry out hundreds of random acts of kindness, helping strangers and giving away a variety of **goods** – anything from **food** to toys and gadgets. David says, 'We can all make the world a better place by doing little things like helping someone with directions or picking up their shopping. And **kindness** is like a virus – it's catching. When you start doing good for others, it makes them want to do the same.'

Recent **research** suggests that doing acts of kindness can also benefit our **health** and well-being. In a **study** in the USA, 95 per cent of people said that they felt good when they helped someone, while 21 per cent said that they felt euphoric. Participating in an **activity** which helped others, such as volunteering, made people feel less stressed. When we're kind, it lifts our spirits and we feel more positive and optimistic.

Grammar: Countable and uncountable nouns

5 Look at the words in bold in the article and find examples of the following.

Countable and uncountable nouns

1 four countable nouns: _____ _____ _____ _____

2 three uncountable nouns: _____ _____ _____

3 two nouns that can be both countable and uncountable: _____ _____

4 one plural uncountable noun: _____

>> For more information on countable and uncountable nouns, see page 171.

6 Some nouns have both countable and uncountable uses, and the meaning may sometimes change. Complete these sentences with the words in the box. Add *a/an* where necessary.

business   coffee   experience   room

1 He's only just left college. I don't think he has enough _____ for this job.

2 Some scientists now say that _____ is good for you – even though it contains caffeine.

3 We do _____ with a number of Italian companies.

4 Do you think there's _____ to put another desk in this office?

5 Well, I'm glad that meeting's over. Do you fancy _____?

6 The house is in a good location but all five _____ are very small.

7 I got stuck in an elevator for two hours. It's _____ I'd rather forget.

8 They're considering starting _____ to sell their textile designs on the web.

7 Uncountable nouns can fall into categories. Write the nouns in the box in the table. Add more nouns to each category.

air   dancing   equipment   fog   golf   history   linguistics
machinery   sugar   sunshine

Groups of similar objects:	furniture transport
Fields of study:	psychology politics
Liquids, metals, gases, powders and granules:	petrol gold
Recreational activities:	jogging tennis
Weather words:	rain snow

Speaking: A helping hand

8 The Smile Project is a group that tries to help the local community by carrying out practical acts of kindness such as giving out umbrellas on a rainy day. Work in pairs or small groups and do the following.

1 It's an unusually hot day. Take one minute to brainstorm things that the Smile Project could give away to help elderly people. Evaluate which three ideas are best.

2 Think of ideas to raise the spirits of people who are in the local hospital. Evaluate which three are best.

9 Join with another pair or group. Present your best three ideas for each of the scenarios in exercise 8. When all the ideas have been presented, choose one for each scenario to put forward to the Smile Project.

TALKING POINT
- How do you think society could encourage people to be kind?
- Apart from kindness, what other virtues do you think are important for society?

Word focus: *time* and *money*

1 Some people think that 'time is money'. What do you think the expression means? How is this similar or different from attitudes in your country?

2 Which of these verbs can be used with:

a money **b** time **c** both money and time?

earn save invest make waste spend lose borrow have lend raise collect get receive donate give pay back owe take allocate refund repay deposit run out of can't spare any be worth a lot of

3 Choose the best option to complete these sentences.

1 At the meeting, there was some disagreement about the amount of time and money to *allocate / invest / raise* to each project.

2 The laptop stopped working after a week so he asked the store to *repay / pay back / refund* his money.

3 If we get the equipment for the presentation ready now, it will *take / save / spend* time tomorrow.

4 It can be difficult to persuade banks to *lend / borrow / invest* money to entrepreneurs when they start a new business.

5 The finance director has meetings scheduled all afternoon, so I'm afraid he *has run out of / worth a lot of / can't spare any* time to discuss your report until tomorrow.

6 The volunteers knocked on doors to *collect / donate / deposit* money for charity.

7 The report suggests than some employees *receive / waste / make* a lot of time on the internet.

8 Consumer groups report that some banks still *owe / earn / get* investors millions of pounds in unpaid interest.

Listening: Happy days

4 🔊 **1.27** Listen to a couple describing their experience of buying something and answer the questions.

1 What did they buy?

2 Did they spend much time and money on it? How do you know?

3 What did they decide to do with it?

5 🔊 Look at the pictures. Then listen again. What three expressions describe the pictures?

Word focus: Metaphors – money, water and happiness

6 We often speak about money as if it is water. <u>Underline</u> the water metaphors in these sentences. Then match them to the meanings (a–e).

1 The boat was a drain on our finances.
2 We had to pour money into repairs.
3 We weren't sure whether we could stay afloat.
4 We wondered if the bank would pull the plug on our loans.
5 We felt like we were drowning in debt.
6 Now we've sold the boat, we're keeping our heads above water again.
7 We splashed out and bought it.

a spend a large amount of money (x2)
b be able to pay the bills (x2)
c being unable to pay the bills
d use up a lot of money
e remove the resources that enable survival

7 Look at some more metaphors. What idea connects them?

1 It was getting us down.
2 He was feeling a bit low.
3 It cheered me up.
4 Things are looking up.
5 It lifted everyone's spirits.
6 She looked down in the mouth.

Speaking: Can we buy happiness?

8 Work in pairs. Roleplay a conversation between two friends discussing a business idea that could change their lives. Try to use some metaphors in your conversation.
Student A: Turn to File 25, page 118.
Student B: Look at the information below.

Your friend has a business idea that they want you to invest in. Listen to their ideas and then raise any concerns that you have. Consider the following factors:

- What problems with money could occur?
- How is your partner likely to feel if the project succeeds / fails?

Decide whether to invest and explain to your partner how you reached your decision.

9 Write down five things that you think are likely to increase a person's happiness. Now write down five of the most expensive things that a person is likely to pay for during their life.

Happiness	Most expensive
Falling in love	*A wedding*

10 Work in pairs. Compare your lists. Combine your ideas and agree on the top three items on the 'happiness' list and on the 'most expensive' list. Could any of the items be included on both lists?

11 Which list – 'happiness' or 'most expensive' – do you think these items would appear on for most people?

Taking a year out to travel or study

A huge TV and sound system for a home cinema

A holiday apartment near the sea

Starting a family

Upgrades to business class on international flights

TALKING POINT   What do you think most people would choose if they were offered the choice between more money or more time to do what they wanted?

Reading: Finance a project

1 Someone you know wants to start up a business in your area selling sports equipment and goods. What resources do you think the company will need to get started? How could they raise enough money to start the business?

2 Read the article about Kickstarter and answer the questions.

1 What disadvantages does it mention about raising money from a bank or venture capitalist?

2 What new funding opportunity does the internet make possible?

3 How does Kickstarter work?

4 What must a project do to get funded?

KICKSTARTER

Putting the fun into funding

Do you have a creative business idea but don't know how to find the money to make it happen? Most investors, including banks and venture capitalists, will usually charge high interest for a loan or want a large percentage of any future profits your idea may earn. Now there is an unusual way to raise funds. **Kickstarter** is an organization that uses the **internet** to help people to finance creative projects and get them off the ground through what is called 'crowdfunding' – the use of the web to get a group of individuals to finance a project.

Individuals pitch an idea on Kickstarter's website and explain how much money they need. They also choose a **deadline** for raising the **money** (between one and ninety days). As an incentive, they list **rewards** they will give to **backers**, for example, an artistic project might offer people who give $10 a postcard, $100 a signed print and $500 a **painting**. Visitors to the site can read information about the projects and might then decide to pledge **money** to one of the entrepreneurs if they like the idea.

This isn't an investment – people give money because they think the project is a good idea or because it's **fun**. They don't want a share of the profits. This sounds like free money, so what's the catch? Well, the project only gets funded if it raises all the money it needs by the **deadline**. Projects that fail to reach their goal by the agreed date don't get any money at all.

Grammar: Articles overview

3 Match the rules in the table below to the words in bold in the article. Some of the words go with more than one rule.

Articles
1 The definite article *the* is used for something specific or when there's only one of something.
2 The indefinite article *a/an* is used for things in general or when there is more than one of something.
3 Articles are not usually used: 　**a** with proper nouns (e.g. names) 　**b** for plural people and uncountable things described in general terms 　**c** with abstract nouns (e.g. *beauty*).
>> For more information on articles, see page 172.

4 Look at the examples again and answer these questions.

1 Why is *deadline* used with both the indefinite article and the definite article?

2 Why is *money* used both with the definite article and with no article?

5 Judith is an entrepreneur who wants backers for her idea. Read the information about her and complete the text with *a, an, the* or *no article* 'Ø'.

Hi, there, I'm Judith and I'm [1]_____ events organizer. I'm looking for [2]_____ investment of $6,000 to start my business. I often buy [3]_____ paper cups and plates so I can use them for parties that I organize at work, and they get thrown away afterwards. I know that some of these things can be recycled, but it still seems like [4]_____ waste of resources. So I came up with my idea – the Munch plate. You put your food on it, eat it and when you have finished, you can eat [5]_____ plate. Yes, that's right, these plates are edible. They are made from [6]_____ rice paper and they taste great. This is [7]_____ really exciting project as it eliminates [8]_____ waste. It's ecological and it also means that you could have something to eat on [9]_____ way home from a party. Believe me, [10]_____ eating has never been more fun! I'll use [11]_____ money you pledge to buy equipment and to market my idea.

Judith's target: $6,000 in 60 days.

Pledge $10 and I'll send you a sample plate.

Pledge $100 and I'll send you ten plates and [12]_____ serving bowl.

Pledge $500 and I'll organize a buffet for you and three guests … eating from my edible plates, of course!

---

6 Work in pairs. Discuss the pros and cons of Judith's idea. Would you back the project, and if so, how much would you pledge?

Speaking: Developing ideas

7 Read the comments below where people describe things that they need. Work in pairs or small groups and choose one of the comments. Brainstorm ideas for a product or service that might solve the problem.

> I like going to music festivals but it's so difficult to recharge mobile phones and gadgets when there is no electricity.

> I travel a lot and find it frustrating that travel guidebooks and websites usually have lots of general information. My fellow travellers and I would love to find a way to get information for trips that fit individual personal interests and schedules – without spending hours on research.

> I have a terrible memory and I often embarrass myself at parties and meetings because I forget people's names. Surely I'm not the only person this happens to?

> So many people need to take language exams that I'm surprised there aren't more useful products and services to help them to revise.

8 Choose one of your ideas and develop it.

- Discuss what you need to get your idea started.
- What will you call your product / service / company?
- How much money will you ask for?
- What is your deadline for raising the amount? (1–90 days)
- What rewards will you offer backers for $10, $100 and $500 pledges?

Writing: A web profile

9 Write a profile about your idea for the Kickstarter website. Include information about any rewards or incentives that you are offering.

TALKING POINT   Which of the following sources is most suitable for funding scientific or artistic projects?
big business   the general public   the government   philanthropists

Listening: What workers want

1 Work in pairs or small groups. Look at these aspects of work and discuss how they can contribute to an employee's satisfaction or dissatisfaction in the workplace.

working hours colleagues working environment rewards travel

2 Look at this list of some of the things that employees value in a job. Rank the ideas in the order that you think is most important (1 is most important, 5 is least important).

_____ Opportunity to develop

_____ Flexible working hours

_____ Recognition

_____ The opportunity to contribute ideas

_____ Independence and autonomy

3 How important are the following perks? Rate them from 1 (unimportant) to 5 (very important). Compare your opinions with a partner. What other perks can make a job more enjoyable?

a	the opportunity to travel to other countries	1	2	3	4	5
b	a desk near the window or a pleasant place in the office	1	2	3	4	5
c	free membership of the company gym	1	2	3	4	5
d	use of a company car or subsidized travel on public transport	1	2	3	4	5
e	discounts on company products or services	1	2	3	4	5
f	health and dental insurance	1	2	3	4	5
g	option to take a sabbatical	1	2	3	4	5

4))) **1.28** Listen to an extract from a meeting and answer the questions.

1 What is the aim of the meeting?

2 What three agenda points are mentioned?

3 What action points are mentioned?

4 What was last year's reward to staff?

5 Does the chairperson handle things effectively?

5 ♦)) Complete the examples in the table. Then listen again to check.

Handling meetings	
Asking for contributions:	Any ideas how we can make our staff feel appreciated? *1 Mila, would you like to _____ your _____ on this?*
Keeping to the point:	Let's look at the first point, which is how to make staff feel valued. *2 _____ to _____ you, we're looking at non-monetary rewards.*
Dealing with interruptions:	Mila, would you like to finish your point? *3 We'll get _____ to that in a _____, Janine.*
Suggesting action:	Would you be willing to look into the practicalities of flexible working hours, Mila? *4 Let's _____ another meeting for next Thursday to _____ up ideas.*
Moving on:	Now, moving on to the next point. *5 I think that just about _____ everything on that _____.*
Keeping time:	We don't have a lot of time, so it would be helpful if we could stick to the agenda. *6 Let's try to _____ through the next point _____.*

6 Work in pairs. Discuss these questions.

1 What would you suggest for this year's gift?
2 Can you think of any disadvantages to monetary rewards?
3 Is it better to reward staff with improvements to their working life (such as flexible working) or with gifts / money?

Speaking: Plan a reward

7 Work in small groups. The board of directors want to show their appreciation to three members of staff in cases 1–3 who have performed well, but they don't want to award a cash bonus.

- Have a meeting to discuss the first case.
- Choose one of your group to lead the meeting.
- Decide on an appropriate way to thank the member of staff. You can choose a reward that will help the person professionally or give them a perk that will make their working life more pleasant.
- Discuss at least two options.
- The meeting should take no more than five minutes.
- Move on to the next meeting and change the leader of the meeting.

8 Compare your ideas with another group. Describe the key factors that influenced your choices.

Case 1

Josephine Cotton: Has worked for the company for five years.

She has been doing unpaid work mentoring junior members of staff for the last year.

She is keen to change to flexible working hours, but this has not been possible due to pressure of work, and because there are three other members of staff who are likely to make the same request if we agree. Josephine has also indicated interest in taking a course in management skills, but there are two other people in the office who are scheduled to take the course first.

Case 2

Per Lundson: Has worked for the company for seven years.

He thought of a new system for organizing payments which saved the company more than £50,000.

He has expressed interest in doing a part-time MBA, but the request to fund the qualification was recently turned down. He has also expressed an interest in working as part of the financial team, but a suitable position has not yet become available.

Case 3

David Elliot: Has worked for the company for two years.

He has worked weekends and evenings for a long period to complete a presentation which was instrumental in winning a major new contract.

He has shown interest in learning about operations in the Moscow branch. He has also made a number of requests to move to a single office (at present he shares with two other members of his team), but his manager has concerns that this might cause problems with more senior members of his department who currently share an office.

Reminder

Countable and uncountable nouns page 37 + Grammar reference page 171
Articles overview page 40 + Grammar reference page 172
Handling meetings page 43

Reading: A solvable problem?

1 Choose two groups that you think society should help more. Tell your partner why you chose these groups.

children   the elderly   the homeless   single-parent families
the unemployed   another

2 Read the article about a social enterprise project and answer the questions.

1 What is the main effect of children being hungry in class?

2 How did Carmel finance the second stage of the project?

3 What makes a social enterprise different from a traditional charity?

4 What three things does Carmel ask organizations to care about as much as profit?

3 Find a word or phrase in the article that has a similar meaning to the following.

1 the characteristic of arriving somewhere on time

2 work online from home rather than in an office

3 money given to a charity or organization

4 money that is made by a company or organization

5 a prize given to recognize an achievement

6 leading by example and doing what you tell others to do

4 Can you think of any other ways in which Carmel could have approached the problem?

Magic Breakfast: a social enterprise project

While writing her book, *Change Activist*, Carmel McConnell was shocked to discover that in the UK many children are going to school without breakfast. Without food, it makes it difficult for the children to concentrate in class because they are too hungry to learn. Wanting to help, Carmel began to deliver food to five local schools in London, including products such as bread, tea and juice, and other breakfast items. Head teachers soon noticed an improvement in the children's attendance, punctuality and behaviour.

As a next step, Carmel took a loan out on her house and used some of the money from her book to finance a project she called 'Magic Breakfast'. Today, Magic Breakfast has a staff of three, who work virtually and arrange for food to be delivered to 210 schools, feeding over 6000 children in the UK every morning. The organization has also developed successful partnerships with companies such as Tropicana and Quaker Oats, which supply food and drink to the scheme.

Magic Breakfast may sound as though it is simply a charitable organization, but it is also a social enterprise. This is because of the way that it is funded. Although it is assisted by volunteers and donations, Magic Breakfast is largely financed by its sister organization Magic Outcomes, which runs community-based development and leadership training programmes for companies. The revenues from Magic Outcomes are then used to help run Magic Breakfast.

The project has won a number of awards and helped hundreds of schools, but there's more work to do. An estimated 700,000 children in the UK still go to school hungry. Asked what had inspired her to set up Magic Breakfast, Carmel said that was 'the genuine belief that this is a solvable problem'. She pointed out that while writing *Change Activist*, she was asking people to take action in line with their values, and encouraging businesses to care about more than just profit by advising them to consider the well-being of the environment, their employees and the local community. 'I thought, I'm talking the talk, what about walking the walk,' she said.

magic breakfast
fuel for learning

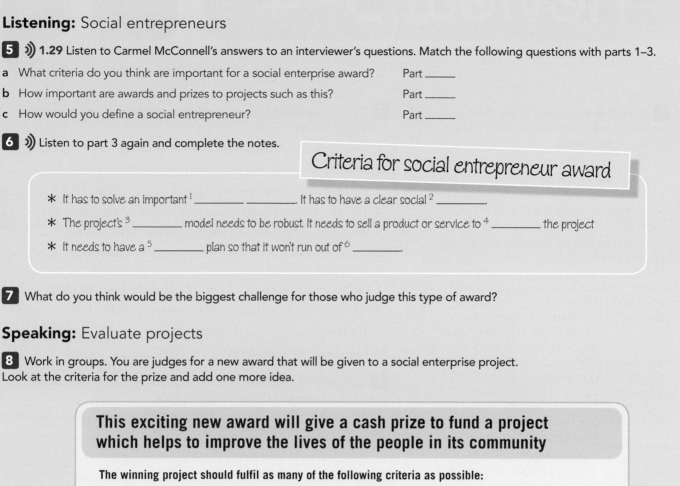

Listening: Social entrepreneurs

5))) **1.29** Listen to Carmel McConnell's answers to an interviewer's questions. Match the following questions with parts 1–3.

a What criteria do you think are important for a social enterprise award?   Part _____

b How important are awards and prizes to projects such as this?   Part _____

c How would you define a social entrepreneur?   Part _____

6))) Listen to part 3 again and complete the notes.

Criteria for social entrepreneur award

* It has to solve an important [1] _____ _____. It has to have a clear social [2] _____

* The project's [3] _____ model needs to be robust. It needs to sell a product or service to [4] _____ the project

* It needs to have a [5] _____ plan so that it won't run out of [6] _____.

7 What do you think would be the biggest challenge for those who judge this type of award?

Speaking: Evaluate projects

8 Work in groups. You are judges for a new award that will be given to a social enterprise project. Look at the criteria for the prize and add one more idea.

This exciting new award will give a cash prize to fund a project which helps to improve the lives of the people in its community

The winning project should fulfil as many of the following criteria as possible:

- it aims to help solve a social or environmental problem
- it includes commercial ideas to fund the project's activities
- it has both short-term and long-term objectives
- it encourages communities to work together
- it includes an educational aspect
- _____

9 Work in groups. Read the information about a finalist for the award. Give the project ten points for each of the criteria above (including your own) that it fulfils.

Group A: Look at Project 1 below. Group B: Look at Project 2 in File 24 on page 118.

PROJECT 1: MOBILITY CENTRE

This project is based in India and helps people who have problems walking. It works with local hospitals to make sure that people with mobility problems are getting medical treatment. The hospitals are provided with the best medical equipment available, and treatment for poorer patients is subsidized by the fees paid by richer patients. Individuals are then given vocational training and support to help them become as independent as possible. Volunteers from the local community visit and provide necessities while the patient recovers in hospital. Local companies are encouraged to employ people with disabilities from the project. The project hopes to set up centres in other areas of India in the future in order to inspire new ways to treat, educate and employ people with disabilities.

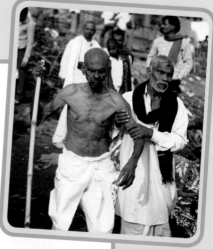

10 Join with another group. Summarize information about your project. Say how many points you awarded, where you awarded them and why.

11 Now decide which project to award the prize to. Present your ideas to the class and explain your reasons for choosing the project. What were your reasons for not choosing the other project?

1 Complete this email. Put the verbs in brackets in the correct tense: either present perfect or past simple.

I'm concerned about our staff's growing lack of enthusiasm for the professional development courses we ¹_____ (begin) to run two years ago.

In the first six months, three out of the four courses on offer ²_____ (be) oversubscribed and attendance ³_____ (be) excellent overall. However, since January this year, attendance figures ⁴_____ (drop) at an alarming rate. Indeed, last month nobody ⁵_____ (turn up) for Mr Thorsen's media skills workshops, and I regret to have to inform you that now he ⁶_____ (decide) to cancel the rest of his programme. This shows that attendance ⁷_____ (become) a serious problem, and we must urgently find out what the causes are. Why ⁸_____ motivation _____ (decrease) so much?

I ⁹_____ (mention) this to Jenny Fruik at a Megatrax meeting a couple of weeks ago, and she ¹⁰_____ (suggest) that we should try and involve our employees more when we discuss what topics to include. Apparently, since Megatrax ¹¹_____ (choose) to let staff design the whole programme themselves, their workshops ¹²_____ (be) a continuing success.

Maybe that's the way to go. What do you think?

2 Complete this text with *a/an* or *the*. Write 'Ø' if no article is necessary.

¹_____ group of ²_____ climbing enthusiasts from our department have decided to take ³_____ part in the Four Peaks Challenge next year. Their task is to climb ⁴_____ four highest peaks in each of the four provinces of Ireland in just 48 hours. This is ⁵_____ unique event which requires ⁶_____ good level of ⁷_____ fitness and which includes ⁸_____ helicopter ride from Mweelrea in County Mayo to Slieve Donard in County Down. They will be training for six months before ⁹_____ event, which should give them ¹⁰_____ opportunity to brush up on their skills and gain more experience.

It's ¹¹_____ big commitment: they have to raise ¹²_____ minimum of €2,000. ¹³_____ money will go to ¹⁴_____ local charity which helps ¹⁵_____ homeless.

3 Decide whether the nouns in bold are countable [C] or uncountable [U] in these sentences.

1 After considerable **discussion**, they finally agreed to our proposal. _____

2 We had a very interesting **discussion** about the future of the Eurozone. _____

3 Please read the **agreement** and sign it. _____

4 There is widespread **agreement** on the need for economic reform. _____

5 What was your first **experience** of living with other people? _____

6 The advice in our booklet reflects the practical **experience** we have gained. _____

7 On this course, students will learn about all aspects of **business**. _____

8 Their firm began as a small family **business** in the late 1980s. _____

9 The **lamb** was playing in the field. _____

10 Fortunately, there was **lamb** on the menu. _____

4 Complete these sentences with the words in the box. Add *a/an* or the plural *-s* with countable nouns as appropriate.

> hope   work   life   space

1 _____ can be difficult when you are unemployed.

2 Geoff is hoping to find _____ as a human rights lawyer.

3 Our library has recently purchased the collected _____ of Dante Alighieri.

4 Remember to leave _____ between each paragraph when you write an email.

5 Ricardo told his brother all his secret _____ and fears.

6 The meeting room isn't huge – there's _____ for about four tables and twelve chairs.

7 They are dreaming of living _____ of leisure on some exotic island.

8 When Yaling first arrived in Sydney, she was full of _____ for the future.

5 Complete each conversation with a discourse marker from the box. Use each marker twice.

> like   I mean   well

1 **A:** What do you think of their proposal?

   B: I'll never agree to it. _____, it's unacceptable, isn't it?

2 **A:** How expensive were the restaurants?

   B: Well, on the seafront lunch was, _____, €15 euros a head.

3 **A:** I hear you went skiing in Slovakia, _____ in Slovenia last winter.

   B: Yeah, that's right. We spent ten days in the Julian Alps.

4 **A:** I suppose Anton was overjoyed with his present?

   B: _____, as a matter of fact he didn't even say *Thank you*.

5 **A:** Will you be in on Sunday evening?

   B: _____, it depends.

6 **A:** How did Claire react to the news?

   B: Mm, she seemed, _____, astonished.

6 Match each sentence 1–8 to a suitable response a–h.

1 I'm afraid we haven't got a lot of time left.

2 Why don't we give our customers the opportunity to shop online?

3 I feel like I'm drowning in debt.

4 The situation is pretty scary, but we're keeping our heads above water.

5 Don't you think the Olympics will be a drain on our economy?

6 Do you know what? I'm off to Kuala Lumpur for a month on the 15th!

7 Is there going to be a staff party this year?

8 Rita seems to be feeling a bit low these days. What's up?

a Your guess is as good as mine. We might get a pay cut instead.

b You're going to Malaysia? Wow! I can't believe it!

c That's good to hear. But do let me know if there's anything I can do to help.

d Oh dear. I'm sorry. Couldn't Aunt Philomena help you get back in the black?

e I'm afraid I haven't got a clue. Those things are just beyond me.

f OK. Let's try to get through the next point quickly, then.

g I haven't the faintest idea. Maybe she's worried about her job.

h We're going to cover e-business later in the meeting, Sophia.

7 Complete these sentences with the correct form of the verbs in the box.

> allocate be deposit donate invest raise
> refund waste

1 A friend advised us to sell our business and _____ all the money in the bank.

2 If you feel like helping out, why don't you try to _____ funds for a good cause?

3 Let's not _____ time discussing problems we know we can't solve anyway.

4 The orchestra has _____ the proceeds of the concert to the famine victims.

5 Their microblogging service _____ worth $1bn a year ago.

6 Their website looks great. It's clear they've _____ a lot of time and energy in it.

7 We guarantee to _____ your money if you are not entirely satisfied with our products.

8 When you take the test, you should _____ the same amount of time to each question.

8 Complete each pair of sentences with the same word.

1 a Don't _____ on that I told you. It's supposed to be confidential.

b Our last gig was a disaster. The worst feeling is having _____ our fans down.

2 a The meeting was very productive and went _____ without a hitch.

b Alex is exhausted and thinking of taking a few weeks _____ work.

3 a We can arrange another meeting next week to firm _____ ideas.

b At last things are looking _____. A lot of people are enquiring about our new product.

4 a I'm afraid we're running _____ of time, so let's move on to the last item on the agenda.

b Some people are beginning to wonder if there is a way _____ of the deepening economic crisis.

5 a Working well as a team is the key _____ success.

b Last year, financial institutions lent over $30 billion _____ new businesses.

6 a The first point we need to discuss is how to _____ staff feel valued.

b I don't want to ask for all sorts of favours and _____ a nuisance of myself.

7 a It's not expensive, but bear in _____ that the price does not include flights.

b Lisa really looks very young in this photo. _____ you, it was probably taken over a decade ago.

8 a Oh, give me a _____, will you? You've already asked me ten times, and the answer is no, N–O.

b It's never easy to _____ bad news to a friend or relative.

9 Match the words according to how the letters in bold are pronounced.

1	w**a**nted	**a**	h**a**ppiness
2	res**ea**rch	**b**	del**ay**
3	**i**ncome	**c**	f**u**rniture
4	fr**a**ntic	**d**	**i**dentify
5	d**i**lemma	**e**	**ow**ned
6	b**u**siness	**f**	redundancy
7	bl**a**me	**g**	s**o**lution
8	afl**oa**t	**h**	s**o**lve

5

A Comparison and contrast
B Making generalizations
C Time management
D **Communication strategies** Being assertive
E **Interaction** Weighing alternatives

The human factor

Comparison and contrast

Reading: Choosing who you work with

1 Work in pairs or in small groups. Tell each other who you think people generally turn to at work when they need help to complete a difficult task.

I think people generally choose …

a the colleague sitting nearest to them.

b someone who has expert knowledge, even if they don't particularly like that person.

c one of their superiors, so that person will see how dedicated they are.

d someone they're sure won't tell anyone that they asked for help.

e someone who is very friendly, even if that person doesn't know a lot about their area.

2 Read the article and answer the questions.

1 To what extent do your guesses in exercise 1 correspond to the research findings?

2 Do you agree with what the article says about likability and competence?

3 Tick (✓) the ideas that are mentioned in the article.

1 Our choice of work partners is motivated by more than two factors.

2 Lovable stars are popular because of their personal feelings.

3 Evaluations of competence are not as important as personal feelings when we choose work partners.

4 People don't want to work with colleagues they deeply dislike, whether competent or not.

5 If you want other people to enjoy working with you, make sure you gain a little extra expertise.

COMPETENT IDIOT AND LOVABLE FOOLS

When given the choice of whom to work with, people will pick one person over another for any number of reasons. For example, if they wish to become more interesting in the eyes of their colleagues, they might decide to associate with a star performer, or if they hope to see their own career develop more quickly, they might want to spend time with someone higher in the hierarchy.

But, according to recent research, competence and likability are considerably more important than any other criteria. Obviously, these two criteria matter, but what is far less obvious is *how much* they matter. Competence and likability combine to produce four types of people: the competent idiot, whose knowledge might be ten times as broad as anyone else's, but who is unpleasant to work with; the lovable fool, who clearly doesn't know as much as the others but is a delight to have around; the lovable star, who's both one of the smartest and most likable members of staff; and the incompetent idiot, who doesn't need a definition.

The research shows that everybody wants to work with the lovable star, and nobody wants to work with the incompetent idiot. Things get a lot more interesting, though, when people face the choice between competent idiots and lovable fools. The study reveals that personal feelings play a much more decisive role in forming work relationships (i.e. not friendships at work but job-oriented relationships) than is commonly recognized. In fact, personal feelings are even more important than evaluations of competence. If someone is strongly disliked, it's almost irrelevant whether or not they are competent – people won't want to work with them anyway. By contrast, the more likable someone is, the more their colleagues are likely to look for every little bit of competence they have to offer.

Generally speaking, a little extra likability goes a longer way than a little extra competence in making someone desirable to work with.

Grammar: Comparison and contrast

4 Complete the examples from the article and read the notes.

Large and small differences

Competence and likability are ¹_____ _____
important _____ any other criteria.

These two criteria matter, but what is ²_____ _____
obvious is how much they matter.

Things get ³_____ _____ _____ *interesting when
people face the choice …*

For large differences, we use *much / a lot / considerably /
far* before the comparative.

For small differences, we use *a bit / a little / slightly*.

---

the …, the …

The more ⁴_____ *someone is,* _____ _____
*their colleagues are likely to look for every little bit of
competence they have to offer.*

We use this form to say that two changes happen together.

… times as … as …

The competent idiot, whose knowledge might be
⁵_____ _____ _____ *broad _____ anyone
else's …*

In comparisons with *times*, we generally use *as … as*, not
~~more … than~~.

> ⚠ '2x' is said as *twice: Jim's office is twice as big as mine.*
> In comparisons with *twice*, we always use *as … as*.

**>> For more information on comparative and
superlative forms, see pages 173–174.**

---

5 Go through the article again and <u>underline</u> the comparative forms not included in exercise 4.

6 Use the information in the first sentence to complete the second one with a suitable comparative or superlative.

1 Your office manager isn't as competent as ours – far from it.

Our office manager _____ considerably _____
_____ _____ yours.

2 I feel less and less confident every time I make mistakes.

_____ more mistakes I make, _____ _____
confident I feel.

3 The registration fee last year was 200 euros, compared to 70 euros in 2005.

Last year's registration fee was almost three _____
_____ high _____ in 2005.

4 I worked less on Wednesday than on Monday.

I didn't _____ _____ much on Wednesday
_____ on Monday.

5 No one in our department is as helpful as Paola.

Paola is _____ most _____ person in our
department.

6 I have rarely worked with a more likable colleague.

He is one of _____ _____ _____ colleagues I've
ever worked with.

Speaking: Working together

7 Study the background information in File 26, page 119. Why does Avatec need to hire consultants? What do the four examples show?

8 Work in pairs. Student A: Turn to File 85, page 131. Student B: Turn to File 97, page 134.

TALKING POINT In your country, what qualities do people generally value most in a work colleague?

Reading: Cultural values

1 What key cultural information do foreign business people need to know about your country?

Consider for example the following categories:

greeting people   business meetings   communication styles   gift giving   dining etiquette

2 Work in pairs or in small groups. Read these extracts from three country profiles and discuss which country you think each extract might be about.

As in many other cultures, people prefer to do business with those they know and trust, so they generally like to spend time building a personal relationship.

They do not need as much personal space as many other cultures and tend to stand relatively close to you while chatting or talking business.

As a foreigner, you will be expected to be punctual for meetings. However, do not expect all of them to arrive on time.

By and large, people respect age, which is considered a sign of wisdom. Therefore, make sure you greet the most senior members of the group first.

Most people in this culture are very individualistic. As a rule, their thought process is very methodical, and they like to examine each aspect of a project in great detail. This process can often take a long time but, once the planning is over, generally speaking a project moves very swiftly. Deadlines are expected to be met.

For the most part, people do not like surprises, so abrupt changes in business transactions are not usually welcome.

On the whole, this is a very egalitarian society where the status of women, both in business and in society, has improved dramatically over the last two decades.

In this culture, a great deal of communication takes place over lunches and dinners, which are a crucial part of business life. Remember that dinner is often served after 9:00 p.m., so it might be a good idea to have a nap in the afternoon.

During meetings and negotiations, people sometimes tend to express their ideas at the same time or interrupt each other when they are very involved in the conversation.

3 Check your ideas in File 72, page 128. Any surprises?

4 The country profiles contain generalizations. Do they overgeneralize and oversimplify? If you have had direct experience of any of the three cultures mentioned in exercise 2, which statements would you confirm? Which ones would you refute?

5 Look at the three country profiles again. Which statements also apply to your own *business* culture?

Word focus: Generalizations

6 Look at the profiles in exercise 2 again. <u>Underline</u> the expressions we can use to limit the generalizations we make.

They <u>generally</u> like to spend time. (Instead of *They like to spend time.*)

7 Use the phrases below to make some generalizations about some other groups of people. Choose groups from the list in the box. Write five sentences.

> business people   teenagers   footballers   accountants
> police officers   politicians   nurses   teachers   American people
> British people   men   women

Business people generally appreciate reliable and efficient service.
Most teenagers enjoy having their own space and privacy.
The majority of star footballers earn a small fortune.

(Business people)	generally often tend to are (more / less) likely to are (more / less) inclined to		like … want … prefer … enjoy … appreciate … dislike …
The majority of Most For the most part, Generally speaking, Roughly speaking, On the whole, By and large, As a rule,	(business people)		
…	is probably seems to be	important to	(business people).

> ⚠ Use *most of* before nouns that have a determiner (e.g. *the, my, these, those*):
> *Most of the people we spoke to said …*
> When there is no determiner, don't use *of*:
> *Most people …* NOT ~~Most of people …~~

8 Work in pairs or groups. Read your sentences to one another. Do you agree with them? Are the generalizations fair? Why?/Why not?

Speaking: Culture quiz

9 Work in pairs. Look at the statements about British culture below and tick (✓) them if you think they are true or put a cross (✗) if you think they are false. Whenever you can, make brief notes about the evidence you have to support your answer.

Some facts and generalizations about British culture

1 Privacy is very important to the English, so asking personal questions should be avoided.

2 If you're invited to someone's home, you should try and arrive at least 15 minutes before the arranged time.

3 After a meeting or a teleconference, it is usual to receive a summary of what was decided and the next steps to be taken.

4 Gift giving is not part of the business culture.

5 British people tend to make their own abilities or achievements seem unimportant.

6 On average, people spend over two hours per day watching TV.

7 A large number of university students are heavily in debt by the time they graduate.

8 About half of households in the UK had internet access in 2010.

9 The majority of British citizens who choose to emigrate go to the United States, Italy or Greece.

10 Work with another pair. Compare and discuss your answers to exercise 9. Then check them in File 33 on page 120. Any surprises?

11 Work in pairs or in small groups. Write similar generalizations to those in exercise 9, but this time about your own country or about another country you know well. Write six to ten statements, including two or three false ones. Swap lists with another group, read the statements and decide whether they are true or false. Finally, get feedback from the other group.

Writing: Email – cultural information

12 A colleague from India is going to spend one year in your country. You are responsible for his/her induction. Write an email in which you provide key information about your culture.

> **TALKING POINT**   If you had the opportunity to live in another country for three years and do exactly the same job, would you take this opportunity? Why?/Why not? Where would you choose to go? Why?

Listening: Managing one's time

1 Discuss these questions.

1 Can time be 'managed'?

2 What would life be like without deadlines? Do we really need them?

3 What sort of things often cause us to waste time? How can we avoid them?

2 Complete these questions with the words in the box.

> aside behind commitments
> prioritize management set

1 Do you _____ yourself clear goals?

2 Do you make a note of all your _____?

3 Do you ever set time _____ for planning?

4 Do you _____ the things you have to do, or do you deal with them as they appear?

5 How often are you _____ schedule?

6 How effective would you say is your time _____?

3 🔊 **1.30** Listen to six people answering the questions in exercise 2. Match each interview (A–F) to the appropriate question (1–6).

Interview A _____   Interview C _____   Interview E _____

Interview B _____   Interview D _____   Interview F _____

4 🔊 **1.31** Listen to some extracts from the same interviews and complete the sentences.

1 I _____ to write everything down, otherwise I forget. And if I _____ things _____, I can put my memory to better use.

2 I know I don't always _____ my priorities _____.

3 Missing a _____ is probably one of the worst things that could happen to me at work – that's why I always try hard to be _____ schedule. In fact, I'm happiest when I can be _____ of schedule.

4 I spend about an hour every Monday morning planning the week ahead. I think it's time _____ _____. Planning gives me a _____ of direction.

5 At the start of the week I usually have three or four clearly _____ and _____ goals.

6 As a rule, I try to _____ first with the tasks which are both _____ and important.

5 Work in pairs. Take it in turns to ask each other the questions in exercise 2. When you answer, give details about your time management using ideas from exercise 4.

6 Work in pairs. Discuss these questions.

1 People can be behind schedule for lots of different reasons. How many can you think of?

2 Why do some people try to be ahead of schedule all the time?

GARE
ST-LAZARE

SNCF

corail
ter

7))) **1.32** Listen to extracts from phone conversations with four people who have a time management problem. Match each person to their specific problem.

1 Suzi   **a)** always tries to beat the clock; completes assignments weeks ahead of schedule

2 Ramesh   **b)** unable to say 'no'; takes on far too much work

3 Fadila   **c)** has unrealistically high standards; does top-quality work but takes more time than is available

4 Stefan   **d)** keeps putting things off and making excuses for doing so; ends up in a panic to finish things at the last minute

8))) **1.33** Complete the expressions. Listen to check or look at the audio script on page 144.

1 I haven't got all the information I need to make an informed choice. It may _____ _____ while.

2 **A:** I was just wondering … You know, that translation … _____'s it coming _____?

    B: Fine. I'm _____ _____ it.

    A: *How _____ can you do it?* Erm … I mean, you know it was due in the day before yesterday?

3 **A:** *When can I _____ it?*

    B: I'll see _____ I _____ _____. I'd say by the end of the week, definitely.

4 **A:** Oh! Yes … Um, Lynne … I'm afraid I haven't _____ _____ _____ it yet. Sorry.

    B: Mm. I know it's been rather hectic lately, but … *what's _____ so long?*

9 Work in pairs. Discuss these questions.

1 How would you rank the four questions in *italics* in exercise 8 as regards their forcefulness (1 = most forceful, 4 = least forceful)?

2 What would motivate someone to use more rather than less forceful wording?

Word focus: Expressions with *time*

10 Match these sentence halves.

1 It's about time   **a** all I want to do is have a drink, sit down and relax.

2 In five years' time   **b** before we're all under video surveillance at work.

3 For the time being,   **c** I'll know whether I've got the job.

4 This time tomorrow   **d** I'll probably be living in Canada.

5 By the time I finish work,   **e** my husband and I are living with my parents.

6 It's only a matter of time   **f** I finished that report.

11 Use each of the sentence beginnings (1–6) in exercise 10 to make at least two sentences which are true for you.

It's about time I started learning how to design a website.
I think it's about time I got promotion.

> *i* The phrases *It's about time / It's high time / It's time* (+ subject) are followed by a verb in the simple past but the sentence always has a present or future meaning.

Speaking: Time matters

12 Work in pairs. Look at the four people and their problems with time management in exercise 7. Which one is most like you? Which one is least like you?

13 Work in pairs. Roleplay a conversation. Student A: Turn to File 34, page 120. Student B: Turn to File 71, page 128.

TALKING POINT   What does 'being late' mean in your culture? How is it regarded? And what does it mean to you personally?

5 Communication strategies Being assertive

Listening: Handling difficult people

1 Some people can be difficult to get along with at work or in life in general.
Read about some different personality types. What's the best way of handling them?

The hothead

Hotheads get angry and lose their temper easily, which can make them terribly difficult to work or live with. They might start shouting or get aggressive and nasty when people don't do what they want.

The whinger

Whingers are always complaining. They don't like things the way things are, but they don't want to change anything either. They just want to tell you how badly everyone treats them and why every new idea will fail.

The people pleaser

It's easy to like these people, but they're difficult to work with because they can't say 'no'. They're notoriously unreliable because they take on more work than they can handle, which means delays and broken promises.

2 1.34 Listen to a counsellor's suggestions for dealing with the personality types in exercise 1. Match them to the correct person.

Suggestion _____ = The hothead

Suggestion _____ = The whinger

Suggestion _____ = The people pleaser

3 Listen again and/or look at the audio script on page 144.
Do you think the counsellor's suggestions would work?

Reading: A difficult colleague

4 Your colleague, Martina, is feeling very cross with someone she works with. She is planning to send this email to her boss, but she's asked you to read it before she hits 'send'. Discuss these questions.

1 What kind of personality do you think Martina is? And what about Bruce? Why?

2 What do you think Martina should do? Should she send this email or make some changes first? If so, what amendments should she make?

Hi Peter

Bruce is driving me crazy. Since joining the company, I've introduced hundreds of useful measures to streamline the production process and reduce costs. Bruce has opposed all my proposals from day one. He has a million different reasons why every change is a bad idea and he's incredibly difficult to work with.

The last straw came this morning when he was really rude. I was explaining how important it was to stay ahead of the competition and he accused me of 'never thinking anything through' and stormed out of the room.

You need to speak to him and tell him to change his attitude.

Martina

5 Martina calmed down and made some changes before she sent the email. Do you think it is better or worse? Why?

Hi Peter

I'm concerned about Bruce. Since joining the company, I've introduced many measures to streamline the production process and reduce costs. I'm sure Bruce has the company's best interests at heart. However, I feel his frequent opposition to the changes has been unhelpful.

The latest example of this came this morning when I was explaining how important it was to stay ahead of the competition and Bruce reacted negatively.

I'm hoping you can help us resolve these differences.

Many thanks

Martina

6 A professional tone is generally neutral. It aims to present both sides of an argument. It is polite and is free of exaggeration while at the same time being assertive. Find examples of these four things in the amended email.

Speaking: Handling conflict

7 Work in pairs. Compare how Speakers A and B react in difficult situations. What are the main differences? Who is more effective? Why?

Situation 1

A: You keep being late. You really upset me. And you disrupt the work of the whole team.

B: When you are late, I get upset because the rest of the team have to wait for you and they find it difficult to get on with their work if you are not there.

Situation 2

A: You always want to work with Fred. You're so unfair. You're not good enough to work with me anyway. Everyone knows that.

B: When you insist on working with Fred, I often feel treated unfairly, because I have the impression you don't appreciate my abilities.

8 Work in pairs. Discuss how you could change these 'you' messages into assertive 'I' messages like the ones Speaker B uses in exercise 7.

1 You're a typical computer geek. You live in your own world and you think everything is simple. But you just can't explain anything when someone needs help.

2 That's so typical of you. You always borrow things from me, you never bother to ask, and then you never bother to return them. You're so inconsiderate!

9 Work in pairs. Take turns to be A and B and roleplay dealing with a difficult person.

Student A: Look at the information below. Student B: Turn to File 41, page 121.

You prefer talking about problems to solving them. Your partner is going to ask you to make some changes to some PowerPoint slides. It's your job to make those changes, so you should agree in the end. Before you do, however, you complain a lot and come up with all sorts of excuses. For example:

- You are incredibly busy this week.
- People around here are always making changes.
- You think you might be coming down with a cold, or perhaps the flu.
- You need an assistant.
- You've told management you need help lots of times but they don't listen.

10 Tell the class about your discussion. Did you both feel satisfied with the outcome?

Reminder

Comparison and contrast page 49 + Grammar reference pages 173–174
Being assertive page 53

Reading: Paper addicts

1 Answer these questions.

1 How much does a pack of 500 sheets of printer paper cost?

2 In a typical working day, approximately how many sheets of paper do you use in total (for printing, photocopying, etc.)?

2 Read the article. How similar is the situation described to that in your workplace?

PRINTING MANIA

Has the 'paperless office' become a distant dream? For years, technology has promised to free companies from the tyranny of paper-based information, only to trigger a surge in print volumes.

That is good news for printer and paper manufacturers, but bad news for the environment.

Printers guzzle both paper and electricity at a frightening rate. Besides, the average employee wastes a huge amount of paper.

Finally, printers place a heavy burden on a company's bottom line. On average, the costs of buying office printers and keeping them up and running typically represent between one and three per cent of total annual revenues.

3 Find words and phrases in the article which mean the same as the following.

1 to cause a sudden increase in

2 consume a lot of something quickly

3 put a lot of pressure on

4 the profit or the amount of money that a company makes or loses

5 money that a business or organization receives over a period of time, especially from selling goods or services

Listening: What are the options?

4 ◉)) **1.35** Listen to a departmental meeting where cost-saving measures are on the agenda. Number the options in the order in which they are mentioned.

_____ password- or card-controlled printing

_____ double-sided printing

_____ encouraging responsible printing behaviour

_____ online invoicing

5 Discuss these questions in pairs or in small groups.

1 Of the four measures in exercise 4, which one would you say is …

- the most effective way to reduce paper waste? Why?
- the least effective way to cut costs? Why?
- the least popular among employees? Why?
- the easiest to implement? Why?

2 What other ways of cutting paper consumption can you think of?

3 Reducing paper waste is only one way of cutting costs at the office. What other measures can you think of? Make a list, and rank them in order of practicality.

Speaking: Cost-cutting

6 Read these notes to prepare for a cost-cutting meeting.

Rivexal is a medium-sized medical technology company which manufactures medical supplies and laboratory instruments. Recently, it has merged with Lambro, a successful global company. One of the consequences of the merger is that cost-savings are now high on Rivexal's agenda.

The general manager has called a preliminary meeting with departmental heads to put forward a number of ideas and weigh alternatives.

By the end of the meeting, three ideas – no more, no less – will be selected.

Possible ways of saving costs	
give more employees the opportunity to work from home to reduce office costs	use teleconferencing to reduce business travel costs
fine employees who do not put their PC in sleep mode when leaving their desk	use laptop and tablet PCs instead of desktop PCs to save on electricity
use multi-function devices (i.e. printer / copier / scanner / fax all in one) to reduce power consumption	install CCTV cameras to make sure nobody uses printers for personal use or takes office stationery home
replace low-level employees with unpaid interns	use filtered tap water instead of bottled water for water coolers
use quality inkjet printers instead of laser printers	use energy-saving light bulbs only

7 Work in groups of four. Roleplay Rivexal's cost-cutting meeting.

Student A: look at the information below. Student B: Turn to File 35, page 120. Student C: Turn to File 59, page 125. Student D: Turn to File 92, page 133.

Student A

You are the general manager, so you speak first. State the purpose of the meeting, and give the floor to one of the participants. Make sure everyone contributes.

Your cost-saving idea:

Replacing low-level employees with unpaid or minimally paid interns is the idea you're most in favour of. So, prepare your arguments to defend it.

The two ideas you dislike most are teleconferencing and working from home (so … prepare your arguments against these ideas).

Be as assertive and neutral as possible at all times.

8 Compare your decisions with those of other groups. Which three ideas are the most popular?

9 Work in pairs. Play the 'double challenge game'.

Student A: look at the information below. Student B: Turn to File 37, page 120.

Student A

You start. Ask your partner a question about the first topic in the first box below. Listen to your partner's answer. It is then your partner's turn to ask you a question. Answer the question truthfully and in some detail. Somewhere in your answer, use the first expression from the list below (see second box).

Continue the activity until you have asked your partner a question about each topic, and you have used all the expressions when answering your partner's questions.

Topics to ask a question about
1 dealing with people who lose their temper easily
2 cutting costs
3 being assertive
4 deadlines
5 choosing work partners
6 time management

Expressions to use
1 … far less …
2 … a bit more …
3 … Generally speaking, …
4 … inclined to …
5 … It's only a matter of time …
6 … This time next month …

Interaction

6

A Past simple and past perfect
B Honesty and deceit
C Between the lines
D **Communication strategies** Compliments
E **Interaction** Breaches of trust

Nothing but the truth?

Past simple and past perfect

Reading: The canoe man mystery

1 Read the first part of a true story about a man who disappeared. What do you think happened to him?

On 21 March 2002, John Darwin went canoeing in the sea and didn't come back. He was 53 years old and he'd been married for 29 years to Anne, a girl he'd met on the bus going to school. They had two grown-up sons, and they lived comfortably in the north of England. John drove a £40,000 Range Rover and they had an investment portfolio with 12 homes that they rented out. John told his family that they would be millionaires by the time he was retired.

When Anne reported he was missing, the coastguards launched a large-scale search. As they couldn't find him, Anne had to break the news to their two sons. They were devastated. John's broken canoe washed up on the beach six weeks later. His body was never found.

2 Answer these questions.

1 What happened after John went canoeing? 2 Do you think the Darwins had enough money for a good lifestyle?

3 Read about John's wife, Anne. Why were her sons concerned about her?

After John had been missing for more than a year, he was officially declared dead. Anne received life insurance money and a widow's pension and she continued to live in the house they'd bought together. On the anniversary of John's death, she bought a bunch of roses and threw them into the sea. She kept one rose from the bunch next to her bed. Her sons were worried that she didn't sleep or eat enough. She didn't seem to be able to overcome her grief.

4 Read what happened next. Do you think this story will have a happy ending?

On 1 December 2007, John Darwin walked into a police station in London and said, 'I think I may be a missing person.' He explained that he had lost his memory and couldn't remember what had happened to him. Anne was in Panama at the time and the family called her to tell her the news. Anne later told journalists that she had always prayed for that moment. Her sons were amazed and elated and they had an emotional reunion with their father. It was a huge news story and the public were delighted for the family.

5 Read two more facts about the case. How do these facts change your view of the story so far?

FACT 1 In November 2007, Anne sold her house in the UK and moved to Panama. A few weeks later, John walked into the police station.

FACT 2 Two weeks before he disappeared in 2002, John had applied for a £20,000 loan. The bank turned him down.

Grammar: Past simple and past perfect

6 Complete the grammar notes. Write the names of the tenses.

Past simple and past perfect

We often use the past ¹_____ tense to tell stories in chronological order:

*Anne **sold** her house in the UK and **moved** to Panama.*

(First Anne sold her house. Then she moved to Panama.)

But sometimes we talk about one past event, and then refer to an earlier time. Here we use the past ²_____ tense to talk about the earlier event and the past ³_____ tense to talk about the later one.

*Two weeks before he **disappeared**, John **had applied** for a £20,000 loan.*

(First John applied for a loan. Then he disappeared.)

We often use the past ⁴_____ tense to report what someone said in the past.

*Anne later told journalists that she **had always prayed** for that moment.*

>> **For more information on the past simple and past perfect, see pages 158, 160–161.**

7 Look back at the story in exercises 1, 3 and 4 and <u>underline</u> two more examples of the past perfect in each one. Identify the earlier and later events.

8 Work in pairs. Complete a different part of the story each, and then check your answers with your partner's help. Student A: Turn to File 40, page 121. Student B: Turn to File 81, page 130.

Speaking: Judge for yourself

9 Discuss these questions.

1 Why did the police arrest John?

2 Which parts of Anne's story do you believe? Which parts don't you believe and why?

3 If you were John and Anne's children, who would you feel most angry towards: your mother or your father?

4 Should John and Anne be able to profit from selling their story to newspapers or writing a book about it?

10 Work in pairs or small groups. Discuss these questions. Then turn to File 36 on page 120.

1 What do you think Anne and John were doing in Panama?

2 Why did John walk into a police station? Why didn't he avoid the police?

3 Should Anne and John be punished, and if so, how?

4 How do you think the children felt about it?

TALKING POINT What famous cases of insurance fraud, or fraud in general, have you heard about? Is not paying a parking fee fraud? What about travelling by train without a ticket? Or not telling a shop assistant or waiter who undercharges you? Should people be punished for such acts?

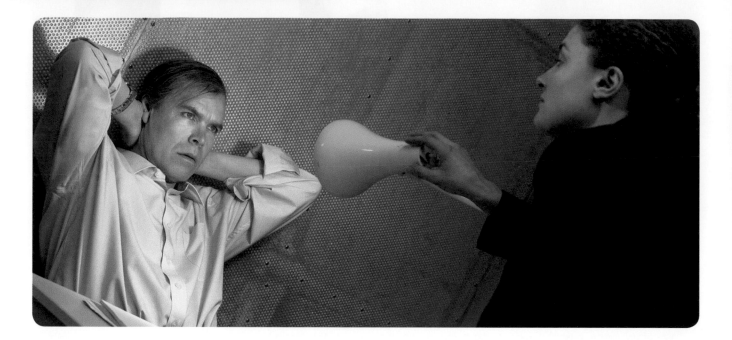

Listening: Can you spot a liar?

1 Are you good at telling whether someone is lying? Do you know any people who are good or poor liars? What makes them good or bad at it?

2 How can you tell whether someone is lying? Decide whether these things are reliable indicators. Then compare your answers with a partner.

1   They fidget (move about nervously).   yes / no
2   They blink (open and shut their eyes) more often.   yes / no
3   They try not to look you in the eye.   yes / no

4   They wave their hands around more.   yes / no
5   They pause a lot when they're speaking.   yes / no
6   Something else.   what?

3))) **1.36** Listen to an interview with Jim Kulver, a retired detective, and find out if you're right. Then answer these questions.

1   What other indicators are there?

2   What is 'reverse storytelling'? Does Jim think this technique has a future?

4))) Complete the sentences. Then listen again and check your answers.

1   Telling a _____ from a _____ person is a rather difficult task, isn't it, Jim?

2   The first time the journalist answered, he _____, and the second time, he _____ the _____.

3   I mean, people who have no intention of misleading or _____ anyone.

4   For example, _____ sometimes try to distance themselves from the _____.

5   _____ a story is hard enough, but telling it backwards is extremely demanding, especially if you've just _____ it _____.

Word focus: Truth and lies

5 Match these sentence halves.

1   Because of the politicians' failure to detail the spending cuts,

2   I explained that the cat had eaten my credit card,

3   Jill's students may look angelic,

4   The CEO has pleaded not guilty to the charges

5   The newspaper's April Fools' claim that gorillas could use iPads

6   Two former employees were accused of preparing false documents

7   Bertrand was convicted of

8   The inconvenient truth about infidelity is that it involves

a   obtaining money by **deception**.

b   intended to **deceive** regulators and auditors.

c   **deceit** and betrayal, neither of which is conducive to a good relationship.

d   but appearances can be **deceptive**.

e   and accused witnesses of **fabricating** their stories.

f   but they thought I was just **making** the whole thing **up**.

g   a lot of people felt they had been **misled**.

h   **took in** huge numbers of readers.

6 Work in pairs. Discuss these questions.

1 Do you agree that appearances can be deceptive? Can you provide an example from your own experience?

2 In what ways can advertisements be misleading?

3 Have you ever been taken in by a deceptive advert? If not, do you know anyone who has?

4 On what occasions did you make up excuses when you were a schoolchild? Were your teachers ever taken in?

5 Which crime is more serious in your opinion: obtaining money from a friend by deception, or stealing money from a relative?

6 What are some of the reasons why witnesses sometimes fabricate the evidence they give at a trial?

7 Match each conversation beginning to the correct response.

1 There's some good news, you know. We're all going to get a pay rise.

2 Sorry I'm late. There was an unscheduled staff meeting, and then …

3 I've worked as an accountant for Crosby & Meyer.

4 I've just handed in my resignation.

5 I'm going to the CEO's birthday party tomorrow.

6 I've just told the boss what I really think of the new schedule.

a You're joking. You said last week you'd just been promoted to assistant manager.

b You just made that up. If anything, we might just get the sack.

c You can't fool me. The only thing you are ever able to tell him is how perfect everything is here.

d Pull the other one! You can't even do basic multiplication.

e Oh, **come off it!** Your problem is, you can't ever be on time.

f I don't believe you! I know she's not coming back from Canada till next week.

8 Answer these questions.

1 What do the phrases in bold in exercise 7 express?

2 What could be the relationship between the speakers?

3 In what situations would using these phrases be inappropriate?

Speaking: Call my bluff

9 Professor Wiseman, who has researched the psychology of deception, designed 'the lying experiment' to assess our lie detection skills.

Try the lying experiment with a partner. Take it in turns to ask and answer questions about the best holiday or trip you've ever had.

1 Student A should ask Student B questions first. They should ask about:

• where and when they went.
• how long they stayed, and where.
• who they went with.
• what was special or surprising about the trip.

2 Student B should answer Student A's questions twice. One time they should tell the truth and another time they should lie.

3 Student A should guess which version is true and which version is a lie.

10 Write three sentences about yourself. Two of them should be true and one false. Write about something unusual you can do or have done.

I once shook hands with the prime minister.
I used to play the drums in a band.
I can knit.

Show your sentences to your partner. Your partner will ask you questions about each statement to find out which one is untruthful. Use a phrase in bold from exercise 7 whenever appropriate.

Which prime minister are you talking about?
Where and when exactly did you meet him/her?

TALKING POINT • Why do children sometimes tell lies to their parents? Is this justifiable?
• Why do parents sometimes not tell the truth to their children? Is this justifiable?

Word focus: Connotations

1 Do these words evoke in you positive or negative feelings, or do you just perceive them as neutral? Tick (✓) the appropriate box each time.

	Positive	Negative	Neutral
old			
rich			
slim			
cosmopolitan			
laid-back			
liberal			
bureaucrat			
complicity			
idealism			
rebel			

2 Work in pairs or in small groups. Compare and discuss your answers to exercise 1.

3))) **1.37** Listen to the first part of an interview with Professor Roy Wilkinson about the connection between words and emotions. Answer the questions.

1 What's the problem with dictionaries, according to Roy Wilkinson?

2 How does he explain the difference between *slim* and *skinny*?

3 What does he want to illustrate through these two example sentences?

a Peter's quite laid-back as a manager. His style encourages people to be careless and to miss deadlines.

b Rosa's quite laid-back as a manager. That's why her employees are so happy and efficient.

4))) Listen to the first part again and complete these extracts.

1 Dictionaries give us the _____ _____ of words, but they don't often tell us about the connotations words have.

2 Language is full of pairs like *slim* and *skinny*. Consider, for instance, *bureaucrat* and _____ _____, *rebel* and _____ *fighter*, _____ and *thrifty* – the first word in each pair being the one with negative connotations.

5))) **1.38** Listen to the second part of the interview. Tick (✓) the statements that are true and rewrite the ones that are false.

1 Fortunately, words never have different connotations when they're translated into other languages.

2 The Chinese word for *old* does not have negative connotations.

3 According to Professor Wilkinson, knowledge of connotations is more important to translators than to the general public.

4 Words influence people in different ways depending on their connotations.

6 Choose the more appropriate option in these sentences. Consider the context provided by the sentence and use a good dictionary if necessary.

1 Jane soon found her office job boring and started looking for something more *difficult / challenging*.

2 Luke was just one of those faceless *bureaucrats / public servants* who thrives on red tape.

3 A *chubby / fat* little baby was playing on the rug.

4 France and Italy are *noted / notorious* for their excellent cuisine.

5 I'd have liked to ask many more questions, but I didn't want to seem *curious / inquisitive*.

6 All of Charlie's teachers had always praised him for being so *determined / uncompromising* and ambitious.

Reading: Lies, big and small

7 Work in pairs or small groups. Discuss when it may be all right to tell lies. Provide concrete examples as well as convincing arguments.

8 Read this article about lying. Which of the ideas presented in the article are the same as the ones you expressed in exercise 7?

Philosopher Sissela Bok, author of *Lying: Moral choice in public and private life*, defines lying as giving some information which you know or believe to be false, with the intention of deceiving someone.

One question which has troubled both philosophers and ordinary people for centuries is whether or not there are certain circumstances under which it may be appropriate to tell lies.

An example that often comes to mind concerns extreme situations, where it is immediately obvious that telling the truth would have terrible consequences. Imagine that some friends of yours take refuge in your house because they are unjustly accused of something. You know that they are innocent. Someone knocks on your door. They are looking for your friends, and there is no doubt that their intentions are evil. What do you answer when those people ask you if you know where your friends are?

There are other circumstances where certain forms of lying are justified, like in games and negotiations. We all know of games which could not be played without lying, or at least pretending, but of course in such games both parties know the rules and play by them. Similarly, in business negotiations both parties involved understand that statements such as 'We can offer a 10 per cent discount only on orders exceeding 100 units' or 'I'm afraid we'll have to look for another supplier, then' are often just meant to keep the bargaining moving.

Finally, we also need to consider so-called 'white lies', i.e. innocent lies which are not intended to deceive but rather to make the other person feel good.

The problem with white lies, of course, is that they may encourage us to tell bigger lies under the pretext that we don't want to hurt anyone.

9 These sentences were removed from the original article. Where do they fit in?

1 However, these are examples of mutually agreed deception.

2 Even if you think the sweater you get as a birthday present looks horrible, you'll probably just say, 'Oh, how lovely!'

10 Discuss these questions.

1 What alternatives to lying can you think of in extreme situations similar to the one described in the article?

2 What other types of white lies can you think of?

3 How do you feel when you find out that someone has told you a white lie because they didn't want to hurt you?

Speaking: A matter of principle

11 Work in pairs. Rank the following 'lies' in order of seriousness, starting from the most serious one.

- a postgraduate student copies whole sections from various dissertations and deliberately omits to quote his sources
- a salesman claims expenses he never incurred
- a traveller with goods over the duty free allowance walks through the 'Nothing to declare' channel at customs
- an advertisement claims that 'Orion washing powder washes brighter'
- an employee rings in sick because it's a sunny day and he fancies going fishing
- an estate agent airbrushes all the photos of properties for sale in order to make them look more attractive to prospective buyers
- a doctor tells one of her patients that his condition will improve, knowing that in fact it can only deteriorate

TALKING POINT People sometimes preface what they say with a phrase like *As far as I know … / To the best of my knowledge … / This still has to be confirmed, but …*, etc. What is the usefulness of such phrases for the speaker / writer and for the listener / reader?

Listening: Compliments and responses

1 Work in pairs. Answer these questions.

1 When did you last pay someone a compliment? Who was the recipient? What was the occasion? What were your exact words? How did the recipient react?

2 Have you ever received a compliment you didn't expect?

3 What is the difference between complimenting and flattering?

2 Compliments, and how people respond to them, can vary a lot from one culture to another. Discuss these questions.

1 In your culture, what do people usually pay compliments about?

2 Who pays compliments more often:

... men or women?

... adults or adolescents?

... bosses or subordinates?

Do they pay compliments about the same things?

3 ᐳ) **1.39** Listen to five conversations and decide whether the statements about each one are true (T) or false (F).

1 **a** Gina bought a new smartphone a month ago.

 b Gina had had her old phone for a long time.

 c Gina's friend hasn't got GPS on his phone.

2 **a** It seems that Anna's friend now has a beautiful office.

 b Bob's office shares no similarities with Anna's.

 c Bob hasn't been into Anna's office.

3 **a** Both Helen and Svetlana are married.

 b Svetlana's husband doesn't really like her coat.

 c Svetlana likes her colleague's coat.

4 **a** Someone helped Albert with his presentation.

 b Albert says his daughter gives great presentations.

 c Albert's daughter is starting art school next year.

5 **a** Maria's car is very uneconomical to run.

 b Maria is not unreservedly enthusiastic about her car.

 c Ron doesn't go to work by car.

4 ᐳ) Listen again and complete the sentences in the box.

Compliments and responses
1 **A:** It _____ fantastic! **B:** I really needed something different. I'd had my previous one for almost a decade!
2 **A:** I really _____ _____ _____ you've decorated your office. It looks gorgeous! **B:** Oh, _____ _____, Anna. I'm _____ _____ you like it.
3 **B:** ... Wow! _____'_____ a really nice coat. **A:** I like yours, _____. Very _____ design.
4 **A:** _____ _____ _____ presentation! I enjoyed every minute of it. **B:** Very _____ _____ _____ to say so. But I can't take _____ _____ for it. It's my daughter who designed the slides.
5 **A:** Nice car! **B:** It's _____ _____, but it really guzzles petrol. It consumes over 20 litres per 100 kilometres.

5))) **1.40** Listen to the intonation people use when they pay someone a compliment.

6 Turn to one or two people in your group and compliment them on something. Sound as genuine and enthusiastic as you can!

7 People tend to use a limited number of strategies when responding to compliments. Match each strategy below to the corresponding example in exercise 4.

a   accepting the compliment

b   returning the compliment

c   giving an explanation

d   making the praise sound less important

e   sharing the praise with other people

8 Work in pairs. Read these conversation extracts. Do any of Speaker B's responses sound bizarre or inappropriate to you? If so, why?

1 **A:** I like your new boots.
  B: Oh, thank you.

2 **A:** What an interesting poster! It's beautiful.
  B: Please take it.

3 **A:** Your English is really good.
  B: No, it isn't. I know it's awful.

4 **A:** That was a great performance. Well done!
  B: I'm now the best one in the club.

9 Work in the same pairs. Give each other information about conversations 1–4 in exercise 8. Student A: Turn to File 42, page 121. Student B: Turn to File 83, page 131.

10 Work in pairs. Read these compliments. Why do you think the recipient may have felt embarrassed by the compliment each time?

1 Lisa, office assistant, to her head of department during a coffee break:

'I like the way you get us to give the best of ourselves. You're so motivating.'

2 Eddy, student of English, to his English teacher at the end of a class:

'The lesson today was very interesting. You are a very good teacher.'

3 Pierre, new employee, to one of the receptionists at his workplace:

'What a beautiful dress! You're looking great.'

11 Turn to File 43, page 121 and read the commentary about exercise 10. What are the differences and similarities with your culture?

Speaking: Making people feel good

12 Someone pays you the following compliments. Prepare your responses, using different strategies. Then work in pairs and practise complimenting and responding.

1   You've had some friends over for supper. After the meal, one of them says, 'That was absolutely delicious.'

2   A colleague overheard you speaking English on the phone and says, 'I'm really impressed. Speaking English seems to be second nature to you.'

3   Your line manager says, 'I've gone through your project proposal. It's truly excellent.'

4   A colleague says, 'I heard your son won this year's Liszt piano competition. He's so brilliant!'

5   A colleague says, 'What a beautiful briefcase you have!'

6   You've just taken some foreign business visitors round your town. At the end of the tour, one of them says, 'That was great. You're a fantastic guide.'

13 Who would you most like to receive a compliment from? Do you have any soft spots – things you secretly love to be complimented on? Which of these things would you prefer to be complimented on? What would you like to add to the list?

1   Something you have achieved, or the success of a family member

2   A possession like your home or your car, or your appearance

3   A particular skill you have, or your taste in art or clothes

4   Being pleasant to work with, or the way you tackle problems

5   Your creativity, intelligence or attitude to life

6   Your progress in English

Writing: Email – paying a compliment

14 You've just watched a web presentation given by an old friend of yours who now works abroad. You thought the presentation was excellent. Write an email to your friend to compliment him/her on the presentation, focusing on three specific aspects that you particularly enjoyed.

Reminder

Past simple and past perfect page 59 + Grammar reference pages 158, 160–161.
Compliments page 64

Reading: A man with a secret

1 Discuss these questions.

1 Imagine you won a huge amount of money on the lottery. Who would you / would you not tell?

2 Look at the headline and the picture in the article. What do you think the story is about?

2 Read the article. How accurate were your predictions about the story?

In love with a SECRET MILLIONAIRE

A millionaire who'd been hurt in the past by women interested only in his money hid his £10m lottery fortune from his girlfriend until they got engaged. After more than a year of cheap dates and a holiday in a seedy two-star hotel, Joe Johnson revealed his secret to girlfriend Lisa only after she'd agreed to marry him. Lisa's world was turned around when the man she'd fallen in love with, who wore shabby clothes and drove a wreck, turned out to be a secret millionaire with a property portfolio, a fleet of expensive cars and money to fly around the world in private jets. Now Joe has turned his amazing story into a book, *The Secret Millionaire*.

Joe said: 'In many ways, winning the lottery had been one of the loneliest things that had ever happened to me. I met a couple of women after winning my fortune, but they were more interested in my money than me. Just before I met Lisa, I had spent £200,000 on one ring for a woman I had loved. I thought she loved me, too, but a week later she left me – with her ring.'

When Joe took Lisa to one of his three homes, a £900,000 14th century former monk's grange in Moreton, he said he was looking after it for a rich friend. Had Lisa entered the garages, she would have found Joe's two £90,000 Porsche Carreras and his £65,000 Range Rover.

Lisa, 40, was a single mother with a five-year-old son when she first met Joe Johnson in October 2000. She was working in a café where he would come in for breakfast every day.

'After some weeks of talking, he asked me out for a meal,' Lisa said, and they split the bill, which they continued to do on many more dates to come.

After dating for more than a year, Joe proposed to Lisa and a week later revealed that he had won £10 million on the Lotto in 1998.

3 Answer these questions.

1 Why did Joe hide his fortune from his girlfriend?

2 When did Joe tell Lisa he was a millionaire?

3 What had happened to Joe just before he met Lisa?

4 What ploys did he use to hide the fact that he was a millionaire?

5 How do you think Lisa felt when she realized she'd been lied to for more than a year?

6 Would you be interested to read Joe's book? Why?/Why not?

Listening: A different perspective

4 Work in pairs. Imagine that you have the opportunity to interview Lisa. What questions would you like to ask her? Write down six questions.

5))) 1.41 Listen to Lisa. Are any of your questions answered?

6))) Listen again and complete these sentences.

1 When Joe first _____ _____ _____ _____, I was furious. Our whole life together had been _____ _____ _____ _____.

2 I _____ betrayed.

3 It was only when he explained how badly _____ _____ _____ before, by women who just wanted him for his money, that I started to realize why _____ _____ to such lengths to hide his fortune from me.

4 I can say _____ _____ _____ that I fell in love with a man who I believed had nothing.

5 I kept having to stop myself from offering to split the bill like _____ _____ _____.

Word focus: Phrasal verbs with *turn*

7 Find three examples of *turn* used as a phrasal verb in the first paragraph of the text in exercise 2. Match them to these definitions.

a to happen, especially unexpectedly _____

b to change (something) for the better _____

c to change (something) to become something else _____

8 Look at these sentences and match the verbs to the explanations below.

1 Experienced presenters know their voice is an instrument, so they **turn** the volume **up** or **down**, raise or lower the pitch, speed up or slow down as appropriate.

2 Two weeks before he disappeared, John had applied for a £20,000 loan, but the bank **turned** him **down**.

3 A big crowd **turned out** to support the race.

a increase / decrease the amount of sound _____

b went to attend an event _____

c refused, rejected _____

> *i* Some of the examples reveal a typical feature of phrasal verbs, namely that they often have multiple, unrelated meanings.
> This is one of the reasons why they are better learnt in context.

9 Complete these sentences with the correct form of an appropriate phrasal verb from exercises 7 and 8.

1 Veronica was offered a top job at an investment bank, but she _____ it _____.

2 The internet company called Clio Hi-tech Systems has been exposed as a fraud, and the CEO _____ _____ to be an 18-year-old kid who was taking people's money and not shipping them anything.

3 New models and new ideas have _____ our company _____ and saved it from closure.

4 Makers of big corporate aircraft _____ _____ in force last week to display their wares at Jet Expo, Russia's business aviation show held in Moscow.

5 Can you _____ the TV _____, please? I'm trying to work.

6 Pat _____ her garage _____ a laboratory and started experimenting with various chemicals.

Speaking: Mediating

10 Work in groups of three on three different situations involving an alleged breach of trust. Take it in turns to play the role of employee, superior, and mediator. Student A: Turn to File 60, page 125. Student B: Turn to File 91, page 133. Student C: Turn to File 101, page 135. Work on Situation 1 to begin with, then move on to Situation 2 and finish with Situation 3.

11 Work in new groups and compare the outcomes your original groups had for each situation.

Review 5-6

1 Cross out the option which is wrong or doesn't make sense in each sentence.

1 The price of oil is *slightly / considerably / the more* higher than this time last month.

2 The more we discuss this issue, *the less / the much / the more* likely we are to find a solution.

3 This model is three times *as fast as / faster than / as fast than* the original version.

4 The client was informed that the product is *as / slightly / a little* smaller than in the catalogue.

5 They admitted that the project was *far more / a lot more / the most* difficult than they expected.

6 The August schedules look as though they'll be *as busy / a lot busier / less busy* than we predicted.

7 The price of air travel is *a slight / a little / a bit* more expensive compared to last year.

8 Sea temperatures have fallen by *as little as / as far as / more than* two degrees.

2 Choose the correct forms to complete these sentences. Sometimes more than one form may be possible.

1 This building cost five _____ as much as the construction company predicted.

   a time **b** timed **c** times

2 The company sold far more copies of the DVD _____ expected.

   a that **b** than **c** as

3 The less we invest in research, the _____ likely we are to lose our share of the market.

   a more **b** most **c** much

4 This year, we had _____ as many applications for each job vacancy as last year.

   a twice **b** double **c** two times

5 The weather report says this summer will be _____ drier than last year.

   a much **b** far **c** more

6 In business, experience can be _____ more important than qualifications.

   a even **b** lot **c** much

7 The hotel will be three times as high _____ the tallest building in the city.

   a of **b** as **c** than

8 The passengers were warned that it might be _____ expensive to exchange currency on board the ship.

   a much **b** much more **c** a lot more

3 Complete this article. Put the verbs in brackets in the correct tense: either past simple or past perfect.

Last week, Neela Safar [1]_____ (find) a paper bag containing more than £40,000. Only a week before she discovered the money, Neela [2]_____ (start) work as a volunteer at an organization which helps to keep the city clean. She told journalists that she [3]_____ (finish) for the day and was on her way home when she spotted the bag. 'I didn't take my usual route home,' she said. 'I was on my bike and [4]_____ (go) down this street because I thought it might be a short cut.' She soon realized that she [5]_____ (lose) her way and so she [6]_____ (stop) to ask directions. 'But there [7]_____ (not be) anyone around,' she said. 'Suddenly I [8]_____ (see) a large bag in the road and went over to pick it up so I could put it in a bin.' However, she decided to check what was in it first, and that's when she [9]_____ (discover) it was full of money. She immediately handed it into a police station and was told that the owner of the money [10]_____ (report) it missing earlier that morning and never expected to see it again. The businessman, who does not wish to be named, [11]_____ (be) to the bank and then lost the package on his way home. He couldn't believe his luck when he heard that the package [12]_____ (find) by someone who not only liked to keep the streets clean but was honest as well. He showed his appreciation by giving Neela a £1,000 reward.

4 Complete these sentences with the words in the box.

by for likely more roughly seems speaking to

1 _____ and large, most of our department seem to be happy with the new procedures.

2 Generally _____, most workers have a positive attitude.

3 It _____ to be easier to attract new customers if you have a website.

4 People are far more _____ to buy cosmetics when they are on special offer.

5 _____ speaking, 50 per cent of travellers had experienced delays.

6 People are _____ inclined than they used to be to research products online.

7 Market research shows that shoppers tend _____ prefer colourful displays.

8 The product range attracts lots of interest, but _____ the most part, there have been few actual sales.

5 Read the compliments 1–6 and then put the words in the correct order to make responses.

1 You did really well in the presentation this afternoon.

   so / of / kind / that's / you / very / say / to

2 Thanks for my present – I love it.

   glad / so / I'm / like / you / it

3 You're looking very well.

   looking / too / you're / thanks / great / and

4 That's a lovely jacket – I love the colour!

   for / had / old / I've / thing / this / years

5 Well done on your success on this project.

   team / credit / so / hard / the / the / can't / worked / whole / well / I / very / full / take

6 That's an interesting watch – I haven't seen one like it before.

   grandfather / belonged / bought / my / it / India / in / to / who / it

6 How is the letter *i* in bold pronounced in these words? Complete the table with the words in the box.

> combine consider delighted design
> fabricate findings likely printer prioritize
> recipient widow wisdom

gift /ɪ/	dining /aɪ/

7 Choose the correct option to complete these sentences.

1 He applied for promotion but his manager turned him *round / down*.

2 Sometimes the newspapers seem to make stories *up / off*.

3 You don't look well – perhaps you're coming *across / down* with something.

4 Did a lot of people turn *out / off* for the marketing seminar?

5 Would your team be willing to take *away / on* more responsibility?

6 The TV programme played a trick on viewers, but I wasn't taken *off / in*.

7 When our team gets together, we come *up / round* with some great ideas.

8 Eventually, his invention was bought by a technology firm for millions and his life was turned *away / around*.

8 Complete this crossword puzzle.

Across

4 An employee who has the skill and knowledge to perform a task is _____.

6 After she retired, she received a _____.

7 There are five hundred _____ of paper in the packet.

9 Many people get embarrassed when someone pays them a _____.

11 It's important to _____ clear objectives at the start of a project.

12 Some bosses have a relaxed and laid- _____ management style.

13 A long, narrow boat for one or two people

16 He sometimes does silly or idiotic things, but he isn't a _____.

18 It's useful to _____ tasks and do the most important one first.

Down

1 I'll order the parts today, but they may _____ a while to arrive.

2 It can be annoying when someone takes the _____ for someone else's work.

3 The couple decided to get _____ in May and get married in December.

5 Many people make the _____ of thinking that Sydney is the capital of Australia.

6 'Don't be late for the meeting – it's important to be _____.'

8 A person who gets angry easily might be called a _____ head.

10 Some people say she's thrifty with her money, while others say she's _____.

14 It's _____ time you got up. It's 8:30 and you'll be late for work.

15 Come _____ it! That can't possibly be true.

17 A person who refuses to tell the truth is a _____.

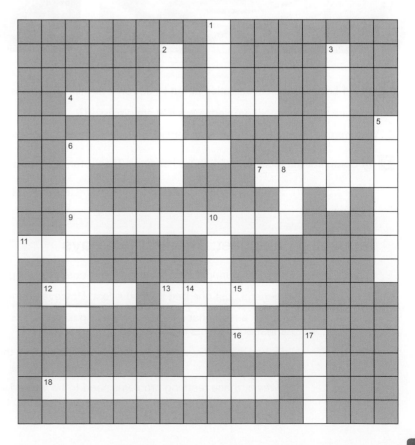

7

A Mixed conditionals
B Risk assessment
C Complaints
D **Communication strategies** Negotiating
E **Interaction** Problem solving

finding fixes

Mixed conditionals

Listening: What went wrong?

1 Look at the photos of an Olympic stadium and an airport under construction. What kinds of things could go wrong on large projects?

2))) **2.1** Listen to the conversation about Heathrow's Terminal 5 and answer the questions.

1 What are the three main problem areas that are discussed?

2 Why weren't adequate systems tests carried out before the airport opened?

3))) Complete the factsheet with these headings. Then listen again and correct any figures that are wrong.

Airport traffic   Cancellations   Losses   Luggage   Technical faults

Terminal 5 Factsheet: **The first five days**

1 _____   Problems during the opening five days cost the company $16 billion.

2 _____   In general, just one bag in 5000 is lost. However, during the opening week, 2300 bags were misplaced.

3 _____   Delays caused chaos for thousands of passengers. Some passengers never reached their destination. Almost 5000 flights never left the ground.

4 _____   Life was also difficult for passengers moving around the terminal. Out of 295 lifts, there were problems with 208.

5 _____   However, these teething problems need to be viewed in context. Heathrow is one of the busiest airports in the world with more than six or seven million people passing through the airport each year.

Grammar: Mixed conditionals

4 Look at the examples from the conversation and match them to the descriptions in the box.

a If I'd identified the problems before they happened, I'd be very popular now.

b If they'd finished the building on time, there wouldn't have been so many difficulties.

c If I listed all the problems, we would be here all day.

d Would you have been as understanding about the problems if you were a busy traveller?

Second, third and mixed conditionals

1 We can use the second conditional to talk about imaginary or unreal situations.
if + past simple, would + base form of the verb

2 We can use the third conditional when we imagine a different past from the reality, and to express criticism or regret.
if + past perfect, would have + past participle

3 We can use mixed conditional 1 to describe the past result of a present or continuing condition.
if + past simple, would have + past participle

4 We can use mixed conditional 2 to describe the present result of a past condition.
if + past perfect, would + base form of the verb

> **i** It is possible to replace *would* with *might / could* to show possibility. We can use *should have* to give advice about or criticize a past condition.

>> For more information on second, third and mixed conditionals, see page 168.

5 Identify the type of mixed conditional in these sentences. Why are they used in each situation?

a If money and time were never a problem, our last three projects would have been a success.

b The company wouldn't be in financial difficulties now if the CEO had listened to the advice of the project manager.

---

6 Look at the notes from a report and the sentences below that are related to them. Complete the sentences using the verbs in brackets and mixed conditionals 1 and 2.

1 didn't relocate sales to Mumbai ➞ costs not lower now

If we _____ (move) the sales department to Mumbai, we _____ (have) lower costs now.

2 last year's sales figures weren't high ➞ global financial situation steadier

Last year's sales figures (possibly) _____ (be) higher if the global financial situation _____ (be) steadier.

3 some of sales team speak Mandarin ➞ increase market share in China over last ten years

If some of the sales team _____ (speak) Mandarin, we _____ (increase) our market share in China over the last ten years.

4 daily computer problems ➞ replace old IT system

We _____ (not experience) these daily computer problems if the old IT system _____ (replace).

5 keep to budget ➞ not pay high bonuses to managers every year

The department _____ (keep) to its budget in 2011 if it _____ (not pay) high bonuses to the managers every year.

6 not have current departmental problems ➞ management follow correct procedures

We _____ (not have) these current departmental problems if the management team _____ (follow) correct procedures in the past.

7 Complete these statements using mixed conditionals and then compare your ideas with a partner.

1 I would be rich now if I had …

2 I wouldn't be where I am today if I hadn't …

3 If I were a time traveller, I could have …

4 If I hadn't worked last week, I might have …

5 If I had listened to my teachers, …

Speaking: It could have been different

8 ◈ 2.2 You are part of a team from your company visiting South America to check on construction projects in the region. You are in Quito in Ecuador and are about to leave for Lima in Peru. Listen to the travel update. What is the problem?

9 Work in pairs. Choose one of these options.

Travel by boat to Lima. Turn to File 6, page 114.

Hire a car and drive to Lima. Turn to File 100, page 134.

10 Work with another pair. Tell them about the decisions that you made and why you made them.

TALKING POINT When things go wrong, is it more important to take time to evaluate whether things could have been done differently or is it better to move on quickly and put the problem behind you?

Listening: Emergency planning

1 Look at the advertisement for the position of Emergency Planning Officer. What do you think the job would involve?

THE ROCKDALE CENTRE

The Rockdale Centre is a unique location for both business and leisure. Set in an area of outstanding natural beauty surrounded by lakes and mountains, the complex is home to an international conference centre, a luxury hotel and self-catering accommodation.

We are currently looking for a first-rate Emergency Planning Officer who will help maintain the high level of safety and security which the Rockdale Centre is famous for.

2)) **2.3** Listen to the successful candidate talk about his job. Does he mention any of your ideas?

3)) Listen again and answer the questions.

1 Why was he confident when applying for the position?
2 What is the main objective of the emergency team?
3 What types of emergency does he mention?
4 What skills does he say are important in the job?
5 What is the first thing he does if there is an event at the centre?
6 What would he do if there was an emergency?

4 Complete the extract from the listening with the words and phrases in the box.
Look at the audio script on page 147 to check.

> although   in case   in which case   provided that   supposing that   what if   when   unless

I knew I had a chance ^{1}_____ I prepared well for interview and demonstrated that I had relevant experience. … Our main role is to anticipate anything that could go wrong and to make sure that there are procedures in place ^{2}_____ there's an emergency. … ^{3}_____ I'm quite a positive person, I always need to imagine the worst case scenario. ^{4}_____ I do, I won't be able to work out the best way to deal with problems when they occur. For example, ^{5}_____ there's an outbreak of food poisoning or a virus? … ^{6}_____ there's a conference or some other big event taking place in the centre, the first step would be to carry out a risk assessment. …. ^{7}_____ we're confident that we've thought of all the potential problems, we then check that there are appropriate procedures in place to deal with them. … Unfortunately, an emergency will sometimes occur, ^{8}_____, I'll work with my team and the emergency services to take appropriate action as quickly and effectively as possible.

5 Work with a partner and discuss these questions.

1 What characteristics does an emergency planning officer need?
2 What might the pros and cons of the job be?
3 In what circumstances is it particularly important to anticipate problems in advance in everyday life?

Word focus: Connectors

6 Choose the best word or phrase to complete the extract from a risk assessment report.

Risk Assessment

The sporting facilities at the centre will be used for training by the Olympic athletics squad during the first week in April. [1] *When / What if / Although* this is a busy week at the centre, we are confident that it will be possible for the team to train privately and safely. [2] *Provided that / Supposing that / Unless* strategic areas of the sports ground are closed off to the general public, the team will have exclusive use of the athletics facilities for five hours each day. [3] *Unless / When / What if* the team manager confirms that these arrangements are acceptable, the centre can begin informing other clients that there will be restricted use of these facilities during their stay. The coach may also request use of the swimming pool [4] *supposing that / in case / in which case* the opening hours for other guests will be changed for that week. One of the members of the squad is currently attracting media attention. We therefore intend to patrol the site and increase security at each entrance and exit [5] *in case / in which case / although* any press photographers or reporters attempt to gain access. [6] *What if / Provided that / Supposing* that unauthorized persons were found in the centre, they would be escorted from the premises by a member of our security team and warned that further attempts to enter would result in the police being called.

7 Find phrases in the risk assessment with a similar meaning to the following.

1 important parts
2 shut to prevent access
3 limited availability
4 causing journalists to be interested
5 walk around checking the area is secure
6 try to get in
7 people who do not have permission to be somewhere
8 accompanied to the exit

Speaking: Anticipate risks

8 Work in pairs or small groups. You are members of the emergency planning team at the Rockdale Centre. Look at information about an important event that the Rockdale Centre is organizing. What risks need to be taken into consideration? What measures could be taken to reduce the risks?

SOLAR

Ideas can change the world …

Solar is a high-profile international annual event. For three days, leading figures from the world of business and finance join with social entrepreneurs, politicians, scientists and celebrities to exchange ideas, listen to talks and plan for tomorrow. For the first time, this year's event will take place at the Rockdale Centre in …

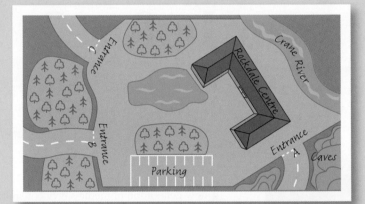

9 🔊 **2.4** Listen to the news report about one of the speakers at the Solar event and make notes. What problems have occurred? What impact could this have on the conference?

10 You have heard that up to 1000 people plan to protest about Lerwood Chemicals at the Solar event. Look at the map and discuss what could be done to minimize disruption and maximize safety for everybody. Which emergency services would you include in your plans?

11 The protest campaign has gathered momentum and up to 20,000 protesters are now expected. Rockdale's emergency team and management team are meeting to decide what action to take. Work in groups of four to discuss the options and decide what to do. Student A turn to File 8, page 115. Student B turn to File 31, page 119. Student C turn to File 46, page 122. Student D turn to File 96, page 134.

12 Report back to the class and explain what action you plan to take. What were the reasons for your decisions?

TALKING POINT What type of emergencies might an organization plan for? What factors can make emergency planning effective or ineffective?

Reading: Consumer power

1 When was the last time that you complained about a product or service? What did you do? How did the company respond?

2 Which form of complaint do you think is most effective? Why?

> email   face-to-face   letter   online review   phone

3 How has the internet changed the way that people complain? Has the power of the consumer increased? Read the article and see if it mentions your ideas.

Do consumers have more power than ever before?

A new generation of media-savvy consumers is using technology to voice their opinions about brands, products and services. Traditional methods of complaint, such as letters or telephone calls to the offending company, are still used. However, many customers are also likely to communicate their dissatisfaction to each other. In recent studies, 83 per cent of people said that online reviews had some influence on their purchasing decisions. Which means a bad review has the power to turn potential customers away. Modern consumers are becoming increasingly aware of their rights and are more likely to negotiate a refund or some type of compensation when transactions are unsatisfactory.

The way that consumers complain as a group is also changing. People are moving away from protests, boycotts and petitions. Something that worries organizations is the speed with which a complaint can become a high profile campaign. Social networking sites allow the failings of a company to be viewed by a huge audience worldwide. A British confectionery company experienced a backlash when it began to use animal products in its chocolate. The Vegetarian Society posted the contact details of the company's customer services department on its website. As a result, the company received 6000 calls and emails from unhappy vegetarian customers. The company swiftly admitted that it had made a mistake and reversed their decision.

4 Work in pairs. Read the article again and discuss the questions.

1 Do you write product reviews, or use reviews when choosing something to buy?

2 Was the confectionery company right to change its decision?

3 How could modern technology be used with protests, boycotts and petitions?

5 Complete the quiz below about consumer complaints using the words in the box.

> boycott campaign compensation protest reliability review

6 Tick (✓) the alternative (a–c) in each case that is closest to your opinion.

Consumer complaints

Are you a kangaroo, a bear or an owl?

1 **A company delivers your new washing machine and damages the floor in your kitchen. Do you …**

a) take photographs of the damage and write to the company demanding ¹_____?

b) feel angry but think it's not worth complaining because the company won't do anything?

c) write an online ²_____ of the company telling people what happened?

2 **Who are you most likely to buy a new laptop from?**

a) the company that offers the best price; you'll return it if it isn't exactly what you want

b) a company that charges more than the rest but is best for ³_____

c) a company that has the best percentage of positive reviews online

3 **Your train is over an hour late. When it arrives, it's hot and crowded and you have to stand up for the whole journey. The ticket inspector wants to charge you more for the ticket as you are now travelling at the busiest time of day. Do you …**

a) pay the extra money but ask the ticket inspector for his name because you intend to write to the rail company to complain?

b) pay the money and complain to your colleagues the next day at work?

c) refuse to pay the money, take a photograph of the ticket inspector with your phone and tell him you are going to use it to make a ⁴_____ about the company's terrible service?

4 **You have taken an important client to a restaurant that you use frequently. Your lunch is cold when it arrives and the service is very slow. Do you …**

a) have a quiet word with the waiter on the way out and negotiate a free meal in the future?

b) say nothing but decide not to take any clients to the restaurant again?

c) write to the restaurant manager and say that you'll organize a ⁵_____ of the restaurant unless they assure you that this won't happen again?

5 **Your mobile phone provider is offering a great new deal for new customers but is increasing the charges for existing customers. Do you …**

a) contact customer services and negotiate a better deal after researching competitors' rates?

b) terminate your contract and move to another provider as soon as possible?

c) start an internet ⁶_____ with an online petition to try to reverse the increase in charges?

7 Work in pairs. Did you answer mostly a, b or c? Look at File 44 on page 122 and read the information. Discuss whether you agree with the analysis. Would you do something different from the alternatives given in the quiz?

8 Complete an additional question for the quiz. Take turns to ask your partner the question. Student A turn to File 45, page 122. Student B turn to File 88, page 132.

Speaking: Having a bad day?

9 Work in pairs. Tell your partner what you would do in this situation.

The morning post arrives. There's a letter from the bank. They accidentally took all your money from your account. As a result, your bills didn't get paid and you have received bank charges.

10 Now look at some more scenarios. Turn to File 48, page 122 and take it in turns to say what you would do. Give reasons for the actions you would take.

11 Choose two of the scenarios. How do you think the different personality types in the quiz would handle these situations?

Writing: Letter / Email of complaint

12 Choose one of the scenarios in exercise 9 or 10. Write a formal letter or email to the company to make a complaint. Give the background to the situation, and say why you are unhappy and what action you want taken.

TALKING POINT

How effective are traditional methods of complaining, such as the phone or letters? Do you think they get better results than modern methods?

Listening: Cooperation and competition

1 What is your definition of a negotiation? Think of three situations in your daily life when you need to negotiate (at home or at work).

2 Look at the diagrams showing two approaches to negotiations. Think of a situation where each approach might be used.

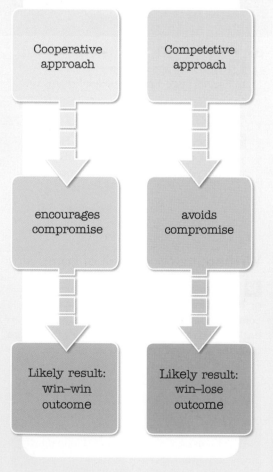

Cooperative approach → encourages compromise → Likely result: win–win outcome

Competetive approach → avoids compromise → Likely result: win–lose outcome

3 Match these headings to the negotiating strategies below.

a Explain your needs
b Listen carefully
c Find out about the other person's perspective
d Encourage the other person to open the negotiation
e Prepare more than one option

1 _____
The other participant may offer more than you would have asked for. Or, conversely, they may ask for less than you planned to give.
2 _____
Ask questions to find out about the other participant's ideas and requirements.
3 _____
If your first choice is not acceptable, be ready to offer some alternatives.
4 _____
Give clear reasons that show why what you want is important.
5 _____
You can miss areas where you might find agreement if you are thinking of what to say next rather than focusing on the other participant.

4))) 2.5 Listen to a conversation and answer the questions.

1 What is the subject of the negotiation?
2 What outcome does Louise want?
3 Is it a cooperative or a competitive negotiation?

5))) Which strategies from the text in exercise 3 do the speakers use? Listen again and check.

6 What options could either party have suggested as a solution?

7 Put these negotiating expressions under the correct headings below.

a   We could lower the price as long as you increase the volume.

b   From my perspective, …

c   Shall we get this in writing?

d   I can certainly see where you're coming from.

e   I'm afraid that doesn't work for me.

f   I'd like time to think about this.

Negotiating
Opening: *I'd like to begin by saying …   Our position is …* 1 _____
Signalling understanding or agreement: *That's a very good argument / point / compromise.* 2 _____
Objecting to a point: *I'm prepared to compromise, but …* 3 _____
Making concessions: *Would it include an extended warranty period if we signed today?* 4 _____
Avoiding decisions: *You've given me a lot to consider.* 5 _____
Closing: *I think we can both agree to these terms.* 6 _____

8))) **2.6** Listen to a conversation between a client and a supplier and answer the questions.

1   Which type of business do the client and supplier work in?

2   What is the negotiation about?

9))) Listen again and answer these questions.

1   What is the restaurant's usual policy concerning food supplies?

2   What is the supplier's usual delivery time?

3   Who does the supplier need to check the delivery times with?

4   What terms do the supplier and customer potentially agree on?

10))) Listen again and/or look at the audio script on page 148 and complete the phrases.

1   Shall we get _____ down to _____?

2   I _____ have some _____ about your delivery times.

3   I understand where you're _____ _____. However …

4   _____ we increased our order by seven per cent, could you _____ your delivery time by two days?

5   It looks _____ we have a _____.

6   Let's arrange another meeting when we've had time to _____ things _____.

Speaking: Fixing the problem

11 Work in pairs. Look at the audio script on page 148 for the training negotiation in exercise 4. Roleplay the situation as a win–win situation.

12 Look at this list of perks. Allocate points depending on how important each perk is for you. The most important get the most points. Choose three perks to allocate three points, three to allocate two points and three to allocate one point.

free health insurance

company shares

large office

annual bonus: 10 per cent of salary

work from home one day a week

company car

flexible working hours

free petrol for work and leisure

school fees paid by the company

13 Work in pairs. Roleplay a negotiation between a CEO and a director and try to get the best result to fix the problem. As the director, use the perks above to try to get what you want. The aim is to score at least eight points with your negotiation.

> **Student A:** You are the CEO.
>
> Your company is having problems with a branch in Lisbon. You want one of your directors to move to Portugal for two years. You know that the person you want for the position will be reluctant as they like their present job and do not want to move their family. Try to choose the perks that will tempt them to take up the position. If they don't go, there is the possibility that they will have to move to a less senior position at a reduced salary.

> **Student B:** You are the director.
>
> You know that your CEO wants you to move to Portugal for two years to run the branch in Lisbon. You are reluctant to go because you like your present job and don't want to move your family. Think of other solutions that could fix the problem. Raise these in the negotiation. If you still have to go, try to negotiate the best perks that you can to make it worthwhile.

14 Think of another perk that you would value in a job. Tell your partner why you think it is important. What would you give up in a job in order to have this perk?

Reminder

Mixed conditionals page 71 + Grammar reference page 168
Negotiating page 77

Speaking: Generating ideas

1 Which of these strategies might be useful to generate ideas when you want to solve a problem? Add another idea to the list.

> brainstorm   go for a walk   listen to music
> talk to a colleague or friend   write lists

2 Add another category to this list. Now think of a recent problem that has occurred in two of the categories.

1 transport
2 the economy
3 the environment
4 _____

3 Work in pairs. Tell your partner about the two problems that you thought of. Try to think of one or more solutions to the problems that your partner tells you about.

4 Look at the rules and play the board game.

5 After the game, discuss which situations you found hardest and easiest to deal with.

1 START
You have overslept and are running late. Your boss is expecting you for an early meeting. What would you do?

2
Your car has broken down and is in a garage. Persuade a friend to let you use their new car.

12
A colleague wants your advice. A faulty product wrecked his demonstration recently. The head of production insists the product is fine and wants him to use the same model in another client demonstration next week.

11
You forgot a meeting. Think of a good excuse (or go back three squares).

13
You bought a watch that is supposed to be waterproof. The shop says that you must have used it in deep water – but you only tested it in the shower. Negotiate a refund.

14
During a presentation the equipment didn't work, some of the pictures were in the wrong order and the slides had spelling mistakes. Say what you could have done differently (or move back one square).

24 FINISH
How will you relax after your difficult day?

23
Tell some friends about your bad day at work. Choose one of the events and tell them what you could have done differently.

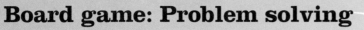
Board game: Problem solving

Work in small groups.

1 Toss a coin to move: heads, move one square; tails, move two squares.
2 If you land on a green square, roleplay a negotiation with the person on your left.
3 If you land on a yellow square, say what you would do or say in the situation.
4 If you land on a white square, follow the instructions.
5 If you land on a coffee break, relax – you don't need to do anything this time.

RULES

3 You realize that you've left important documents at home. What could you have done to avoid the situation?

4 Coffee break

5 You remember that you were meant to phone a client back yesterday but you forgot. You know they'll be angry. What would you say to the client?

6 You grab a quick coffee and spill it on your jacket. Talk to a colleague and get them to lend you their jacket for a product demonstration you have to give.

10 What would you do if you had just finished lunch with a major client, but the restaurant declined your credit card and you didn't have a cheque book or any cash?

9 A major client phones to tell you that he/she is thinking of switching to another supplier. Convince the client to stay with your company.

8 You give a demonstration to a major client, but the product doesn't work. Apologize and explain to the client what was wrong (or go back two squares).

7 Coffee break

15 Coffee break

16 You stop the car for two minutes to drop off a package. When you return, a traffic warden is about to put a parking ticket on your car. Explain the bad day you are having and convince them not to give you a ticket.

17 What would you do if a client came to your office for a meeting, but you couldn't remember their name and you had to introduce them to a colleague?

18 You have a phone message from a difficult client asking you to call, but you don't want to speak to them. Convince a colleague to make the call for you.

22 What would you do if you arrived home from work and found that you'd forgotten the key to your flat?

21 You forgot your best friend's birthday. You're in a meeting all afternoon. Convince your colleague to organize a present for you to give. Offer to do a task for them that you know they don't like.

20 Coffee break

19 Your boss wants you to work late but you have an important social commitment. What would you say?

Interaction

79

8

A Passives overview
B Asking questions
C The media
D **Communication strategies** Clarifying
E **Interaction** Dealing with a problem

Breaking news

Passives overview

Listening: News consumption

1 Which of these ways of following news stories do you use? Which do you prefer?

> TV newspapers radio computer mobile phone tablet

2 Work in pairs or small groups and discuss these questions.

How has technology affected the following?

1 the way that we access the news

2 the speed at which news stories are reported and updated

3 where and when we read, listen to or watch the news

3))) **2.7** A media analyst is giving a talk about the way that news consumption has changed. Listen to part 1 and match the phrases to the topics.

1	I'm here to talk about ...	a	Habits and interaction with the news
2	Firstly, ...	b	Changes to the time spent consuming news
3	I'll start by ...	c	News consumption and technology
4	Then ...	d	Changes in the way news is obtained
5	Finally, ...	e	Opening question about headlines

4))) **2.8** Listen to part 2 and decide if the following statements are true (T) or false (F).

1 Traditional news media are no longer popular.

2 More people watch news stories on TV than follow the news on the internet.

3 Newspapers are more popular than news websites.

4 Women and men use digital media to get news stories to approximately the same extent.

5 Fewer young people use the internet to view the news than people aged 30–49.

5))) **2.9** Listen to part 3 and write notes on the following topics.

1 The way that news was accessed in the past

2 The way that news items are read now

3 Changes in who manages news content

6))) **2.10** Listen to part 4 and answer the questions.

1 How does the speaker suggest that people might use the following? Do you agree?

> mobile phones internet websites newspapers and TV

2 What future challenges are mentioned?

Grammar: Passives overview

7 Which of the following sentences from the talk use the passive form?

1 News consumption has been affected by new technology.

2 News stories can be accessed with digital devices such as smartphones.

3 The proportion of people who get their news online continues to grow.

4 Digital technology isn't used by a particular age group.

5 Have our news habits been changed by the internet?

6 We can check news stories while commuting to work or college.

7 It is thought that the internet will be used as a key news source for those in the 50–65 age group.

8 Individuals might use their mobile phone to read news headlines on the move.

8 Choose the correct alternatives in 1–3 to complete the information about the passive.

The passive

1 We use passives when we are more interested in *who does the action / the action itself*.

2 We use passives when we *want to / don't want to* place emphasis on important information.

3 We use *by / with* to say who or what is responsible for an action and *by / with* to talk about the thing used to perform the action.

In formal contexts, we can use *it* to introduce passive phrases. This suggests a distance between the speaker and the opinion.

It is thought / believed / said that ...

It is expected / understood / reported that ...

>> For more information on passives, see page 169.

9 Look at the examples of the passive in exercise 7 again. Say why you think the speaker uses it rather than the active.

10 Use *by* or *with* to complete the sentences.

1 The headlines were read _____ the newsreader.

2 Can this device be used _____ headphones?

3 The accident was filmed _____ a passerby _____ a small phone camera.

4 It is understood that the fire was started accidentally _____ teenagers _____ matches.

5 The oil was cleaned up _____ dispersants sprayed onto the slick _____ the emergency services.

11 Rewrite the sentences using passive forms. Use an *it* form of the phrase in brackets to introduce the sentence. Only include the agent if it is necessary for the sentence to make sense.

1 (People think that) 80 per cent of the population will use mobile devices by 2020.

> ***It is thought that** mobile devices **will be** used by 80 per cent of the population by 2020.*

2 (People say that) internet service providers improved connection speeds last year.

3 (People believe that) a new media consultancy has carried out the survey.

4 (People understand that) the company is making a statement today.

5 (People expect that) government ministers will attend next week's trade show.

6 (People report that) a major cable company has launched a news website.

Speaking: Giving a talk

12 Work in pairs. Use the information in the Files to prepare a short talk (five minutes) for or against the following statement. Use the outline below to help you structure the talk.

'People should be charged to use news websites.'

Student A: Give a talk agreeing with this viewpoint. Turn to File 50, page 123. Student B: Give a talk disagreeing with this viewpoint. Turn to File 78, page 129.

Introduce the subject	Briefly outline main points	Summarize key points and conclude
• *I'd like to talk about ...* • *I'm here to tell you about ...*	• *Let's start by ...* • *Now we'll move on to ...* • *Next, we'll ...*	• *To sum up ...* • *To conclude ...* • *What should we conclude by this?*

13 Take turns to give your talk to your partner. When you are listening, write down a question or comment and introduce it at the end of the talk.

TALKING POINT Do you think that people would be more or less relaxed if they were unable to access news bulletins for a week?

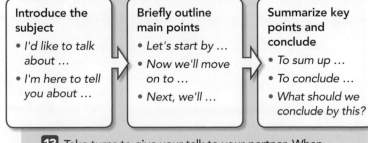

Listening: Interview styles

1 Work in groups. Look at the photos and discuss what is happening in the three television interviews by studying the body language.

2))) **2.11** You are going to hear two interviews with Paul Valera, the founder of the production company, P Valera Productions. Listen to the first interview and answer the questions.

1 What does the interviewer accuse Paul Valera of doing?

2 What are two possible consequences if P Valera Productions is sold?

3 What problems were there in the interview?

3))) **2.12** Listen to the second interview. Which interview was more successful? In which three of these ways does the second interview differ from the first?

The interviewer:

1 uses phrases to show she is responding to what Paul Valera is saying

2 uses interruptions to stop Paul Valera avoiding answering the question

3 doesn't ask questions about controversial subjects

4 doesn't use direct questions to introduce controversial subjects

5 uses a variety of question types

4))) Use information from the second interview to complete the report on the *Business Tonight* website. Listen again to check.

RADIO 9

business tonight

This afternoon, presenter Kirsty Green interviewed Paul Valera, the [1]_____ of P Valera Productions. Mr Valera confirmed that he has recently been in talks with giants of the media [2]_____. The production company makes [3]_____ and [4]_____ series that deal with serious [5]_____. Despite interest in his company, Mr Valera insisted that they would continue to make high [6]_____ programmes and denied that there would be any staff changes to his [7]_____ or management teams. In addition, he guaranteed that there would be no [8]_____ in the company.

Mr Valera made an exclusive statement about his latest project, which is being filmed in the [9]_____ rainforest and which he believes will be one of the most amazing [10]_____ documentaries ever seen on television.

Grammar: Asking questions

5 》) **2.13** Complete the questions from the interviews with these words. Listen to check.

> are haven't isn't tell whether why you

1 The timing is interesting, _____ it?

2 _____ these accusations true?

3 Could _____ _____ me _____ it's true that an offer has been made to buy your company?

4 _____ would I change a winning team?

5 _____ you been working on a secret programme in the Amazon rainforest?

6 Match the questions in exercise 5 to the types of question below.

Asking questions

a Direct questions – to find out specific information

b Embedded questions – to ask questions in a less direct and more polite manner

c Negative questions – to express surprise or disapproval, or to check information

d Tag questions – to verify that the statement that we've made is correct

e Rhetorical questions – a statement formulated as a question but which does not require an answer

>> **For more information on asking questions, see pages 163–164.**

7 Complete the conversation with the correct negative question or tag question.

A: ¹_____ you say that you used to work in Toronto?

B: Yes, for a couple of years.

A: You were based in Montreal for a while, too, ²_____?

B: That's right. I really enjoyed it.

A: Do you remember Sunil and Alice? They worked in the same department as you in Montreal, ³_____?

B: Yes, they did. You don't happen to have their address, ⁴_____? I lost contact with them.

A: ⁵_____ you heard? They'll be at the sales conference in Dubai in May.

B: Really? That's good news. We'll have to arrange to have lunch together, ⁶_____?

8 Make these questions less direct by using embedded questions.

1 Have profits increased this year?
  Can you tell me _____?

2 How much will the materials cost?
  You don't know _____, do you?

3 When does the seminar start?
  Do you have any idea _____?

4 Are interest rates going to rise or fall in April?
  Is it possible to tell us _____?

5 How accurate are these projected figures?
  Could you tell me _____?

6 Will you have finished the report in time for the meeting?
  Let me know _____ or not.

9 You are preparing questions to ask at a meeting. Look at the notes below and write a suitable question in each case. Use embedded questions to introduce difficult subjects and direct questions when you need factual information.

1 estimate for building the new headquarters was incorrect?
  Can you tell me whether the estimate for building the new headquarters was incorrect or not?

2 construction firm was not correctly supervised?

3 mistakes were made?

4 number of contract workers who were employed?

5 amount we'll be over budget at the end of the project?

6 date the new headquarters will open for business?

Speaking: Difficult interviews

10 Work in pairs. You are going to roleplay two interviews for a business news website. Read the information and prepare questions individually. Then roleplay the interviews with your partner.

Interview 1
Student A: You are the interviewer. Turn to File 10, page 115. Student B: You are the interviewee. Turn to File 39, page 121.

Interview 2
Student A: You are the interviewee. Turn to File 94, page 133. Student B: You are the interviewer. Turn to File 51, page 123.

11 Did you find it easier to be the interviewer or the interviewee? When you were being interviewed, which questions did you find it most difficult to answer?

TALKING POINT

What qualities does someone need to be good at interviewing people? Think of an example of a TV or radio presenter who does or doesn't do their job well.

Word focus: TV programmes

1 We can watch TV and films in a number of different ways these days, using laptops, portable DVD players and mobile technology. What do modern programme makers need to consider when making programmes that will be shown on different sized screens?

2))) **2.14** Listen to five extracts from TV programmes. Put five of the following types of programme in the order that you hear them, 1–5. Add two more types of programme to the list.

Documentary	_____	Murder mystery	_____
Costume drama	_____	Arts programme	_____
Sitcom	_____	Reality show	_____
Talent show	_____	Game show	_____
Chat show	_____	Current affairs programme	_____

3 Work in pairs and discuss these questions.

1 Which sorts of programme are most / least expensive to make?

2 Which types of programme attract the biggest audiences?

3 If you worked for a production company, which types of programme would you recommend that they make more of?

4 We can use the words in the box to describe what is happening in a programme. Complete the descriptions with the words.

> about   characters   episode   plot   setting

1 The _____ is an old castle in the mountains. It's very atmospheric.

2 The programme's _____ a fire station and the people who work there.

3 There are two main _____ – they're twins who share an apartment in LA.

4 It's an interesting _____ : a man wakes up in hospital but he's lost his memory and the police think he's a murderer.

5 Last night's _____ was the final part of the series, but it wasn't a very good ending.

Reading: Positive and negative reviews

5 Read the reviews about a TV programme and complete the table to show how the reviewers' opinions differ.

	Review 1	Review 2
Plot		
Main character		
Setting		
Who the show is aimed at		

Review 1

Viewers will immediately be hooked by this new series. The opening episode introduced us to Lara, a troubled and secretive heroine. Forced to leave her job as a nurse in order to find her irresponsible younger sister, Lara arrives at a mysterious house in Scotland. The location is atmospheric, with fog rolling in from the sea. This is a complex and fascinating story, which is beautifully acted. If you like explosions and car chases, then this serial probably isn't for you. However, if you enjoy well written drama made for adults rather than teenagers, then give this a try.

Review 2

Who watches programmes like this? Presumably those over forty who have nothing better to do in the evening. This costume drama opened by introducing the main character, Lara, a nurse who travels to Scotland in search of her missing sister, Eliza. She arrives at a dark and gloomy manor house where most of the action takes place. Eliza, it is reported, is charming and fun loving. Unfortunately, the viewers never get to meet her. Instead, we have Lara, who is aggressive to everyone she meets as well as being unbelievably annoying. The problems with character and setting would be less serious if the storyline was better written. But the opening episode was slow, boring and puzzling. I had no idea what was going on. Watching paint dry would be more interesting than spending another evening watching this.

6 Tell your partner about a programme that you have recently watched and either really enjoyed or disliked. Give reasons for your views. When you are listening, ask questions about the programme.

Word focus: Evolving English

7 The English language continues to evolve. There are over a million words in the English language and a new word is created every 98 minutes. Choose the correct new word or phrase (a–c) to complete the review extracts below.

1 **a** programme leaping   **b** channel hopping   **c** satellite jumping

2 **a** brunch   **b** dunch   **c** linner

3 **a** sofa cabbage   **b** armchair apple   **c** couch potato

4 **a** webiquette   **b** netiquette   **c** interquette

1 As most viewers will have noticed, there was very little to watch last night. As a result, I hardly watched any show for more than two minutes and spent the evening _____ until it was time for bed.

3 While my friends decided to go out to a club, I spent the evening sitting with my feet up, watching old movies on TV. I must admit, now and then it can be very relaxing being a _____.

2 This band knows how to make albums that make listeners feel good. This is the perfect music to play on a sunny morning while having _____ with friends.

4 The new website will be useful to all international business people. One helpful article explains the importance of being polite in all internet communication and contains some very useful tips on _____.

8 Which words in exercise 7 do these things?

a join two words together, e.g. *sitcom* (situation + comedy). Which two words do they join together?

b create a descriptive or visual image, e.g. *murder mystery*

9 Look at these words and phrases (1–8) that have come into use in recent times. Match them to the definitions (a–h).

1	infomercial	**a**	word or phrase that is used a lot in the media or business
2	telethon	**b**	all day and all week
3	multi-tasking	**c**	a long, factual advertisement on television
4	mass media	**d**	data about a person on social networking sites and web pages
5	buzzword	**e**	a charity event broadcast on TV that lasts hours or days
6	digital footprint	**f**	someone who says they like you but also seems to hate you
7	frenemy	**g**	ways of communicating to a large audience
8	twenty-four seven	**h**	do more than one thing at the same time

Speaking: Create a new word

10 Work in groups. Choose two words to join together to make a new word or phrase. Write a definition for each new word.

11 Join with another pair or group. Listen to the new word that they have created.

- You get two points if you can identify the two words that they have joined together.
- You get three points if you can correctly guess the meaning of the new word.

TALKING POINT   Do you think it is a good idea for a language to adopt words or expressions from other cultures / languages / countries?

Reading: Avoid misunderstandings

1 Work in pairs and discuss these questions.

1 In your experience, when are misunderstandings most likely to occur?

   a on the phone **b** in writing (messages / notes / emails)

   c when speaking to someone face-to-face

   Why do you think this is?

2 Who is responsible for making sure that understanding is clear in a conversation: the person giving information or the person receiving information?

2))) 2.15 Listen and match the speakers to four of these topics.

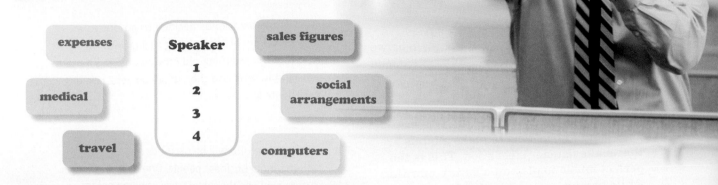

expenses

Speaker
1
2
3
4

sales figures

medical

social arrangements

travel

computers

3))) Listen again. What information might be unclear to the listener?

4 Work in two groups. Group A, brainstorm ways that a person giving information can make sure that they are getting their message across. Group B, discuss ways that the person receiving information can make sure they understand.

5 Look at the tips for clear communication below and complete the information with these headings.

   Forget blame   Be specific   Ask questions to clarify   Check understanding   Summarize and signal   Avoid multi-tasking

6 Do the tips mention any of your ideas? Which tip refers to both the speaker and the listener?

1 _____

- When you're trying to get your message across effectively, it's not a good idea to try to do more than one thing at a time.
- Concentrate on what you are doing at the moment and what you want to say or write.

2 _____

- Misunderstandings can occur when people use vague or approximate language. Give enough information so that your meaning is clear.
- If a misunderstanding occurs, apologize and try saying it again in a different way.

3 _____

- Is there anything in the person's voice or body language that suggests that they are having a problem understanding?
- Stop and ask questions to check whether they need more information or clarification.

4 _____

- Reformulate important information to check that you have understood correctly.
- Use body language such as nodding or verbal responses to show that you understand.

Tips!

5 _____

- Identify areas where you need more information or clarification.
- Use questions to check or ask for more information.

6 _____

- If there is a misunderstanding, work together to communicate effectively.
- Remain polite. Solve the problem rather than focus on who is at fault for the communication breakdown.

Listening: That wasn't what I meant

7))) **2.16** Listen to a phone conversation between two colleagues. What are the three misunderstandings? Which is the only tip heading in exercise 5 that the speakers follow?

8))) **2.17** Now listen to another version of the conversation. What do they do differently? Is there any difference in the speakers' attitudes in the two conversations?

9 Complete the phrases from the second version of the conversation and put them under the correct heading in the table. Use the audio script on page 151 to help you.

1 Could I just _____ a few things?

2 If I understand _____, …

3 D'you see what I _____?

4 That wasn't what I _____.

5 What I was _____ to say was …

6 I _____ you mean …

7 Ah, _____ you.

8 Can you tell me a little more _____ …?

9 Do you _____?

10 That's all _____ now.

Clarifying	
Check the listener understands:	**Reformulate to check (the information you've been given):**
Is that clear?	*So, you're saying that …*
Are you with me?	*Is that correct?*
Clarify meaning (when giving information):	**Ask questions to clarify:**
I think there's been a misunderstanding.	*Can I check what you mean by …?*
Let me put that another way …	*Do you have any more information on …?*
	The other thing I wanted to check was …?
Respond:	
Oh, I see. I see what you mean. Oh, of course.	

10 Work in pairs. Take turns to explain one of the following to your partner. When you're explaining, check understanding and clarify meaning as necessary. When you're listening, ask questions and reformulate the information to check you have understood.

- the rules of a game
- how a device or gadget works
- a process
- a theory
- something else

Speaking: Can I clarify that?

11 Work in pairs. Look at the two messages that have been left on an office desk.

Student A: You have been out of the office all morning. Talk to your colleague and clarify the information in these messages that he/she has left for you.

Student B: You are the colleague. Turn to File 52, page 123 and answer your partner's questions about the information.

Phone message

JH: cancel meeting with paper supplier – Thursday?

Confirm orders for media advertising web TV?

Hope all clear.

Note

New catalogue pictures missing – photographer copies?

Find DVD images.

Check last publication date with the printers

Design department – ask for confirmation of artwork budget 20? 30?

12 Work in pairs and roleplay a telephone conversation to check information.

Student A: You work for a media sales company which organizes advertising for international companies. You received the email below from a client, but some of it is unclear. Phone to clarify the information.

Student B: You work for Diego Tyres. You are the client of a media sales company which organizes advertising for international companies. You sent the email below. Turn to File 53, page 124 and answer your partner's questions about the information.

Hi

I've had some thoughts about possible changes to forthcoming advertising for Diego Tyres.

1 Magazine
Stop advertisements in *That Car!*
Move to *Speed and Travel* from next mth.

Colour not b/w. Full pge not half.
Position = back (if poss).

2 TV commercial
Keep same time slot (8.30) but change day
Thurs → Fri

3 Online
Website - *Car Crazy*? Wrong for our market?
Other possible blogs / websites?

Let me know what you think.

Regards

Reminder

Passives overview page 81 + Grammar reference, page 169
Asking questions page 83 + Grammar reference, pages 163–164
Clarifying page 87

Reading: A safety incident

1 Look at the photos from a brochure offering team-building courses at an outdoor activity centre. Which activity would you most and least like to take part in?

2 Rank the activities in order of how dangerous you think they are (1 = most dangerous, 4 = least dangerous). Compare your ideas with a partner.

3 Work in pairs. Choose one of the activities and carry out a risk assessment, listing at least five things that could go wrong. What could the organization running the activity do to make sure that it is as safe as possible? You can include these topics.

training   safety equipment   emergency procedures

4 Read the news report on a website about an accident at the Waterside Activity Centre and the comments that have been added. Discuss the questions.

1 Has the Waterside Activity Centre got a good reputation for safety? What makes you think this?

2 What problems could the article cause for the activity centre?

3 The activity centre states that it will 'look into the incident'. What is the first step it should take to do this?

Breaking News …
Accident at local activity centre

More problems for the South East's biggest activity centres.

After two previous safety incidents last year, there was more unwelcome publicity for Waterside Activity Centre yesterday, following reports of an accident during a team-building exercise. Initial reports suggest that a team member may have been injured during a caving activity. An ambulance was seen leaving caves near the centre. The injured party has been identified as Sam Hughes, an employee of Centara Insurance. Waterside Activity Centre has said that it will look into the incident and will release a statement at a later date.

JamesDukan@Freeband.com   *two minutes ago*

Wouldn't it be a good idea to wait for more info before jumping to conclusions?

LianC@Linkworld.com   *five minutes ago*

Was there 2 wks ago. Very big groups and the instructor seemed pressurized to get through the activity as quickly as possible.

MiaCal@Founder.com   *ten minutes ago*

Seems a bit harsh JJ. Accidents usually happen due to a combination of factors. I was at Waterside on a training day a few months ago and it seemed pretty chaotic.

JJ@Maze.com   *twelve minutes ago*

Agree KMV. Accidents like this r often due to participants treating it as fun and games and not listening to basic safety instructions.

Kmv@ gomail.com   *fifteen minutes ago*

Surprised to read this. Our company took part in an event there last year and found the instructors very professional, with high safety standards.

Listening: Clarify events

5))) **2.18** Listen to a conversation between the Health and Safety Officer at Waterside Activity Centre and the Training Coordinator at Centara Insurance, the company that employs the injured team member. Answer these questions.

1 Which two things happened to Sam Hughes during the caving trip?

    a became ill

    b got lost

    c broke leg

    d lost torch

2 Which two things are different between Zaheer's account and Sam's account?

    a location of accident

    b length of safety talk

    c number of people in group

    d whether or not group was told to check equipment

6))) Listen again and decide if these statements are true (T) or false (F). Correct any false information.

1 Sam is getting better in hospital.

2 Sam might not have been listening carefully to the safety talk.

3 It took Zaheer 20 minutes to discover that one of the group was missing.

4 There was a quick response in getting medical help.

5 Sam followed signs to get out of the cave.

6 Sam entered an area where visitors were not permitted to go.

Speaking: Analyze the problem

7 Work in two groups. Decide what questions need to be asked to clarify how the accident happened.

Group A: Suggest questions to ask Sam Hughes.
Group B: Suggest questions to ask Zaheer Kumar.

8 Work in pairs, one person from Group A and one from Group B, and roleplay the interviews.

Interview 1

Student A: You are the Training Coordinator. Interview Sam and clarify details. Use some of the questions that you discussed in your group.

Student B: You are Sam Hughes. Turn to File 54, page 124.

Interview 2

Student A: You are Zaheer Kumar. Turn to File 82, page 130.

Student B: You are the Health and Safety Officer. Interview Zaheer and clarify details. Use some of the questions that you discussed in your group.

9 Discuss how an incident such as this could be avoided in the future.

Writing: Memo – make recommendations

10 You are the Health and Safety Officer at the Waterside Activity Centre. Write a memo to your management team.

Outline information on the following:

- what happened
- factors that contributed to the accident (look at the Files again to help you)

Make recommendations to improve procedures in the future. Include ideas about the following:

maximum size of group, safety talk, how to check if a group member is missing, when a missing person search should start, what an instructor should have in case of emergency, who should they contact first / next.

Interaction

1 Complete these sentences using the second or third conditional.

1 If you left the house on time, you _____ (not be) late for work every day.

2 The team _____ (visit) the new headquarters in Rome if their flight hadn't been cancelled.

3 We _____ ([possibly] win) the contract if we'd spent more time on the presentation.

4 If you'd entered the competition, I'm sure you _____ (come) first.

5 The client would have called you back if you _____ (leave) a message when you phoned him.

6 If the seminar finished by five o'clock, they _____ (be) able to meet at the café afterwards.

7 If the building _____ (not be completed) on time, we would have cancelled the launch party.

8 I think people _____ ([possibly] get) in touch with us if our contact details were more clearly displayed.

2 Choose the best option to complete these sentences.

1 If they hadn't changed their marketing strategy last year, they probably wouldn't *be / have been* the market leader today.

2 If *I'd won / I win* the competition, I'd give you half the prize money because you were such a help.

3 If the team *hadn't promised / hasn't promised* such impressive profits, the shareholders wouldn't expect such generous returns now.

4 They should've stopped and helped if they *saw / have seen* that there was a problem.

5 We could be on a beach right now if we *hadn't missed / didn't miss* our plane.

6 If staff wanted a pay rise, wouldn't they *have agreed / agreed* to work longer hours?

3 Choose the correct word or phrase to complete these sentences.

1 The economy may continue to recover _____ we may consider raising interest rates in April.

   a supposing **b** in which case **c** although

2 You can finish early today _____ all the important tasks are completed.

   a provided that **b** unless **c** in case

3 Make sure that you call me _____ you get there.

   a until **b** whether **c** when

4 Employees won't reach their potential _____ they are given adequate support and training.

   a although **b** unless **c** supposing

5 I'll bring a spare key _____ we get locked out.

   a in case **b** in which case **c** as long as

6 It's a very popular restaurant _____ the service can sometimes be slow.

   a unless **b** when **c** although

7 The weather might be fine at the moment but _____ it snows this afternoon?

   a what if **b** in case **c** as if

8 The financial markets are strong but _____ the price of gold suddenly falls?

   a in case **b** supposing **c** although

4 Read this extract from a memo and then rewrite the sentences in *italics* using the passive.

After consultation with the local community, we have decided to purchase land on which to extend our present facilities. [1] *A local contractor has carried out a full survey.* [2] *We intend to invite construction companies to bid for the contract.* The deadline for the submission of bids is 1 October. [3] *We hope the successful company will start the building work as soon as possible.* [4] *We expect that the construction work will continue until next autumn.*

[5] *Reports say that the design of the present offices has caused many problems.* The new building will resolve many of these issues and all staff will have larger workspaces. [6] *However, we expect that the building work may cause a certain amount of disruption.* [7] *We have already made plans for dealing with this.* We apologize in advance for any inconvenience the building work may cause.

[8] *Hilary Rocha is coordinating the project.* Please contact her on extension 3046 if you have any queries.

5 Complete these questions with words or phrases from the box. You do not need to use some of the words or phrases.

> couldn't didn't have haven't if isn't it or not
> say tell whether weren't

1 Could you clarify _____ you paid the money by cash or by credit card?

2 Did they confirm whether _____ they want the order?

3 Can you _____ me the name of the company, please?

4 You have sent the marketing report to the client, _____ you?

5 Viewers would like to know _____ it's true that you signed the document.

6 The view from your office is wonderful, _____?

7 You sent the client the contract, _____ you?

8 You were based in Shanghai for a year, _____ you?

6 Find ten words connected to the media in the word square, to help you complete these sentences.

1 A _____ show is where amateurs can sing, dance or do other things they are good at.

2 The _____ is the main events of a story.

3 The main _____ was played by Johnny Depp.

4 My brother watches TV all day – he's a real _____ potato.

5 When viewers want to laugh, they usually watch a _____.

6 I prefer programmes which analyse business, news and _____ affairs.

7 Several celebrities were interviewed on last night's _____ show.

8 Some people can get irritated when the person they watch TV with starts _____ hopping.

9 The _____ for their film is a spooky old house during a terrible storm.

10 The Belgian detective had to discover who killed the famous artist; it was a rather silly murder _____.

M	C	H	A	N	N	E	L	V	S
S	Y	S	I	T	C	H	P	F	E
V	E	I	H	C	U	O	C	L	T
C	H	T	E	R	D	U	H	W	T
D	W	C	A	P	C	H	A	I	I
C	U	O	S	L	N	I	R	N	N
U	H	M	I	O	E	W	A	G	G
R	J	A	T	T	Q	N	C	H	A
R	M	B	T	M	I	S	T	E	E
A	U	Y	O	C	H	A	E	Y	B
N	P	L	T	N	E	R	R	U	C
M	Y	S	T	E	R	Y	L	A	T

7 Complete this telephone conversation with the phrases a–j.

A: Hi, I'm calling about the statement that I received from your company yesterday. ¹_____?

B: Of course, how ²_____?

A: Well, looking at the statement, if I ³_____, you've charged me twice.

B: Are you ⁴_____ you were charged for the same item two times? ⁵_____?

A: No, that's ⁶_____ . The total of everything I bought has been charged twice. Are ⁷_____?

B: Oh, I think I see ⁸_____. You were charged double the price for one of our products.

A: No, listen, let ⁹_____. I bought ten items and each item cost £35. Your company has charged me for twenty items and has taken £700 from my account.

B: Ah, I'm ¹⁰_____ now. I do apologize. I'll take your details and order a refund …

a saying that

b you with me

c can I clarify a few things

d what you mean

e not what I meant

f me put it another way

g understand correctly

h is that correct

i with you

j can I help

8 Put each word in the box into the correct group according to its stress pattern.

> construction chaos terminal technical cancellation
> assessment leisure understanding connection
> departmental internet controversial mobile
> escorted officer statement headline consumer
> accidental networking

O o	O o o	o O o	o o O o
airport	passenger	procedure	conversation

9

A Making predictions
B Modal perfect
C Breaches of privacy
D **Communication strategies** Indirectness
E **Interaction** Monitoring at work

Security and privacy

Making predictions

Listening: Plastic money

1 Choose *two* questions and discuss them.

1 How do you think credit card security is going to improve?

2 In your opinion, is there going to be more or less credit available over the next couple of years?

3 How do you think the way people pay for the things they buy is going to change in the next few years?

4 What do you think will happen to debit card customers in the years to come?

2))) **2.19** Listen to people in the street answering the questions above. Match each answer to the appropriate question.

Interview A = Question _____   Interview C = Question _____

Interview B = Question _____   Interview D = Question _____

3))) Listen to the interviews again and complete the sentences.

1 I think it's _____ that credit card payments will decrease in popularity.

2 It's _____ _____ that more and more consumers will turn to mobile banking.

3 So, really, _____ _____ whether access to credit will be easier.

4 For those who have credit cards, it _____ _____ be more difficult to spend.

5 Well, plastic cards _____ won't become any safer to use – they'll continue to get stolen or lost.

6 So there's _____ _____ be a great improvement in security in the next few years.

7 The number of credit card customers is _____ to decline sharply over the next few years.

8 It's _____ _____ that debit cards will become everybody's preferred plastic.

4 Which of the predictions in exercise 3 do you think may also be true for your country? How would you rewrite the ones that you think are not true?

I think it's unlikely that credit card payments will decrease in popularity.

→ In my country, credit card payments definitely won't decrease in popularity.

Grammar: Making predictions

5 We use the phrases you completed in exercise 3 to show how sure or not we are about the predictions we make. Put the numbers of the phrases in what you feel is the correct place on the line. Then read the notes below.

sure something
will happen ⟷ sure something
won't happen

Predictions and probability

We can make predictions and express degrees of probability in various ways.

1 We can use these modals (see Unit 2): *may / may not; might / might not; could.*

*Scanners **may / might / could** replace traditional credit cards.* (= it is possible)

*Scanners **may well / might well / could well** replace credit cards.* (= it is more sure – the addition of *well* signals an increased feeling of certainty)

2 We can use *will / won't* together with an adverb.

*It **will definitely** be more difficult to spend.*

*Plastic cards **probably won't** be safer to use.*

*Security **will certainly** continue to be an issue.*

Note that such adverbs normally come after *will* but before *won't*.

3 We often use a lexical phrase: *it's (highly / quite) unlikely that / it's (quite) probable that / I doubt whether / there's no (little / not much) chance of / there's sure to be, etc.*

>> For more information on predictions and probability, see pages 166–167.

6 Complete the second sentence in each pair so that it means about the same as the first sentence. Use between *three* and *five* words, including the word given.

1 I don't think parking meters will ever accept credit cards.

doubt

_____ parking meters will ever accept credit cards.

2 Consumer card usage will drop sharply.

sure

There _____ sharp drop in consumer card usage.

3 Credit cards are going to become less available and more expensive.

bound

Credit cards _____ less available and more expensive.

4 Banks will never value low-end, high-risk customers.

chance

There's _____ ever valuing low-end, high-risk customers.

5 Banks are unlikely to discontinue all their reward programmes.

probably

Banks _____ all their reward programmes.

6 I'm sure credit card fees will increase significantly.

definitely

There _____ increase in credit card fees.

7 I don't think I'll apply for a credit card. I'd be in the red all the time!

unlikely

_____ I'll apply for a credit card. I'd be in the red all the time!

8 Paper money probably won't disappear in the near future.

likely

Paper money _____ disappear in the near future.

Speaking: What does the future hold?

7 Work in pairs. Which of the words or phrases from the Grammar table would you choose instead of *will* in these sentences? Discuss your opinions.

The internet will have very serious problems.

Credit cards will disappear completely.

Most people will choose security over privacy.

Intelligence agencies will be able to scan irises from a distance.

Artificial noses in doorways will identify people by their unique body odour.

Everyone will have a biometric identity card.

A: It's highly likely that the internet will run into serious problems.
B: Why do you think so?
A: Well, …

8 Write your own predictions for the distant or immediate future about three of these topics.

- yourself
- one of your colleagues
- a member of your family
- a celebrity of your choice
- a political figure of your choice
- your favourite football team
- the euro
- the Chinese economy

Then work in pairs and discuss your predictions.

A: I'll definitely start learning to play tennis.
B: Really? Why tennis?
A: Well, I …

TALKING POINT • Do you think that living on credit causes too many problems for people – and for countries?
• Were things better when people saved up to buy things?

Reading: Security? What's that?

1 Answer these questions.

1 Where do security breaches usually happen?

2 What famous security breaches have you heard of?

2 Read the article and discuss these questions.

1 What did the UN security guards do wrong?

2 How do you think the actor felt before, during and after this promotional stunt?

3))) **2.20** Listen to Renata Miller, an American marketing executive, give her views on the incident at the UN. How positive or negative do you think she will be?

Grammar: Modal perfect

4))) Read the information in the table. Then listen again and complete the examples.

Modal perfect
We form the modal perfect with modal + *have* + past participle.
We can use the modal perfect to:
1 criticize or comment on past actions.
This security breach [1]_____ *not* _____ *happened.*   *The guards* [2]_____ _____ _____ *the actor's identity.*
2 speculate about events in the past.
The whole idea [3]_____ _____ _____ *a terrible failure.*   *I think the guys behind the stunt* [4]_____ _____ _____ *everything very carefully.*   *It* [5]_____ _____ _____ *easy to find an actor willing to take the risk.*
>> For more information on the modal perfect, see page 167.

5 Complete the modal perfect forms to make meaningful sentences.

1 I can't access my online account. I _____ _____ keyed in the wrong password.

2 Good thing you didn't press those two keys together. You _____ _____ erased all the data from your hard drive!

3 Last month, ten people managed to enter the building without a pass. The head of security _____ _____ been too pleased with the guards on duty!

4 I'm afraid it's too late to sign up for the computer course. You _____ _____ done it last week.

5 Milo _____ _____ been utterly exhausted. He literally fell asleep at his desk!

6 You _____ _____ given him your password. What if he wasn't from the IT department as he claimed to be?

KFC at the UN?

A man impersonating the Kentucky Fried Chicken founder Colonel Sanders managed to enter the UN headquarters in New York and shake hands with a senior official.

Dressed in the fast food icon's familiar white suit and black bow tie, the actor evaded tight security to gain access to the restricted areas of the complex. He even posed for a photograph with the president of the UN General Assembly, before the alarm was raised and he was ejected.

A spokeswoman for the UN said that an investigation had been launched into the security breach, which was dreamt up by KFC as a publicity stunt. 'It should not have happened,' she said.

Word focus: Compound nouns

6 Match a noun from Box A to a noun from Box B to make compound nouns. Then use them to complete the article below.

A	B
football	workers
girl	word
family	friend
pass	teams
office	names

A sweet way into people's PCs

A survey of ¹_____ _____ found that 71 per cent were willing to reveal their ²_____ for a bar of chocolate. Workers were asked a series of questions which included 'What's your password?', to which 37 per cent immediately gave their password. If they initially refused, the researchers made a comment like 'I bet it's to do with your pet or child's name'. At this, a further 34 per cent revealed their passwords, but realized within seconds that they had been taken in, and said they should have been more careful. Many explained the origin of their passwords, such as 'my team – Arsenal', 'my ³_____'s name – Sarah'. The most common password categories were relatives' or close friends' ⁴_____ _____, followed by ⁵_____ _____ and pets. One of the most common passwords was … 'password'!

7 Read the KFC article again and find at least five compound nouns.

8 Discuss these questions.

1 How many different internet passwords do you use? How do you remember them?

2 How would you evaluate these passwords in terms of safety and usability?

a mariedeschamps (= user's first name + surname)

b vwgolf&4701 (= user's car + & + last four digits of number plate)

c 21August1990 (= user's date of birth)

d ginger (= user's cat's name)

e f@23rfq$nsq%&zx495

f intermilan (= user's favourite football team)

g IMyours4ever

Speaking: Stories from keywords

9 Work in groups of three. Take it in turns to ask and answer questions about three real stories of security breaches.

Story 1:
Student A: Turn to File 11, page 115. Students B and C: Turn to File 28, page 119.

Story 2:
Student B: Turn to File 49, page 123. Students A and C: Turn to File 56, page 124.

Story 3:
Student C: Turn to File 90, page 132. Students A and B: Turn to File 95, page 134.

10 Work in groups of three. Reflect on the different people in your stories.

1 How would you criticize the following people?
- Haisong Jiang
- the Newark Airport authorities
- the Salahis
- the White House security officers
- the Slovak authorities
- the Irish police

  Haisong Jiang shouldn't have gone into the secure area.

2 Speculate about how the following people felt after the event.
- Haisong Jiang
- the passengers at Newark Airport
- the Salahis
- the White House social secretary
- the Slovak authorities
- the Slovak electrician

  Haisong Jiang must have felt sorry for what he did.
  The passengers can't have been too pleased about the delays.

TALKING POINT
- What could organizations do to help employees with internet security issues?
- What do organizations do to ensure the personal security of their staff?

Listening: A Bigger Brother

1 Discuss these questions.

1 How important is privacy when you are a high-school student?

2 What do schools and parents sometimes do that makes teenagers feel their privacy is being invaded?

3 Should school authorities carry out any kind of surveillance on children?

2)) **2.21** Work in pairs or in small groups. Look at these keywords from a radio news item and try to predict what the news item is about. Then listen and check.

> school   webcam   laptop   lawsuit   home

3)) Listen again and answer these questions.

1 What was special about the laptop the school district gave the students?

2 How did the student and his parents discover that the computer was equipped with security software?

3 How did the school authorities justify their actions?

4 How widespread does this kind of surveillance technology seem to be?

4 Discuss these questions.

1 Were the student and his parents right to go to court?

2 Would the school's actions be legal in your country?

Word focus: The law

5 Choose the correct option to complete these sentences from the radio news item. Then go to the audio script on page 152 to check your answers.

1 The parents of a high-school student from Philadelphia have *made / filed / complained / faced* a lawsuit against the school district.

2 He was *charged / sentenced / judged / accused* of bad behaviour in his home.

3 The only evidence the school was able to *present / judge / make / examine* to support the accusation was a photograph taken from the webcam embedded in the laptop.

4 Blake's lawyers have also expressed serious concern over the officials' actions and said they could face criminal *trials / cases / charges / verdicts.*

6 Match these sentence halves.

1 If you don't withdraw your allegations,
2 It's highly likely that the case will be heard
3 The former interior minister denied
4 The company faces a number of lawsuits
5 The prosecuting lawyer managed to prove
6 She produced evidence that

a that the defendant intended to cause bodily harm.
b her bank account had been accessed fraudulently.
c over its failure to protect its workers.
d he'll certainly contact his lawyer.
e charges of corruption and money laundering.
f in the Court of Appeal.

7 Complete this extract from a newspaper article with the verbs in the box.

> brought   charged   faced   heard   intervened   removed

Google executives face Milan trial

In 2006, an incident at a school in Turin caused outrage in Italy. Four boys were filmed teasing another boy, who has Down's syndrome. A three-minute mobile phone recording of the incident was uploaded to Google Video, where it was seen by thousands of users over almost two months before being ¹_____ by Google after the Italian government and police ²_____. An Italian prosecutor then ³_____ criminal charges against four Google executives. The four executives were ⁴_____ with criminal defamation against the disabled boy and with breaching the Italian privacy code. They ⁵_____ up to three years in prison if found guilty of charges of defamation and of failing to protect the boy's privacy. The case was ⁶_____ at the Milan criminal court in February 2010.

8 Go through exercises 5, 6 and 7 and complete this record of some of the collocations that you came across.

1 to f_____ a lawsuit (against somebody)
2 to f_____ a lawsuit
3 to p_____ evidence
4 to p_____ evidence
5 to f_____ charges

6 to d_____ charges
7 to b_____ charges (against somebody)
8 to w_____ allegations
9 to h_____ a case

Speaking: What's your verdict?

9 Work in pairs. Consider carefully the Blake Robbins vs. Lower Merion School District case in exercises 2 and 3.

- First, discuss the case. What do you think the outcome was?
- Then, compare your verdict against the actual court ruling (File 57, page 124). Any surprises?

10 Work in new pairs. Consider the Google case in exercise 7.

- First, discuss the case. What do you think the outcome was?
- Then, compare your verdict against the actual court ruling (File 22, page 118). Any surprises?

11 Work in small groups. Telecommuting (i.e. working at home using a computer connected to a company's main office) is a rapidly growing trend in a number of countries. It is said to be 'the future of work'. But how should employers monitor telecommuters?

- Discuss the pros and cons of equipping telecommuters' computers with a webcam which would allow employers to monitor them.
- Make sure you look at the issue from both the employer's and the employee's point of view.

> **TALKING POINT**   Some people say 'If you have nothing to hide, you have nothing to worry about'. What do *you* think?

Listening: Requests

1 Work in pairs. Look at these situations and answer the questions.

1 At work: Marianne's computer has just frozen and she doesn't know what to do about it. She asks Geoff, a colleague, for help. What could she say?

2 At work: Rick has a problem changing his computer password. He calls someone from the IT department for help. What could he say?

3 Shopping: Anya, the customer, has decided to buy the Vectra anti-virus software package. What could she say to the shop assistant?

2))) **2.22** Listen to the conversations for the three situations in exercise 1. Work in pairs. Did the people say what you expected? The conversations were all natural except for one. Which one do you think it is and why?

3))) **2.23** Listen to someone talking about the way English speakers make requests in exercise 2. Some things she says are correct and some are wrong. Which ones are wrong?

4))) Listen to the first part of the commentary again and complete the summary.

In most English-speaking countries, the way in which we express requests is influenced by at least three ¹_____:

- the ²_____ between the interlocutors (the greater the social ³_____, the more formal the language)
- ⁴_____ relationships (do the interlocutors have ⁵_____ ⁶_____ and power, or is one inferior and the other superior?)
- the ⁷_____ of the request (are you asking for a big or a small ⁸_____?)

Think about your culture. Are requests influenced by the same or other factors? In what ways?

5))) **2.24** Listen to four conversations between colleagues and decide what the requests are about. Number the topics 1–4 as you hear them.

- working overtime
- working during the coffee break
- translating a letter from Russian into English
- sending out conference invitations
- installing computer software
- editing some photos
- copying a computer program
- checking a translation

6))) Listen to the conversations again and complete the examples in the table.

Indirectness: request openers and softeners
1   **A:** ¹_____ _____ bother you, ²_____ _____ you do something for me? Would you ³_____ _____ a look at it when you have a minute?   **B:** ⁴_____ at all.
2   **A:** I know you're very busy, but do you think ⁵_____ _____ go through this translation for me?   **B:** No problem.
3   **A:** I ⁶_____ if you could ⁷_____ do some overtime on Thursday and Friday, ⁸_____ .   **B:** ⁹_____ _____ _____ , I've got to be home by six Thursday evening. We've got a family reunion.
4   **A:** ¹⁰_____ I ask you something? ¹¹_____ it be all right if I copied it onto my laptop?   **B:** I'd ¹²_____ to help you, but I'm ¹³_____ it was only a trial version.

- Instead of starting a request simply with *Could you*, we often use an 'opener' (e.g. *I wonder if you could / Do you think you could*, etc.). We may also use a 'softener' before the opener to show we understand that the hearer might be inconvenienced by our request (e.g. *I know you're busy / Sorry to bother you*, etc.).

- Sometimes, instead of expressing a request literally, we just give the hearer a hint:

A: It's rather cold in here. (= *Could you shut the window?*)

Speaking: Sounding less direct

7 Work in pairs. Look at these requests, which are not expressed directly.

What are these people requesting? Can you 'decode the hints'?

> **1** Oh no, my printer's jammed!

> **2** Those biscuits look delicious.

> **3** It's dark in here, isn't it?

> **4** Erm ... Have you got a minute?

8 Work in pairs. How would you turn these requests into 'hints'?

> **1** Do you think I could borrow your camcorder for the weekend?

> **2** Can I help myself to some fruit?

> **3** Would you mind helping me move this desk over there?

> **4** Could you lend me 20 euros?

9 Here is an extract from a conversation between two managers discussing surveillance. Put the lines in the correct order.

_____ *A: Don't worry about the unions. We always win them over.*

_____ *A: I doubt it. Cameras are a powerful deterrent. And they are the cheapest solution.*

_____ *A: Right. But first we need to think about our bottom line. We need to stop employee theft, so we need to increase surveillance.*

_____ *A: We should install CCTV cameras everywhere. It's the best solution. What do you think?*

_____ *B: I don't think that's true. Cameras may be relatively inexpensive, but installing the whole system costs a small fortune.*

_____ *B: That's true, but we need to think about the well-being of our staff, too.*

_____ *B: Well ... erm ... I'm not sure. The unions definitely won't like the idea.*

_____ *B: Yes, but what I'm saying is, there are better ways of doing that than CCTV cameras.*

10 <u>Underline</u> the phrases in exercise 9 that Speaker B uses to disagree with Speaker A.

Indirectness: disagreeing

In conversation, we don't often use phrases like *I agree* or *I disagree*, and we usually avoid direct confrontations like *You are wrong.*

We often disagree by saying *Yes, but …*, and then asking a challenging question or raising an objection.

However, we sometimes want to express our opinions more forcefully (e.g. *Yes, but what I'm saying is … / I don't think that's true.*).

---

11 Work in pairs. Rewrite this conversation to make it more appropriate by using suitable requests and ways of expressing disagreement where necessary.

A = project manager; B = research assistant

A: Hi, Nathan. I want to have a word with you about our project.

B: Sure. What's up?

A: Well, we're running behind schedule. So you and the rest of the team will be working on Saturday morning. OK?

B: What? Saturday? No way.

A: I know it's not easy, Nathan. But make a special effort this time. We really need an extra project meeting.

B: Plan it for Thursday instead.

A: Impossible.

12 Work in the same pairs. Practise your new dialogue, and add four lines at the end (B / A / B / A). Then work with another pair and take it in turns to perform your dialogue.

13 ◀)) **2.25** Listen to another version of the conversation in exercise 11. How is it different?

Reminder

> **Making predictions** page 92 + Grammar reference pages 166–167
> **Modal perfect** page 94 + Grammar reference page 167
> **Indirectness** pages 98 and 99

Word focus: Easily confused words and expressions

1 Reflect on your experience as a language learner. Answer these questions.

1 Which English words and phrases do you tend to confuse with other English words and phrases? Write them down.

2 Which English words and phrases do you tend to confuse with words and phrases in your mother tongue? Write them down.

2 Work in small groups. Compare your lists. Tell each other what you do in order to try and stop confusing those words and phrases.

3 Complete each sentence with the best word.

1 I think use of the internet for private purposes during office hours is bound to _____ the quality of an employee's work.

   a effect **b** accept **c** affect **d** except

2 An employer should have the right to _____ the use of electronic communications by an employee.

   a control **b** overview **c** test **d** oversight

3 _____ my opinion, video monitoring of teachers is a guarantee of quality.

   a By **b** In **c** From **d** According to

4 At work, we _____ being watched all the time, so nobody complains.

   a used to **b** used **c** use to **d** are used to

5 Companies should _____ employees to send and receive personal emails at least during breaks.

   a make **b** allow **c** grant **d** let

6 In my country, the number of complaints against improper monitoring procedures at work has _____ considerably.

   a raised **b** rose **c** risen **d** arose

7 I think all managers should get some _____ from an IT expert on how to monitor their employees' electronic communications at work.

   a advise **b** advising **c** advises **d** advice

8 How much monitoring is necessary at work depends _____ the amount of trust between workers and management.

   a on **b** for **c** at **d** from

9 A lot of people complain about being monitored at work _____ they think nothing of sharing details of their private lives on social networks.

   a despite **b** however **c** in spite **d** although

10 If you are responsible and work _____ all the time, you don't need to worry about being monitored.

   a much **b** hardly **c** a lot of **d** hard

4 Read the completed sentences in exercise 3. Tick (✓) the ones that you agree with. Then work in small groups to compare and discuss your answers.

5 Rewrite the sentences in exercise 3 that you don't agree with so that they express your own opinion.

Listening: Employee monitoring

6))) **2.26** Listen to an extract from a radio documentary programme about internet monitoring in US firms. Complete the extract with the missing statistics.

According to a US survey:

- more than [1] _____ per cent of employers monitor their workers' website connections
- [2] _____ per cent of firms use software to monitor external (incoming and outgoing) email
- only [3] _____ per cent take advantage of technology tools to monitor internal email conversations that take place between employees
- [4] _____ per cent of employers have implemented a written email policy
- almost [5] _____ per cent of employees report sending and receiving inappropriate and potentially damaging content (e.g. jokes, gossip, confidential information about the company, etc.)

7 Make predictions about internet monitoring in your country based on the US statistics in exercise 6.

The number of employers who monitor their workers' website connections will certainly go up.

It's unlikely that employees will agree to having their internal email conversations monitored.

Speaking: The boss never blinks

8 Exchange information in pairs to find out more about how employers can monitor their staff.

Student A: Turn to File 58, page 125. Student B: Turn to File 87, page 132.

9 Reifert Ltd is a private pharmaceutical research company which employs 250 people. Many of them have access to data and information that should not be divulged.

Read the notes about the company's workplace monitoring policy.

Current measures:

* all employees' incoming and outgoing emails are monitored, as well as all their website connections

* all internal and external phone calls on company telephones are monitored

* video surveillance is used for security purposes only (e.g. laboratories, warehouse, parking lot, etc.)

Possible future measures:

* monitoring of blogs and social networking sites to find out what employees might be saying about the company

* ban on the use of private mobile phones during working hours (a new hotline could be made available for urgent personal messages)

* use of video surveillance for performance evaluation purposes as well

* recording the time employees spend on bathroom and smoking breaks

Now work in pairs. The aim of your discussion is to:

- review the current monitoring measures and decide whether to keep all of them.
- decide which new measures you want to introduce, and provide convincing arguments for them.

Student A: Turn to File 61, page 126. Student B: Turn to File 89, page 132.

Writing: Memo – monitoring measures

10 Work in the same pairs as in exercise 9. Draft a memo to staff.

In your memo, you should explain:

- why the current measures are being kept.
- if relevant, why any of the current measures are being dropped.
- which new measures are being introduced and what their purpose is.

10

A Verb patterns
B Extreme adjectives and adverb usage
C Giving feedback
D **Communication strategies** Motivation
E **Interaction** Managing change

Flexible thinking

Verb patterns

Reading: My life, your choice

1 Things can change during a career. Look at the list and add three more items. Which two things do you think are the most positive changes? Which change could be most stressful?

starting a new job   learning new skills
taking a sabbatical   moving department
promotion prospects   retirement

2 Look at the title of the blog on the right. What do you think *crowdsourcing* might be? What words does it join together?

3 Blogger Mathew Harding is starting an experiment with his career. Read his blog and check what *crowdsourcing* means. Answer these questions.

1 What were Matthew's ambitions when he was a student?

2 What is the main problem he has with his job now?

3 What field does he think he would like to move into?

4 Has he got enough money to cover the costs of training to be a doctor?

5 What is the experiment he wants to do?

4 Work in pairs. Discuss the pros and cons of each of Matthew's possible choices. Decide which of the two options to vote for – red or green. What do you think will happen if he takes this action?

If you pressed the red button, turn to File 29, page 119 and find out.

If you pressed the green button, turn to File 62, page 126 and find out.

5 Work with a different partner. Find someone who voted for a different option to you. Explain why you chose your option. Summarize what happened when Matthew followed your choice.

Can crowdsourcing solve my career dilemma?

Before leaving college, I planned to have a long and successful career and imagined *becoming* the youngest CEO of a global multinational. I expected *to get* a job quickly and have many happy years of training and promotion before *retiring* young at the age of 55. That was the plan, anyway.

Many of my friends found it difficult to get even a job interview, but I was lucky *to find* a position soon after *completing* my electronics exams. I have my own office, a regular salary and good promotion prospects. But there's a problem. Although I enjoy *working* with my colleagues, the work itself no longer interests me. I've realized that I want *to work* in the medical profession. I considered *discussing* the situation with my line manager but it's not easy *to talk* to him. Anyway, it's no use *trying* to explain anything to him, he'd probably just point out that it would be crazy to *leave* a good job. Besides, how could I afford to *train* as a doctor even if I got a place on a course? I need to *make* a decision soon.

You might have heard of crowdsourcing: it's a way of *using* the internet to get ideas from a large group of people. So, as an experiment, I'm going to hand decisions about my career over to you intelligent blog readers out there. I look forward *to hearing* from you. I'll follow whatever you decide *to tell* me to do. Here's the first decision I'd like you to make for me. Press the button next to the action you think I should take. I'll keep you posted about what happens.

On Monday morning I'll ...

continue in my job at the electronics company. I'll attempt *to save* most of my salary so that I can go back to college and retrain when I'm older.

risk *explaining* the problem to my manager. I'll ask to *work* part-time for six months and do voluntary work in the medical profession to see if it is a career that I really want to *pursue*.

Grammar: Verb patterns

6 Match the verb patterns to the examples from the blog.

Verb patterns	
1 Verb + -*ing*	a I planned to have a long and successful career
2 Preposition + -*ing*	b before retiring young at the age of 55
3 Idiomatic expression + -*ing*	c I was lucky to find a position
4 Verb + infinitive with *to*	d I considered discussing the situation with my line manager
5 Adjective + infinitive with *to*	e it's no use trying to explain

>> For more information on verb patterns, see page 170.

7 Look at the other verbs in *italics* in the blog. Which pattern are they examples of?

8 Complete this advice from a careers expert with the correct form of the verb in brackets.

> If you are thinking of ¹_____ (change) career, it's worth ²_____ (speak) to a trained career guidance expert for advice. It can be difficult ³_____ (make) the right decision.
>
> Before ⁴_____ (give up) a secure position, it is important ⁵_____ (do) some research. Think about why you want ⁶_____ (move) – are you genuinely interested in ⁷_____ (learn) the new skills that a career change may require? Or is it that you want to avoid ⁸_____ (deal) with a problem in your present position?
>
> Change can only be successful when it is carried out for the right reasons.

Speaking: A fresh start

9))) **2.27** Sasha is talking about her career. Listen to what she says and complete the notes.

> Sasha's present job: _____
> Her problem: _____
> Solutions she mentions:
> 1 _____
> 2 _____
> Type of career she is considering:
> _____

10 Work in pairs. Think of five tips to give Sasha about making a career change.

Before …   You should consider …   It might be worth …   Don't forget, you're good at …   It can be difficult …

11 Work in different pairs. Roleplay a conversation between Sasha and a colleague to discuss her dilemma.

> **TALKING POINT**   For what reasons might someone visit a careers guidance expert?
> At what stages in a career might it be most useful to do so?

Word focus: Extreme adjectives

1 When you are telling a story or anecdote, what verbal and non-verbal signals show that the person listening is interested? How can you tell if someone isn't interested in what they are hearing?

2))) **2.28** Listen to an anecdote about a motorbike and answer the questions.

1 How did the manager like to keep the office?

2 Why did the two friends bring the motorbike indoors?

3 What happened to surprise them?

4 What influence did the incident have on the speaker's career?

3 The speaker often uses the word *very* with adjectives. What effect does repeating *very* have on the story? Suggest other words the speaker could use.

4 We can use an extreme adjective in place of *very* + ordinary adjective, e.g. *fantastic* in place of *very good*. Match the ordinary adjectives (1–10) to the extreme adjectives (a–j).

1	big	a	spotless
2	hungry	b	furious
3	cold	c	hilarious
4	bad	d	exhausted
5	funny	e	filthy
6	tired	f	awful
7	angry	g	excellent
8	good	h	huge
9	clean	i	freezing
10	dirty	j	starving

5))) **2.29** Listen to another version of the story and answer the questions.

1 How is the ending different in this version of the story?

2 What effect does the use of extreme adjectives have?

6 Work in pairs. You are going to tell your partner an anecdote. Use one of the ideas in the Files or tell an anecdote of your own. Student A: Turn to File 64, page 126. Student B: Turn to File 98, page 134.

Grammar: Adverb usage

7)) **2.30** Two former colleagues meet at a seminar and catch up on news. Complete the conversation with the words and phrases in the box. Then listen and check.

> joking same remember rightly chance ages
> regards mind you up to

A: Excuse me, could you tell me what time the next seminar starts?

B: Oh, Martine, is that you? It's me, Lars.

A: Oh, Lars, hello. How are you? I haven't seen you in ¹_____. What have you been ²_____ _____?

B: I've been incredibly busy, actually. I set up my own business and it's going really well. It's hard work but I enjoy it very much. How's everyone in the department?

A: ³_____ as ever. Donald from Accounts has been promoted.

B: You're ⁴_____! He was completely useless at his job.

A: I know, but amazingly, he's now on the board of directors.

B: You can't be serious! ⁵_____ _____, he always was rather good at office politics.

A: They quickly realized their mistake. But it's too late now.

B: What about Jasmine? If I ⁶_____ _____, she wanted to leave to become a professional musician. She plays the violin absolutely brilliantly, doesn't she?

A: That's right. She's doing well, too. There's talk of her moving to Sydney to work in the Australian branch.

B: That's hardly surprising. She's extremely intelligent, isn't she?

A: Look, the talk's about to start. Hopefully, we'll get a ⁷_____ to talk later.

B: Unfortunately, I have to drive to the airport straight after the seminar. You'll give my ⁸_____ to everyone at the office, won't you?

A: Of course. It was great to catch up.

8 Complete the exercises in the table.

Adverb usage

1 Underline the word that the adverb describes in these examples from the conversation in exercise 7.
  a) He was completely useless.
  b) They quickly realized their mistake.
  c) She plays the violin absolutely brilliantly.

2 Look at the things that adverbs can modify. Match them to the examples (a–c) in 1.
  1 Adverbs can modify adjectives.
  2 Adverbs can modify adverbs.
  3 Adverbs can modify verbs.

3 Find one more example in the conversation of each of types 1–3.

4 Adverbs can also be used to describe a complete idea or a clause in a sentence. Match the sentence halves from the conversation.

1 Unfortunately,	**a)** we'll get a chance to talk later.
2 Amazingly,	**b)** I have to drive to the airport straight after the seminar.
3 Hopefully,	**c)** he's now on the board of directors.

>> **For more information on adverb usage, see pages 174–175.**

! Extreme adjectives and adverbs like *excellent*, *useless* and *brilliantly* cannot be qualified by *very*. You can use *really*, which can be used to modify both extreme and ordinary adjectives and adverbs.

Words that can be used instead of *really* to modify extreme adjectives and adverbs include *quite*, *completely*, *absolutely*, *totally*.

9 Find and correct six mistakes in this text.

We discovered a new restaurant last night. It was very excellent, and the food was amazingly good. The chef cooked everything absolutely brilliant. We enjoyed very much the meal. Mind you, the service was useless totally. The main course was really late and when it arrived, it was completely freezing. So we immediately sent it back to the kitchen. The chef rushed over to our table and started shouting furious. It's hard surprising; after all, he has a reputation for being temperamental. Hopefully, we'll go again next week – you should come, too.

Speaking: Catching up

10 Work in pairs. You are at a business convention when you meet an old colleague or college friend. Look at the information and roleplay the conversation. Student A turn to File 65, page 126. Student B turn to File 99, page 134.

> **TALKING POINT** People sometimes tell anecdotes, stories and jokes to break the ice when they meet in business situations. Do you think that this is useful or do you prefer to get straight down to talking about business?

Word focus: Describing characteristics

1 Do these relationships work better if the participants have similar characteristics or different characteristics?

friends   work colleagues   romantic partners
travelling companions

2 What characteristics do you think a manager values in staff? What characteristics might staff value in a manager?

3 The adjectives in the table can all be used to describe people. Match an adjective in column A with an opposite adjective in columns B and C.

A	B	C
calm	assertive	anxious
conscientious	moody	careless
late	punctual	grumpy
pleasant	outgoing	prompt
reserved	slapdash	sociable
unconfident	stressed	self-assured

4 ᴐ)) **2.31** Listen to two managers discussing their concerns about Jozef, an employee. Tick (✓) the adjectives in exercise 3 that they use.

5 ᴐ)) Listen again and answer the questions.

1 When did changes in Jozef's behaviour begin?

2 What reason (apart from his latest project) could there be for the change in behaviour?

3 What action do you think the manager should take?

6 Work in pairs. If you were an employer, which four characteristics would you most value in a worker? Which three could be a problem? You can choose from the adjectives in the table in exercise 3 or others that you know.

Word focus: Linking

7 Complete the table with the linking words in the box.

although furthermore since whereas consequently
besides moreover despite owing to as well as
not only that

Contrast	Addition	Cause / Result
however	in addition	as a result

8 Choose the best linking word or phrase to complete this internal report about Jozef.

Jozef has always been one of the most effective members of the team. ¹ *Furthermore / However*, he is conscientious and shows great potential. ² *Besides / Despite* having little experience in the travel industry, he has quickly attained an excellent level of expertise. ³ *As well as / However*, recently there have been concerns about his performance at work. ⁴ *Whereas / Since* in the past he has been punctual and reliable, he has started to arrive late. ⁵ *In addition / Although* he has had a lot of time off. ⁶ *Since / Owing* to this, his colleagues have had to take on some of his workload. ⁷ *Despite / Furthermore* some of his team have reported that he has started to show signs of stress recently. ⁸ *Consequently / Besides* I requested a meeting with Jozef to discuss these matters. ⁹ *Although / Moreover* he was reluctant to discuss the problem at first, we were eventually able to clarify the matter. ¹⁰ *As well as / Since* working on a number of difficult projects, Jozef has also been looking after an ill relative and is in the process of moving house. I recommend that we now arrange professional support and stress management to help him.

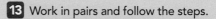

Speaking: Performance review

9 In what ways can a manager give feedback to staff about positive or negative performance? Is feedback more useful when it is formal or informal?

10 In some organizations, employees have regular performance reviews. Match the aims of a review (1–5) to the explanations (a–e). Do you think all the aims should be included in a performance review?

1 Feedback   **a** identify training requirements

2 Goal setting   **b** tell the employee about their recent performance

3 Evaluation   **c** offer incentives to reward performance

4 Motivation   **d** specify objectives for the future

5 Development **e** discuss ability to work effectively

11 Work in groups of three. Look at these two opinions on performance reviews. Which is closer to your opinion? Can you think of any alternatives to traditional performance reviews?

> (Pros)
>
> Employee finds out what their manager thinks of their work and how to improve.
>
> Provides information about who to promote, reward or offer training to.
>
> Cons
>
> Tends to focus on short-term goals and performance.
>
> Rewards individual performance rather than teamwork.

12 Discuss three alternatives to traditional performance reviews. Summarize your information and tell the other people in your group about it. Discuss the advantages and disadvantages of each method. Which one do you prefer? Which combination of methods could work well together? Student A turn to File 30, page 119. Student B turn to File 66, page 126. Student C turn to File 93, page 133.

13 Work in pairs and follow the steps.

A line manager and a departmental manager are meeting to discuss an employee.

1 Look at the roles below and then read the information about Nadim in File 67 on page 127.

Student A: You are Nadim's line manager. You feel that positive changes in his behaviour mean that he should be offered greater responsibility. Try to find evidence to support your view and make notes.

Student B: You are the departmental manager. You feel that any major decisions about Nadim, such as giving him extra responsibility, should be postponed until his next performance review in six months' time. Try to find evidence to support your view and make notes.

2 Have a meeting to discuss Nadim's past and present performance. Discuss any changes in his actions and attitude.

- Identify the areas where he needs support or training.
- Decide whether to offer Nadim a place on an important team project which could lead to promotion.

14 Join with another group and summarize what you decided in your meeting. Give reasons for your decisions.

Writing: Summary – review follow-up

15 Write a summary of the meeting you had. Summarize the main points and confirm the following.

- any improvements in Nadim's work or attitude since his previous performance review
- any training which you intend to offer him to help his career development
- whether or not to offer Nadim a place on the new team project. If so, what improvements would he need to make?
- any other points that were made or decisions that were reached

TALKING POINT   What rewards can a company offer an employee for good work? Should an organization impose penalties for unsatisfactory work?

Listening: Revise plans

1 Discuss the following questions.

1 To what extent do you think workers should be allowed to personalize their workspace, for example, their desk, personal office or cubicle?

2 Would you prefer to work in an open-plan office or in an individual office?

3 What changes to your workspace would make it easier for you to do your job?

2 Work in pairs. Discuss the advantages and disadvantages of the personal workspaces in the photos. Which would you most and least like to work in?

3))) **2.32** You are going to hear a team leader make an announcement to his team. Listen and choose the correct alternative a–c.

1 The team leader recently had a meeting about
  a new offices for his staff.
  b designs for a client.
  c a contract for telecoms services.

2 Mayhew Telecoms thought the team's efforts
  a were too colourful.
  b didn't follow the brief.
  c fulfilled what they were asked to do.

3 Mayhew's requirements have changed due to
  a a reduced budget.
  b a competitor offering a better price.
  c problems with the schedule.

4 The new brief is expected to affect
  a the technology and deadline.
  b the size and quantity.
  c the style and what the items are made from.

5 A member of staff at the meeting suggests that
  a they cancel the contract.
  b they change the design slightly.
  c they get paid overtime.

6 The team leader proposes that the team
  a stays late to discuss the problem.
  b works at the weekend.
  c takes the rest of the day off.

4))) Listen again and complete phrases 1–6 below. Then match the headings in the box with A–E.

> Encourage suggestions   Empathize
> Say what needs to be done   Thank the team
> Use motivating language

Motivation

A _____   I realize that this must be ¹_____ for you all.
B _____   You're doing really well.   You did an excellent job.   ²_____ on, we can do this.
C _____   What we need to focus on now is …   Let's concentrate on ³_____ this …
D _____   That's certainly worth ⁴_____, but …   I'm looking forward to hearing your ideas.
E _____   I'd like to thank you for your ⁵_____.   I really ⁶_____ all your efforts.

5 Use the correct form of a verb from box A with a phrase from box B to complete the sentences.

A	B
be	together to get this done
pull	with fresh ideas
come up	a break
revise	every confidence
need	beyond our control
have	the designs

1 The project leader _____ that the the team will meet the deadline.

2 We have done everything we can to win this contract and now the final decision _____.

3 After news about the budget cuts, they decided to _____ to make them more cost-effective.

4 Everyone _____ after all the overtime you've done to finish the job.

5 If the R&D team _____, they'll all be rewarded for their efforts.

6 We might have _____ in the meeting if we hadn't been so exhausted.

Speaking: Encourage the team

6 You are a team leader. Read the information below and answer the questions.

1 What objections do you think your team might raise about the situation?

2 What information will you choose to stress when you are telling the team about the delay?

3 How can the team use the three desks effectively?

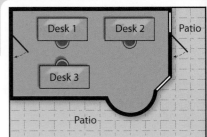

Your team has been promised a large, new open-plan office. Construction is scheduled to finish this week and everyone is packed and ready to move. Unfortunately, the construction company has hit a problem, and the move will be delayed for ten weeks. In the meantime, your team will need to use a very small temporary office.

Naturally, your team will be extremely disappointed with the news. There is an additional problem: the temporary office has space for three desks and there are six people in the team. However, you will be given a budget to purchase any equipment or furniture which might help.

7 Work in pairs. Take turns to present the information to your team.

When you are the team leader, try to present the information in a way that will motivate the team.

When you are listening, raise questions or objections at the end of the presentation.

8 Work in groups. You are members of the team. You frequently have team meetings and conference rooms are rarely available. The team leader has asked you to look at three options (A–C) which might help with the space problem in the temporary office. Discuss the options and choose the one you think would be most useful.

A

Have your meetings in the open air and boost creativity. Great for team building as you need to cooperate to drive successfully. Seats up to seven people.

B The ultimate space saving furniture. Easy to put up and take down, two people can sit in the large hammock at the same time. Suitable for indoor and outdoor use.

Sit with a laptop and work in comfort or get together for relaxed meetings. These bean bags are easy to move around, and when not in use they can be stored in a corner.

C

9 Present your ideas to another group and give reasons for your choice. Say why you think the other options would not be suitable.

Reminder

Verb patterns page 103 + Grammar reference page 170
Extreme adjectives and adverb usage pages 104–105 + Grammar reference pages 174–175
Motivation page 108

Word focus: Idioms connected to change

1 Look at two quotes about change. Do you think that they present helpful views?
Which do you think best describes the attitude to doing business in your country?

> *'Change does not always mean that things improve. Without careful consideration, the result can be conflict or confusion.'*

> 'After you've done a thing the same way for two years, look it over carefully. After five years, look at it with suspicion. And after ten years, throw it away and start all over.'

2 Match the idioms (1–6) connected to change to the correct meanings (a–h).
Two of the meanings are not used.

1 *It's simply change for the sake of change.*

2 *If it ain't broke, don't fix it.*

3 *Let's ring the changes.*

a like to do things the way that they have always done them
b do something different when there's no need to
c do something differently
d keep things as they are if they work well
e make important changes to avoid problems later
f constantly change their ideas
g decide not to make a change until options are discussed
h do something outside the usual routine as it's refreshing

4 *A change is as good as a rest.*

5 *Some people are always chopping and changing.*

6 *People can get set in their ways.*

3 Complete these sentences with your own ideas. Then discuss your ideas with a partner.

1 When a change occurs suddenly, it can be …

2 A change in routine is often …

3 Changing your mind is sometimes …

Listening: A change of plan

4 Read the information about Holden Lodge and answer the questions.

1 What facilities are you likely to find in a state-of-the-art leisure complex?

2 What do you think of the logo and slogan? Are they effective?

Holden Lodge, a former country house hotel in large grounds, has been purchased by Landwing Holdings. A spokesperson for Landwing announced plans to turn Holden Lodge into a state-of-the-art leisure complex.

5 🔊 **2.33** Work in groups. You are a member of the team developing Holden Lodge. Listen to the CEO address the team and make notes about what he wants you to do.

6 Use your notes from exercise 5. You have ten minutes to carry out the CEO's orders.

7 🔊 **2.34** While you are working on the project, you are asked to be part of an urgent conference call with the CEO. Listen. What changes does he want you to make? Try and make the changes in five to ten minutes.

8 🔊 **2.35** When you get back to the office, there is a brief message from the CEO. Listen and try to complete the tasks in less than five minutes.

Speaking: Presenting plans

9 In your group, organize your notes and look through the information you have gathered. Which points do you think are most important?

10 Prepare a presentation about your plans for Holden Lodge. You may wish to use this outline to help structure your ideas.

> **Describe what it is:** *Holden Lodge is a …*
> **Target clients:** *Membership is aimed at …*
> **Outline plan:** *We intend to attract clients by …*
> **Suggest ways to use the building / grounds:** *In addition, we plan to maximize profits by …*

11 Join with another group and present your plans for Holden Lodge.

12 Discuss which parts of the other group's plan you think would work best.

Interaction

1 Put the words in the correct order to make sentences.

1 currency / that / I / devalued / be / doubt / our / will

2 spend / able / We / be / to / more / won't / definitely

3 competition / There / job / sure / the / fierce / is / be / top / to / for

4 to / card / is / The / scheme / fail / identity / government's / bound

5 since / will / in / This / renovations / certainly / hotel / the / ratings / rise

6 replace / the world's / the US / China / power / well / economic / top / might / as

2 Complete the modal perfect forms to make meaningful sentences.

1 Tina has switched her computer off. She _____ gone home early.

2 It _____ been hard for those guys to withdraw money from Jim's account. He'd left his card in the ATM with the 'Would you like another transaction?' message still on!

3 Anita _____ worked very hard on this project. I know how dedicated she is.

4 It was stupid of me to give them my credit card details! I know I _____ done that.

5 It's too early to tell, but it looks like I _____ made a mistake.

6 I simply overlooked the section about insurance. I _____ studied the contract in more detail.

3 Choose the correct options to complete this text.

After ¹work / working for six months as an intern for a multinational company, Francesca Lawson was offered a position in the Research and Development department. She hoped ²learn / to learn about the latest fibre optics technology as that was the area that she wanted ³to specialize / specializing in. Instead, she discovered that she was expected ⁴carry / to carry out basic routine tasks and administrative duties. She felt that it was no use ⁵to complain / complaining to her manager because whenever staff raised any issues with their work, he simply told them that they were lucky ⁶to have / have a job. At first, she considered ⁷to leave / leaving the company, but after ⁸taking / to take advice from her mentor, she decided ⁹to speak / speaking to the HR department about the problem. She explained that she enjoyed ¹⁰to work / working for the company, but felt that her skills were not being used to their full potential. She was relieved ¹¹to discover / discovering that the HR manager was sympathetic to her problem and was able ¹²making / to make practical suggestions to improve the situation.

4 Match each hint (1–6) to a suitable request (a–f). Use each request once.

1 It's so hot today. I'm really thirsty!

2 My car's broken down again.

3 Are you in a hurry?

4 These toner cartridges are so difficult to install.

5 This new PC is a mystery to me.

6 There's a bit of a draught, isn't there?

a Can I ask you to show me how to start this program?

b Would you mind closing the window?

c Sorry to bother you. Do you think you could give me a hand?

d I was wondering if you could give me a lift to the office tomorrow.

e Could I have a glass of water, please?

f Can I ask you a couple of questions? It won't take long.

5 Replace very + the adjective in italics in these sentences with a suitable extreme adjective.

1 The supplier was very *angry* when they cancelled the order.

2 The inside of the hire car was very *dirty* so they decided to complain.

3 Unsurprisingly, at the end of the marathon all the runners were very *tired*.

4 I'm going to call the heating engineer because my apartment is very *cold*.

5 The table in the restaurant wasn't free until 10:30, so we were all very *hungry* by the time we ate.

6 During the presentation, the speaker told a story which the audience thought was very *funny*, but I didn't get the joke.

7 The hotel room was perfect – the furnishings were really comfortable and everything was very *clean*.

8 The candidate for the post should speak at least three languages and have very *good* analytical skills.

6 Complete these sentences with the words in the box.

for of in down up on

1 He's working _____ a project to help the environment.

2 She pretended to be a celebrity but no one was taken _____ by her act.

3 The judge accused the gang _____ stealing credit cards.

4 Have you signed _____ for the talk on mobile technology?

5 Do you want a coffee or shall we get straight _____ to business?

6 After the press conference, they posed _____ photographs with the president.

7 Choose the word in each list where the letters in bold are <u>not</u> pronounced in the same way as in the others.

1	a g**u**y	b s**i**gn	c d**u**ty
2	a l**e**gal	b k**i**nd	c just**i**f**y**
3	a fra**u**d	b la**w**yers	c cho**i**ce
4	a evaluat**e**	b div**u**lge	c doc**u**mentary
5	a prom**o**tion	b alth**o**ugh	c butt**o**n
6	a **ch**ance	b es**c**aped	c Australian
7	a pl**ea**sant	b l**ea**der	c l**ei**sure
8	a opera**ti**on	b relation**ship**	c brea**ch**es

8 Complete this crossword puzzle.

Across

1 Allowed by the law.

4 A _____ of appeal deals with cases in which people are not satisfied with a decision.

6 Retract (e.g. allegations).

7 By _____, seat belts must be worn by all passengers.

8 Very often, victims of crime are reluctant to bring _____ against their attackers.

11 Make sure nobody else knows your _____ name and password.

12 Opposite of *admit*.

15 If a case is _____ in a court of law, all the facts about it are presented in order to make a legal decision.

16 Opposite of *innocent*.

17 A _____ of conduct is a set of rules that employees, companies or professional people agree to follow in the way they behave and do business.

18 Two human rights organizations were able to _____ evidence that the men had been put under police surveillance.

Down

1 British English for *attorney*.

2 Ron's friend _____ into trouble with the law.

3 The criminal investigation was _____ by the US Attorney and the FBI.

4 Two top executives were _____ with criminal defamation and with breaching the German privacy code.

5 The judge decided to stop the _____ when it emerged that witnesses had been threatened.

8 The lawyers will only be paid if they win the _____.

9 A man is under _____ following the suspicious death of his business partner.

10 The men received a six-month suspended _____ for violating privacy.

13 Eventually, you'll have to _____ for yourself whether it was right or wrong.

14 I always have to _____ with the neighbours in my appartment block about whose turn it is to clean the staircase.

9 Choose the correct word or phrase to complete these sentences.

1 It was a top-of-the-range device but when I used it, was _____ useless.

   a completely   b very   c real

2 The office was so noisy that he found it _____ impossible to work.

   a quiet   b quietly   c quite

3 The product launch went _____ and the client is delighted.

   a absolute brilliant   b absolutely brilliantly
   c absolutely brilliant

4 We _____ realized that we had gone the wrong way and turned the car round.

   a quick   b quickly   c quite

5 The board has an emergency meeting on Friday morning so, _____, I'll need to postpone our appointment.

   a unfortunately   b really   c hopefully

6 It's _____ surprising that they missed the plane – the traffic was terrible.

   a hard   b hardy   c hardly

7 Someone in the audience started talking _____ on their phone during the performance.

   a loud   b loudly   c louder

8 Before I call the police, are you _____ sure that you didn't leave your wallet at home by mistake?

   a very   b complete   c absolutely

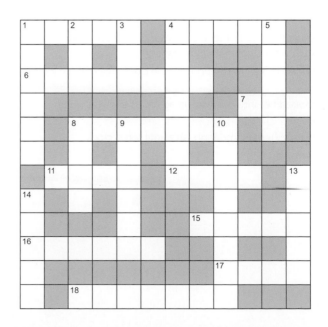

Information files

File 1, 1B, page 7

Student A:

Ask your partner questions to make them say exactly the same words as on your cards.

| Blue. | It depends. | Twice a day. |

| He's an actor. | Because it's sweet. | In 2016. |

File 2, 1C, page 9

Student A:

As you know, all business correspondence can be formal, neutral or informal. It depends who you are writing to. It depends on your relationship with your reader. When you are in doubt, a friendly, neutral style usually works best.

Complete the 'Opening' column with the expressions from the box. Then check your answers with your partner.

> Dear Tony,   Hi Tony,   Dear Mr Adenuga,
> Dear Tony Adenuga,

	Opening	Closing
Informal	Tony,	Talk soon,
↓	_____	See you soon,
		Bye for now,
		Best,
↓	_____	All the best,
		Regards,
↓	_____	Best regards,
		Best wishes,
Formal	_____	With best wishes,

Now discuss these questions.

Do you ever

- start an email with no greeting?
- end an email with no closing (i.e. you just sign off with your name or initials)?

File 3, 1C, page 9

Student A:

This is just to confirm the arrangements we have made for Mrs Kuchelstein, your Product Manager.

If you need more information, please don't hesitate to get in touch.

I've booked her into the Astoria again, as she was quite pleased with it.

Fortunately, her first meeting isn't until ten o'clock.

Dear Angela

File 4, 1D, page 11

Student A:

Topic 1	You are passionately involved in this issue, so you argue strongly that it is absurd to raise the retirement age when so many young people are out of work.
Topic 2	You have no strong opinion, but you believe a national health service is a good thing.
	You notice that someone is not saying much, so you try to draw them into the discussion.
Topic 3	You don't really feel like contributing anything to this discussion, so let the others argue. Don't say anything unless someone asks you.

File 5, 1E, page 12

Students A1 and A2:

Part 1

Work together. Put these words and phrases in the correct order to make questions.

You both need to write down all three questions.

> **1** Mehrabian's types of communication valid all findings are for ?

> **2** use good do voice presenters how their ?

> **3** and gestures about do what posture presenters can ?

Part 2

Use the article to work out the answers to questions 1–3 together. Make sure you remember the answers as you need them for Part 3.

Part 3

Each one of you now works with a partner from the other pair. Ask your new partner your three questions. Help or correct your partner whenever necessary.

Then answer your partner's questions.

File 6, 7A, page 71

Your boat journey runs into problems due to bad weather. It stops in the port of Salaverry. which is 548 km from Lima.

You decide to wait until the boat can sail again. Turn to File 18, page 117.

You accept an offer from a fellow traveller on the boat to share a hire car to Lima. Turn to File 27, page 119.

File 7, 1E, page 13

Student A:

First, just listen and complete the text on your own. Then compare your text with Student B's and check your answers. Underline all the expressions the speaker uses to structure his presentation. Finally, go to the audio script on page 138 to check the underlined expressions.

[1]_____ _____ _____ that back and neck problems are one of the top ten medical problems in Western countries? Twelve years ago, because of my job and my research, I was spending an average of 12 hours a day sitting at a desk. My spine was stiff. I could hardly bend any more. That's [2]_____ _____ _____ to take up Tai Chi. I'd read somewhere that it could do a lot of good to your joints, so why not give it a try?

Today, I'd like to talk to you about this ancient Chinese martial art called Tai Chi.

My talk is [3]_____ _____ _____. I'll start with a little historical background. Then I'll move on to the health benefits of Tai Chi. And finally, I'll describe what it's like to practise in a club.

Let me start then with an overview of the history of Tai Chi. First, I'll take you back to the origin – 12th-century China. Then I'll say [4]_____ _____ _____ about how and why Tai Chi evolved into a number of different schools. And thirdly, I'd like to explain how this art reached the rest of the world. …

This leads me to [5]_____ _____ _____, which is why Tai Chi can bring so many health benefits to so many people. I'd like to consider three areas that we can develop through Tai Chi: the muscles and the joints, the internal organs, and your powers of concentration. …

[6]_____, what is it like to practise in a club? What do you notice when you just observe a Tai Chi session? Three things: an instructor, demonstrating the moves and guiding the students; a group of people imitating the instructor and practising; and last but not least, an atmosphere of calm, concentration and congeniality. …

[7]_____ _____ _____, I'd like to sum up the main points of my talk. …

I'd like to conclude now [8]_____ _____ _____ of something I said at the beginning. …

File 8, 7B, page 73

Student A:

You are on the management team.

You want the Solar event to be cancelled. If anything goes wrong, the publicity could damage the Rockdale Centre. Think of reasons to support your argument.

File 9, 2E, page 22

A, C, D and E are real services. B and F and G may also exist, but we just don't know about them yet.

File 10, 8B, page 83

Interview 1

Student A:

You are the interviewer.

You work for a business news website. You are going to interview the CEO of a Telecoms company which has been in the news due to reports of financial problems. The CEO has walked out of interviews in the past when the questions have been too direct or aggressive.

Try to confirm whether the following is true:

• Reports suggest that the company is about to make a loss for the second year in a row.

• Some people have suggested that the CEO should quit.

• Shareholders recently voted against the board of directors' financial strategy.

• Last night some members of the board resigned.

You want the following facts:

• Amount the company lost last month?

• Shareholders having an emergency meeting? When? Subject of the meeting?

• How many board members resigned? More plan to go?

• Reports that the company plans to close? True?

File 11, 9B, page 95

Student A:

Step 1: Read the story carefully.

Step 2: Students B and C will try to guess what the story is about. Answer their questions with 'yes' or 'no'. Do not answer any questions that you consider to be grammatically incorrect (ask your teacher if you are not sure).

When Students B and C have asked a maximum of five questions each, tell them the story.

Story 1

This story happened at Newark Airport, one of America's busiest airports, on Sunday night, 3 January, 2010. A man breached the security by going through an unattended screening checkpoint and walking on the wrong side of the terminal. After this incident, Terminal C was shut down for more than seven hours, 100 flights were grounded and all the passengers were re-screened.

The man responsible for this security scare was Haisong Jiang, a 28-year-old university student. Jiang illegally went into a secure area in order to give his girlfriend one last farewell kiss. She was returning to Los Angeles after spending the festive season with him.

Jiang was later arrested and questioned. His arrest exposed the defects in the security of the airport.

Information files

File 12, 2A, page 15

1

Your department holds a long meeting every week where everyone gives a status update. People are unhappy because the meetings are boring. They don't start until late and everyone is tired. How can you change the meetings to make them more interesting and make sure that everyone gets home on time?

2

You have been asked to help with a national campaign to encourage people to eat more vegetables. The last campaign was unsuccessful because people didn't like being told what to eat. You want your campaign to encourage children and families to improve their diet.

3

Many of the employees in your department have desk jobs and they don't move around much. Everyone needs to take more exercise and quite a few need to lose weight. What changes can you make around the office to promote a more active lifestyle?

4

Your town wants to improve recycling in the area. At the moment, fewer than 30% of households recycle regularly. What ideas would make recycling fun and easier to do at home?

5

Your CEO wants employees to suggest ways to improve attendance at work. What can you do to reward those who come to work regularly, or to discourage those who take time off when it isn't necessary?

File 13, 3B, page 29

Many people think discourse markers are just sounds and words that we say to fill spaces. Some people think they are a sign of careless speech or poor education. However, well-educated speakers utter these words and sounds a lot, too. They can signal a speaker's intentions in different ways, and help listeners understand better. For example, *So* and *Well* can signal the introduction of a new topic:

So, shall we start?

Well, shall we move on?

Well can also warn listeners that what follows may be a little unexpected:

A: Is Vic all right?

B: Well, in fact he's rather disappointed.

We can also use *Well* to give ourselves a little time to think what to say next.

File 14, 2B, page 17

Problem 1: real-life solution

Some large companies like Google and 3M allow their developers and engineers to work on their own projects for 20% of their time. Atlas Sian, an Australian software company, has occasional days where it tells its developers they can work on whatever they want. They call them Fed-Ex Days because you have to deliver something overnight, so you have to share the results with colleagues within 24 hours. Lots of ideas for new products and fixes for existing products have been developed on Fed-Ex Days.

Problem 2: real-life solution

At the Zappos call centre, employees have no script. The calls aren't timed or monitored. Employees are simply told they should solve the problems any way they want and just get it done. Zappos has one of the best customer service ratings of any company in the US.

File 15, 2D, page 21

1

You work in a furniture store and your boss won't give you your bonus until you make one more sale. A customer in the shop is interested in a sofa, but they can't make up their mind whether to buy. The store closes in fifteen minutes.

Student A: You are the sales assistant.

Student B: You are the customer. You don't want to rush into a decision.

2

Your company has decided to work with a charity that helps with local community projects. They want every employee to give 10% of their salary to the charity every year. Every member of staff needs to agree to take part before the scheme can go ahead.

Student A: You are a member of staff. You don't want to give 10%.

Student B: You are a member of the charity asking people to take part in the scheme.

3

Your old school is organizing a day when ex-pupils come to talk to students about their time at school and what they have done since leaving. A teacher phones to persuade you to take part in the event next month.

Student A: You are the teacher.

Student B: You are the ex-pupil. You don't want to take part.

4

A manager wants to have a 'creative day' once a week to boost productivity in your department. Suggestions for activities include wearing a silly hat at your desk, singing instead of speaking in meetings and using dance to communicate product ideas.

Student A: You are an employee in the department. You don't want to take part.

Student B: You are the manager who wants to try the idea.

File 16, 2B, page 16

Mostly A:

You work hard and are motivated. Yet sometimes your prime motivation may be fear of failure. This can be effective as it keeps the objective in focus. But you also need to have confidence that success will come from your ability. It can be as important to recognize when you are doing a good job as it is to identify where you can improve performance.

Mostly B:

You are focused and self-motivated. You respond well to a balance between challenges and rewards. Sometimes these rewards might be small treats that you give yourself. At other times they will be more significant professional gains such as promotion or a bonus. The challenge of the task is also important and can sometimes be sufficient in itself, without reward.

File 17, 3A, page 27
Student A:

You are the office manager. Look at the email you sent your PA and rank the tasks in order of importance (1 = most important).

Hi Sam,

As you know, I'll be away for ten days. Here's a reminder of the things that need to be taken care of – could you deal with them as soon as possible?

• Update health and safety regulations on the basis of the new Ministry guidelines. Send all departmental managers a copy of the revised document for discussion/approval.

• Check stock levels of all office supplies. Anticipate needs and order accordingly.

• Contact three or four IT companies. Find out which software solution is best for our needs (the choice is between Pegasus, Sage and Microsoft Dynamics). Get a written quote.

• Contact our usual maintenance company and ask if they can look at all our photocopiers and printers. Ideally, the maintenance work should be done over one weekend next month. If not possible, look for someone else.

• Find out how employees feel about the monitoring and recording of long-distance phone calls.

• Go through applications for the post of Customer Service Advisor. Shortlist five candidates, and arrange interviews with them for the week after I get back.

When you have read the email, phone your PA.

• Ask a general question to start off with.
• State the purpose of your call.
• Find out which of the three most important tasks have been done and which haven't.

Have you _____ yet?

• For things that have been done, ask follow-up questions to enquire about the results.
• For things that haven't been done, possibly enquire why, and ask when the PA intends to do them.

File 18, 7A, page 71

The delay means that when you finally arrive in Lima, they have given your hotel room to another guest.

You go to tourist information to ask about accommodation. Turn to File 73, page 128.

You meet someone in a café who gives you the number of his cousin's bed and breakfast. Turn to File 86, page 131.

File 19, 3C, page 31
Student A:

1 Work on your own. You have now identified the problems that your predecessor was up against while organizing the event. Decide what went wrong in each area 1–3. Choose problem (a) or (b), or invent your own problem (c).

1 The budget:
  a spouses and children have to pay an admission fee
  b the budget for the event has just been halved
  c _____
2 The venue:
  a the company cafeteria is available but is too small
  b the meeting room is quite large but is booked the morning after the event
  c _____
3 Promotion:
  a there's a noticeboard, but few people read the announcements
  b the company used to send out invitations, but that's not cost-effective
  c _____

2 Tell your partner about the problems in areas 1–3.

3 Now listen to your partner and make a note of the problems in areas 4–6.

4 Entertainment: _____

5 Catering: _____

6 Registration: _____

4 Work on your own again. Think of a solution to problems 4–6.

5 Work together with your partner again. Ask and answer questions about the problems each of you had to deal with, and the solutions you've come up with.

Information files

File 20, 3D, page 32

1 *pretty low* = rather unhappy, depressed.

2 *heavy-going* = difficult to understand.

3 *Mind you* = We use *Mind you* when we say something that is almost the opposite of what we have just said, or that explains or emphasizes it (e.g. *He looks very young in this photo. Mind you, it was taken years ago.*)

4 *to wind someone up* = to annoy someone.

5 *Fingers crossed* = Let's hope that …

File 21, 3D, page 33

Student A:

Step 1: You start. Ask your partner the questions on the left. Make sure you get the correct response and a different way of saying *I don't know* each time.

You ask:	Your partner replies:
What shall we get Olga for her birthday?	_____ What about a nice engraving or something like that? I think she likes modern art.
How can I install Apps on my iPhone?	_____ Ask Suzana, she's our techie.
What's your greatest worry?	_____ Losing my job, probably.
Hey, who won the match?	_____ I didn't watch it.
What time does the bus arrive?	_____ I always take the underground, you see.

Step 2: Answer your partner's questions. Think of another way of saying *I don't know* and choose the appropriate answer from the box.

Your partner: I haven't seen Simon this week. Any idea what's up?

You: I'm not really sure, but I think he's off sick.

> _____ You know what the traffic can be like.
> _____ Why don't you look at the instructions manual?
> _____ Helping people and learning from them.
> _____ I think he's off sick.
> _____ I don't even know anyone by that name.

File 22, 9C, page 97

> Google Inc. executives received a six-month suspended sentence for violating privacy, according to a ruling by the Milan court.
>
> David Drummond (Google's senior vice president of corporate development and chief legal officer), Peter Fleischer (global privacy counsel) and George Reyes (a former chief financial officer) received the sentences, according to a ruling by Judge Oscar Magi.

File 23, 3E, page 35

Student A:

Step 1: Before you join with Student B, think how you are going to give the four pieces of news below in an indirect way (see the audio script on page 142 if you need help), and be prepared to answer your partner's challenging questions!

> • You have overspent your budget.
> • The office cafeteria will soon close down.
> • One of your customers has just cancelled a huge order.
> • You have to ask some of your employees to take early retirement.

Step 2: Work in pairs. You speak first. Break your bad news to your partner. Start with the first item. Listen to your partner's reaction and respond. Then move on to the second item.

Step 3: Now listen to your partner's news, react in the most appropriate way and then ask challenging questions.

Do you mean that …? / Are you saying that …? /

So if I understand correctly … / You mean, …?, etc.

File 24, 4E, page 45

> **Project 2: Amazon conservation project**
>
> This project manages community forests in Brazil. It arranges for classes from local schools to have lessons outside in the jungle. The aim is to increase students' knowledge of their local environment and encourage them to take a role in its conservation in the future. As well as working with the children, trained environmentalists work with parents, teachers and the local community to provide them with the skills that they will need to manage the community forest together. A marketing campaign encourages local and environmental companies to sponsor a class to help pay for the tools and training needed while they take part in the project.

File 25, 4B, page 39

Student A:

You want to turn one of the following ideas into a business. You want your partner to join you in this project and invest some money. Choose one project and explain why it is a good idea.

> • *Start a music studio* You have found an old house in a good location. You want to buy it and install the latest equipment to make it into a modern music studio.
> • *Buy and sell paintings* You have found a painting that you want to buy. It's expensive, but you think that you can sell it for a good profit. You will invest the money in buying more paintings.
> • *Business traveller assistance* You would like to use your knowledge of your local area to help people who are visiting on business. You could arrange accommodation, transport, translation services and local information.

File 26, 5A, page 49

Background information

You and your partner are consultants who have been hired by Avatec, a medium-sized American-owned company located in Slovenia.

Although Avatec is a successful company, recently the general atmosphere has deteriorated a lot. For example, several employees have asked to be moved to a different office; many have criticized certain colleagues for their attitude; some are taking sick leave for no apparent reason, etc. The directors are concerned that this might soon affect performance. They have hired you to look into the situation and come up with possible solutions.

The problems

You have spent a considerable amount of time getting written feedback from Avatec's employees and having face-to-face conversations with over 50 of them. You have then selected the comments which in your view best reflect the overall cause of the problem the company is facing:

• 'Within departments, people tend to form cliques. Of course the result is that other people feel excluded. It's not good for our morale.' (*Karen, Admin*)

• 'There is little communication, but there is a lot of envy and competition between the various departments.' (*Damjan, Human Resources*)

• 'There are very talented people here of course, but unfortunately some of them just seem to pursue their own goals. So other employees feel they can't approach them.' (*Alex, Logistics*)

• 'Some people seem to be very popular with colleagues, even with the boss, but their work is often below standard. Nobody seems to care. There's something wrong there.' (*Nada, Sales*)

File 27, 7A, page 71

Your fellow traveller insists on stopping in a small town on the way to Lima to go to a family wedding.

You accept his invitation to go to the wedding before continuing your journey. Turn to File 18, page 117.

You decide to try to hitchhike the last 100km to Lima. Turn to File 38, page 120.

File 28, 9B, page 95

Students B and C:

Look at the words in the box. They are words from a story. You have to try and guess the story by asking Student A 'yes' or 'no' questions.

Student A will only answer questions that are grammatically correct.

Story 1

> airport   kiss   screening checkpoint   shut down   student

File 29, 10A, page 102

Red button

Thanks for voting. Well, I guess you'd like to know what happened next. As you suggested, I didn't quit my job. It was pretty difficult. In addition to working in a job that I had little interest in, I was also saving almost all my salary. I soon got used to travelling to work by bus to save money on petrol. I managed to earn enough to do the first year of a degree course in medicine. I applied to university and was delighted to be offered a place. My line manager wasn't happy with me, but I was surprised to discover that my departmental manager was really supportive. When I explained that I wanted to retrain in the medical profession, he suggested working part-time in my old job to pay for my course. I admitted having a problem with my line manager and moved to a new position in a different department. So I'm studying for my qualification part-time and paying for my education from my wages. I like studying, but the funny thing is, I like to spend time in the office as well. This experience has taught me that it's worth speaking to somebody before making a career move, but it must be the right person. Things have worked out better than I thought they would. Thanks for your vote!

File 30, 10C, page 107

Student A:

Read about this alternative to the traditional performance review. Summarize the key points for the others in your group.

MBO (Management by objective)

• Managers and employees set objectives together.

• Employees are given a deadline to achieve agreed goals.

• Manager and employee decide to review goals monthly, quarterly or annually.

• Reviews check whether employees have achieved goals, not how they have achieved them.

File 31, 7B, page 73

Student B:

You are on the management team.

You want to arrange a meeting between the protest leaders and Carl Hamilton during the event to try to improve the situation. Think of reasons to support your argument.

File 32, 2D, page 20

Calvin starts off by asking for something outrageous and then decreasing the size of his requests until he asks for the cookie he really wants. He says *She's on to me* because his mother sees through his plan and does not agree to his request.

File 33, 5B, page 51

Answers

1 Generally true.

2 False. – It is generally advisable to arrive on time or 10 to 15 minutes after the arranged time.

3 Generally true.

4 Generally true.

5 Generally true.

6 True.

7 True.

8 False. – About three quarters.

9 False. – The majority go to Australia, Spain or France.

File 34, 5C, page 53

Student A:

You are a manager. Last week, you asked your assistant to make all necessary arrangements for an in-house training seminar due to take place fairly soon. You want to find out if the following tasks have been dealt with:

• book a room

• contact the presenters to ask what equipment they will need

• ask the presenters for an outline of the seminar

• put up a notice on the board

• send an email to all employees concerned.

You were expecting this information a few days ago, but your assistant seems to have a time-management problem. Now you need to find out:

• exactly what has been done

• why certain things haven't been done yet

• when exactly your assistant intends to deal with them – do not accept vague answers.

Secret agenda: Can you determine what sort of time-management problem your assistant has? (See exercise 7.)

File 35, 5E, page 57

Student B:

Your cost-saving ideas:

Choose what you think is the simplest idea from the list in exercise 6. This is the only idea you are prepared to accept. You are not going to try very hard to push it through, because you have been with the company since Day 1 and you don't want to see any changes.

Your task is to find arguments against any of the ideas your colleagues put forward.

File 36, 6A, page 59

This is what happened to Anne and John. Do you think their prison sentences were too long, too short or just right? Why?

• John and Anne had bought some land in Panama and they planned to build a holiday resort. They had promised 20 local families jobs working in their hotel.

• Nobody is sure why John walked into the police station. Some people think he needed a new passport so he could move to Panama permanently. Others think he had had an argument with Anne.

• Anne and John had to pay back the insurance and pension money they had received. John was sent to prison for six years and three months. Anne was sent to prison for six years and six months.

• Their children say they don't want to have anything to do with their parents ever again.

File 37, 5E, page 57

Student B:

Your partner will ask you a question. Answer the question truthfully and in some detail. Somewhere in your answer, use the first expression from the list below (see first box).

It is then your turn to ask your partner a question. Ask a question about the first topic to begin with (see second box).

Continue the activity until you have asked your partner a question about each topic, and you have used all the expressions when answering your partner's questions.

Expressions to use
1 … many more …
2 … slightly more …
3 … By and large, …
4 … tend to …
5 … It's about time …
6 … For the time being …

Topics to ask a question about
1 time management
2 deadlines
3 dealing with people who complain all the time
4 wasting paper
5 working in a team
6 popular colleagues

File 38, 7A, page 71

When you arrive in Lima, you are exhausted. You go to your room and discover that it is above a disco and very noisy.

You put the pillow over your head – you just want to sleep. Turn to File 47, page 122.

You complain to the manager about the noise. Turn to File 55, page 124.

File 39, 8B, page 83

Interview 1

Student B:

You are the CEO of a Telecoms company. Your company has been in the news because of reports of financial problems. You are going to be interviewed for a business news website. Prepare for the questions you think the interviewer might ask. You can use the information below and also invent information where necessary. You do not respond well to very direct or aggressive questions.

- Your company made losses for two years in a row – last month it lost $1.2 million.
- You intend to continue leading the company.
- Tomorrow there's an emergency meeting with the shareholders to listen to their concerns.
- You've begun talks with the board to rethink the company's financial strategy.
- Two members of the board resigned yesterday – no further resignations are expected.
- Competitors have started untrue rumours that the company will close.
- You believe the economic situation is improving and that shareholders will see a profit next year.

File 40, 6A, page 59

Student A:

Step 1: Work on your own. Read the whole story and complete the first part with the past simple or past perfect of the verbs in brackets.

Step 2: Work in pairs. Listen to your partner read out the first part of the story and check your answers. Then read out the second part for your partner to check his/her answers.

On 5th December 2007, someone [1]_____ (discover) a photograph on the internet. It [2]_____ (show) John and Anne buying some property together in Panama and it was dated 2006 – five years after John had disappeared. The police [3]_____ (arrest) John and charged him with fraud.

Newspaper reporters [4]_____ (contact) Anne and she [5]_____ (confirm) the photo was real. Soon after, she admitted that John [6]_____ (fake) his death so they could claim insurance money and pay off their debts.

But Anne also claimed that when John first disappeared, she thought he was dead. 'I genuinely thought he [7]_____ (have) an accident,' she said.

She also said she didn't know he was alive until 11 months later. He turned up at her house unexpectedly and she almost didn't recognize him because he had grown a beard to disguise his appearance. She begged him to go to the police, but he refused. Instead he moved into the house next to hers and they lived together secretly for years.

Anne insisted that their children did not know anything about it. She said, 'They thought John was dead. Now they are going to hate me.' Anne returned to the UK on 9th December. She was arrested and charged with fraud and money laundering.

File 41, 5D, page 55

Student B:

Your partner is incredibly difficult to work with because they are always complaining. You need them to make some changes to some PowerPoint slides by Friday. You can sympathize a little with them if you think it will help, but then you should try to move the conversation forward. Identify the problems and encourage your partner to think of solutions.

Use a professional neutral tone. For example: do not exaggerate; be assertive, not aggressive, so use 'I' messages.

File 42, 6D, page 65

Student A:

Read the commentary about conversations 1 and 2 in exercise 8. Jot down a few notes if you wish. Prepare to tell your partner as much as you can remember without looking back at the commentary.

1 A: I like your new boots.
   B: Oh, thank you.

In most English-speaking countries, a simple 'thank you' is usually enough in response to a compliment. Many people, though, often add a comment, e.g. 'Oh, thank you. I bought them at C&A.'

Note that in a number of other cultures, more than a simple 'thank you' is expected in response to a compliment.

2 A: What an interesting poster! It's beautiful.
   B: Please take it.

Speaker B's reply will seem strange if Speaker A doesn't know that in some cultures (e.g. in a number of Arab countries), you should avoid complimenting someone on one of their possessions because they would then feel compelled to give it to you.

File 43, 6D, page 65

Situations (1) and (2) have one thing in common: the complimenter and the recipient of the compliment are not of the same status – the complimenter has a lower status – and this restricts the range of compliments that can be paid.

In (1), the head of department probably did not expect to be praised for her professional qualities by an office assistant, at least not in public.

Similarly in (2), the teacher may have felt that it was inappropriate for a student to give feedback on her performance, especially in public. It would be all right for the teacher's supervisor to do that. It would also be all right for the student to compliment the teacher face-to-face, or of course when completing a feedback form.

Of course it's not only status, but also how well people know each other which determines how appropriate a compliment might be. In (3), Pierre being new to the company, the receptionist may have perceived his compliment as too familiar or flirtatious.

Information files

File 44, 7C, page 75

Mostly a

You are a bear.

You know your rights and you make sure that you get them. You don't have a problem with confrontation and you choose the most appropriate person in a company to get results. If there is a problem, you try to sort it out quickly and effectively.

Mostly b

You are a kangaroo.

When you experience bad service or unsatisfactory goods, you vote with your feet. You're unlikely to speak to the company to complain – you simply don't use them again. You're more likely to discuss the bad service with colleagues, friends and family and warn them not to use a company that you have had a bad experience with.

Mostly c

You are an owl.

You know the power of the internet and use it both to research whether an organization is reliable and also to tell others about your experience as a consumer. You don't have a problem confronting bad service face-to-face, but you believe that the consumers' real power is through communicating to a company in writing or online.

File 45, 7C, page 75

Student A:

You ordered a watch online as a present for a friend's special birthday. When it arrives in the post, it looks nothing like the picture on the website. You know that your friend will hate it so you rush out and buy another expensive present to replace it. Do you …

a _____?

b _____?

c _____?

File 46, 7B, page 73

Student C:

You are on the emergency team.

You want to stop Carl Hamilton from attending the event. It would go ahead – but without him as a speaker. Think of reasons to support your argument.

File 47, 7A, page 71

You sleep very badly. The next morning, you finally arrive to inspect the construction project. But you are so tired that you fall asleep in an important meeting. The project leader is upset and complains to your boss.

File 48, 7C, page 75

You took the morning off work to wait for the delivery of a new wardrobe, but it didn't arrive. You paid extra to have it delivered in this time slot.

When you arrive at work, there's an email from a supplier to say that the delivery that they promised will be 24 hours late. This causes big problems for the project you are working on.

You pop out to buy a sandwich from a fast food chain. When you take your first bite, you realize that there is a small piece of plastic in it.

You leave to go on a business trip. When you arrive at your destination, you discover that the airline has lost your suitcase containing the clothes and laptop that you intended to use in an important presentation you need to give the next day.

File 49, 9B, page 95

Student B:

Step 1: Read the story carefully.

Step 2: Students A and C will try to guess what the story is about. Answer their questions with 'yes' or 'no'. Do not answer any questions that you consider to be grammatically incorrect (ask your teacher if you are not sure).

When Students A and C have asked a maximum of five questions each, tell them the story.

Story 2

This story happened at the White House in November 2009. It was the first big social event organized by the Obama administration. More than 300 guests, including Cabinet members, diplomats and Hollywood celebrities, had been invited to a dinner in honour of visiting Indian Prime Minister Manmohan Singh.

Tareq and Michaele Salahi, a couple from Virginia, were not on the guest list but they managed to crash the event because a Secret Service checkpoint did not follow proper procedures.

The day after, Mrs Salahi's page on her Facebook site showed her posing for photographs with the Vice President, the White House chief of staff, the mayor of Washington DC and even three US marines.

As a result, White House security systems were put under review.

File 50, 8A, page 81

Student A:

People should be charged to use news websites.

Use five of the points in the box and at least one idea of your own to give a short talk on the subject. Use the active and passive form as appropriate.

- News isn't free – reporters and writers are expensive to employ.
- Visitors to news sites will pay for news content they can trust.
- Most news sites are good value for money – some cost less than a cup of coffee to join.
- Some news sites use a system where visitors can see a certain number of news stories; if they want to view more stories, then they pay more.
- People will be attracted to news sites that have specialist information, such as financial news.
- Other specialist content websites charge viewers, so why shouldn't news websites?.
- Soon it will be normal to pay to access all news websites. Research suggests that more than 50% of visitors will agree to pay.

File 51, 8B, page 83

Interview 2

Student B:

You are the interviewer.

You work for a business news website. You are going to interview the Managing Director of a pharmaceuticals company which has been in the news because of reports that a new medicine is unsafe. The Managing Director has walked out of interviews in the past when the questions have been too direct or aggressive.

Try to confirm whether the following is true:

- Company first knew about the problem a year ago.
- Three of the top scientists on the project have suddenly left the company.
- Reports that the government has warned doctors to stop using the medicine immediately.
- Some patients want compensation from the company.

You want the following facts:

- Exact problem with the medicine?
- Amount of people who use it?
- Doctors are still giving the medicine to patients?
- What people using the medicine should do now?

File 52, 8D, page 87

Student B:

Look at the full details of the messages you left on your colleague's desk. Use this information to help you clarify the information that your partner asks about.

Phone message

Jason Hendry called — he wants you to reschedule the meeting with the supplier. Is it possible to have the meeting next Thursday instead? He also wants to confirm what your orders are for the next media advertising campaign. Do you want the campaign to focus on the internet or on TV?

Hope this is clear.

Call Jason Hendry if you need more information.

Note

There are ten pictures missing for the new catalogue. Does the photographer have copies we could have?

You can find a DVD of the missing images on your desk.

Also, could you check with the printers to find the last date that we can get the photographs to them to publish in the catalogue?

The Design department have asked you to send confirmation of their new artwork budget for the catalogue — is it £20,000 or £30,000?

Information files

File 53, 8D, page 87
Student B:

You want to change the advertising for Diego Tyres. Use these details to help you clarify the information in the email that your partner asks about.

1 Magazine
Currently you advertise in the magazine *That Car!* From next month, you want to change and advertise in *Speed and Travel*. You want the advertisements to be in colour not black and white. The advertisement size should be full page not half page. If possible, you want the position of the advertisement to be the back page of the magazine.

2 TV commercial
You want the advertising time to stay the same as it as at present (8.30 in the evening) but you want to change the day that the commercial is broadcast. At present it is Thursday, and you want to change to Friday.

Hi

I've had some thoughts about possible changes to forthcoming advertising for Diego Tyres.

1 Magazine
Stop advertisements in *That Car!*
Move to *Speed and Travel* from next mth.

Colour not b/w. Full pge not half.
Position = back (if poss).

2 TV commercial
Keep same time slot (8.30) but change day
Thurs → Fri

3 Online
Website - *Car Crazy*? Wrong for our market?
Other possible blogs/websites?

Let me know what you think.

Regards

3 Online
You have been advertising your company on a website called *Car Crazy*. However, research suggests that the blog is aimed at 18–24-year-olds, whereas your target market is 25–45. Would it be a good idea to stop advertising on this site and advertise on other blogs or websites instead?

File 54, 8E, page 89

Interview 1

Student B: Sam Hughes

You only need to answer questions that you are asked.

- You were chatting to your colleague while the safety information was being explained. You can't be sure exactly how long the safety talk lasted or what the instructor said.
- You didn't think it was necessary to check equipment before entering the cave.
- In the cave, you realized your torch didn't work. You didn't tell the instructor. Instead you stopped to try to fix it and when you looked up, your group had gone.
- You didn't see the signs back to the entrance because it was dark.
- You saw the 'danger' sign, but you were curious and went to see what was inside. You hadn't been told not to go into 'danger areas'.

File 55, 7A, page 71
Your request is successful. You have a good night's sleep and arrive at the construction project rested and refreshed. The project leader is impressed with your ideas and compliments you to your boss.

File 56, 9B, page 95
Students A and C:

Look at the words in the box. They are words from a story that you have to try and guess by asking Student B 'yes' or 'no' questions.

Student B will only answer questions that are grammatically correct.

Story 2

| couple dinner Indian invited White House |

File 57, 9C, page 97

Blake Robbins was awarded $175,000, which was placed in a trust.

Jalil Hassan, a second pupil who filed a lawsuit against the school authority, was awarded $10,000.

Although the school authorities eventually admitted they had used the webcams to monitor students secretly, the FBI and regional prosecutors chose not to bring criminal charges against the school authority. Explaining why it settled the case, the authority's president said a lengthy trial 'would have been an unfair distraction for our students and staff and it would have cost taxpayers additional dollars that are better devoted to education.'

The remaining $425,000 of the settlement was paid to the boys' lawyer for his work on the case.

6

File 58, 9E, page 101

Student A:

You start. Ask your partner questions in order to complete the first part of the article. Then read the rest of the article to answer your partner's questions.

What can employers listen, watch and read?

Recent surveys have found that a majority of employers monitor their employees. Such monitoring is virtually unregulated. So, unless company policy specifically states otherwise, employers can listen to, watch and read [1]_____ (What?).

Many employers track keystrokes and [2]_____ (What?). Some monitor blogs and social networking sites [3]_____ (Why?).

Employers sometimes monitor phone calls with clients or customers [4]_____ (Why?). Besides, telephone numbers dialled from phone extensions can be recorded by a device called a pen register. It allows the employer to see a list of phone numbers dialled by any extension and the length of each call. This information may be used to evaluate the amount of time spent by employees with clients. The conversations employees have with co-workers can be monitored in the same way that their conversations with clients or customers are.

Many companies use video monitoring to counter theft, violence and sabotage, and some use video surveillance to track employees' on-the-job performance. Most employers inform employees about such practices.

File 59, 5E, page 57

Student C:

Your cost-saving ideas:

Choose two ideas from the right-hand column of the list in exercise 6. Think of strong arguments to support these two ideas.

You have a slight problem listening to people. You are impatient to present your own ideas, so you keep interrupting people who put forward different ideas.

File 60, 6E, page 67

Student A:

Situation 1

You are the manager of a pharmaceutical company who recently discovered during a performance review (PR) that Student B, one of your most brilliant researchers, lied on their CV. You found three discrepancies:

CV: No health problems
PR: had an epileptic fit three months ago

CV: 'project manager'
PR: 'assistant project manager'

CV: 1999–2004 worked for Pfizer
PR: worked for Sikra 2003–2008

Your task is to:

• listen carefully to B's explanations

• decide whether you want to maintain your decision to sack B for breach of trust; if you decide not to sack B, what alternative measure are you going to take, if any? (e.g. demotion / salary cut / transfer to another department / negative reference, etc).

Situation 2

You are the mediator and you speak first.

Student B works as a designer in the IT department of a tour operator and accuses Student C, the CEO, of taking credit for some of his/her work.

Your task is to:

• get both parties to fill you in on the details of this dispute; start with the CEO

• ask probing questions to establish whether this is really a case of taking credit for someone else's work

• help both parties reach an amicable settlement.

Situation 3

You are a salesperson for a furniture company. Everyone knows how successful you are: other people struggle to meet their sales targets, but you always exceed them. You tend to be a bit careless with administrative duties because you have more important things to worry about. Last month, you incurred €55 travelling expenses, but you lost the receipt. To make up for the loss, you got a similar receipt from a friend, but the amount was only €34.

Your task is to:

• listen to the accountant give his/her version of the story

• give your own version

• maintain that no deception is involved here – you just claimed something you are entitled to.

File 61, 9E, page 101

Student A:

You represent management, while your partner is a staff representative. Read the information below.

> You think the current measures are insufficient, and you are concerned about:
> - the decrease in productivity
> - the growing distrust between staff and management
> - the fact that some of your staff have 'friends' and/or former colleagues in rival companies
> - the lack of monitoring of interns working in the laboratory.

Make your case for the introduction of all four new measures proposed.

You strongly believe that, as long as the monitoring policy is clearly explained to all employees, they will certainly welcome the new measures.

When you disagree with the staff representative, avoid direct confrontation but do express your opinions forcefully whenever necessary.

File 62, 10A, page 102

Green button

Thanks for voting. Well, I guess you'd like to know what happened next. As you suggested, I explained the problem to my manager. He wasn't very supportive and refused to let me work part-time. I considered talking to my departmental manager but decided that it would probably be a waste of time. I managed to do voluntary work at a local hospital at weekends and made some good contacts there. After a few months, I decided to leave my old job. I'd managed to save some money so I went travelling and did voluntary work with medical charities in some interesting countries. I got a lot of practical experience. It convinced me that I really wanted to go into the medical profession and I returned home determined to study. I've been offered a place on a course to study medicine, which I hope to start in September. I miss having a regular salary and I don't mind telling you that it's all been more difficult that I thought. But I'm studying full-time so I will get my qualifications sooner than if I worked at the same time. It will all be worth it when I'm a doctor. Thanks for your vote!

File 63, 1B, page 7

Student B:

Ask your partner questions to make them say exactly the same as words on your cards.

Five.	I don't know.	In winter.
She's Spanish.	To find a job.	Yes, I do.

File 64, 10B, page 104

Student A:

Use the following information and any ideas you want to add to prepare a short anecdote. Use extreme adjectives to make it interesting.

> - Last week, your friend was working late on the top floor of a building.
> - The lifts weren't working.
> - She walked down the stairs. It was very tiring.
> - The lights went out. She heard a noise. She was frightened.
> - She ran to an office and hid.
> - She heard a voice. It sounded very angry.
> - It was the security guard. He thought she was a burglar.
> - He was very surprised to find her under a desk.
> - He thought it was very funny and told the story to everyone in the office.

File 65, 10B, page 105

Student A:

You are at a business convention when you see someone that you worked with in the past (or studied with in the past). Start a conversation and find out what they are doing now. Answer their questions about you. You can make up information or use the following information.

> - You stayed at the same company. You have been promoted and are now a director. You are very happy in your job.
> - Answer questions about Carla (a mutual colleague). She left to work for a competitor and took lots of clients with her. Your CEO was very angry.
> - James (another mutual colleague) left to start a restaurant. You went there and the food is very, very good.
> - Remind your ex-colleague about a time when you organized a departmental social event together. It was a karaoke evening and you discovered that your boss had a very bad voice. It was very funny.
> - Suggest going to have a coffee to talk about old times.

File 66, 10C, page 107

Student B:

Read about this alternative to the traditional performance review. Summarize the key points for the others in your group.

> **Self-review**
> - Employees analyze own strengths, weaknesses and successes.
> - They say what areas need to improve.
> - They use a form to give themselves a score in different work-related categories.
> - Manager meets with employee and asks them to explain how and why they decided on their score.

7

File 67, 10C, page 107

Performance review 20 February: Nadim Tariq	
Requirements	1 = Rarely meets requirements 2 = Often fails to meet requirements 3 = Generally meets requirement 4 = Always meets requirements 5 = Generally exceeds requirements
Listens to directions from management	2
Communicates effectively with co-workers	3
Works well in a team	2
Demonstrates ability to learn and use new skills	4
Responds politely and efficiently to customers	2
Demonstrates an ability to generate ideas and solve problems	4
Arrives and leaves work at the appropriate time	1
Dresses smartly	2
Attendance	1
Comments Nadim shows ability and often has excellent ideas. However, there are areas that need to be improved to help him progress in the company.	**Action** A meeting was arranged with Nadim and the following objectives were agreed: • Improve dress style, timekeeping and attendance. • Attend training course on customer care. • Contribute to team tasks more effectively.

April 5
Results of customer satisfaction survey

Customers were asked to rate whether their queries were effectively and politely dealt with

Nadim Tariq
Score: 98% satisfaction

June 17   Comments from team members on a recent team project

'Nadim has shown huge improvement in his style of dress in the office and often wears a suit.'

'Always on time now. Often works late, too.'

'Not off work so often but still has more days off than rest of the group.'

'Might still need some support in skills for working in a team as he can sometimes follow his own ideas too much.'

'Nadim has started to show great potential. He's showing some good leadership qualities.'

File 68, 1C, page 9
Student B:

With best wishes,
Claude

Marcel, our driver, will be picking her up at Brussels Airport and taking her directly to her hotel.

It's only a five-minute walk from our head office, so she'll have plenty of time to relax before a very busy day.

I'm sorry I wasn't available to take your call yesterday.

I attach a detailed schedule for the day, as well as a map of the area just in case.

File 69, 1D, page 11
Student B:

Topic 1	You have no strong opinion, but you believe it is a good thing to raise the retirement age. You notice that someone is not saying much, so you try to draw them into the discussion.
Topic 2	You don't really feel like contributing anything to this discussion, so let the others argue. Don't say anything unless someone asks you.
Topic 3	You are passionately involved in this issue, so you argue strongly that working from home is just a trend that will not last. People need companies as much as companies need people.

File 70, 1C, page 9

Student B:

As you know, all business correspondence can be formal, neutral or informal. It depends who you are writing to. It depends on your relationship with your reader. When you are in doubt, a friendly, neutral style usually works best.

Complete the 'Closing' column with the expressions from the box. Then check your answers with your partner.

> Best regards,   With best wishes,   Best,   Talk soon,

	Opening	Closing
Informal	Tony,	_____
↓	Hi Tony,	See you soon, Bye for now,
↓	Dear Tony,	_____ All the best, Regards,
↓	Dear Tony Adenuga,	_____ Best wishes,
Formal	Dear Mr Adenuga,	_____

Now discuss these questions.

Do you ever

- start an email with no greeting?
- end an email with no closing (i.e. you just sign off with your name or initials)?

File 71, 5C, page 53

Student B:

Your manager has asked you to make all necessary arrangements for an in-house training seminar due to take place fairly soon. So far, all you've done is book a room and put up a notice on the board – you haven't done anything else. The problem is, some other people have asked you to help and you don't want to disappoint anyone.

- Henry from Accounts asked you to fix his computer.
- Liz from Human Resources asked you to look after Olivera, the new temporary assistant.
- Melinda from Admin asked you to go over a letter she'd translated.

When asked when you intend to deal with the remaining tasks, try to get away with vague answers like, I'm working on it, It may take a while, I'll see what I can do.

File 72, 5B, page 50

The three countries described are:

- Turkey
- Germany
- Spain

File 73, 7A, page 71

The only accommodation available is in a backpacker's hostel. It's very noisy and you have to share a room with three other people.

You take the room and try to get some sleep. Turn to File 47, page 122.

You offer to pay the manager extra for a single room. Turn to File 55, page 124.

File 74, 3C, page 31

Student B:

1 Work on your own. You have now identified the problems that your predecessor was up against while organizing the event. Decide what went wrong in each area 4–6. Choose problem (a) or (b), or invent your own problem (c).

4 Entertainment:

a you could hire a DJ, but there's hardly any room for dancing!

b your boss suggested hiring a magician, but they're all expensive

c _____

5 Catering:

a you feel food and drinks should be free, but what about your budget?

b your favourite catering company has just increased its prices

c _____

6 Registration:

a last year, 56 people registered, but only 48 turned up

b one month to go, and only 23 people have registered so far!

c _____

2 Listen to your partner and make a note of the problems in areas 1–3.

1 The budget: _____
_____

2 The venue: _____
_____

3 Promotion: _____
_____

3 Now tell your partner about the problems in areas 4–6.

4 Work on your own again. Think of a solution to problems 1–3.

5 Work together with your partner again. Ask and answer questions about the problems each of you had to deal with, and the solutions you've come up with.

8

File 75, 1E, page 13

Student B:

First, just listen and complete the text on your own. Then compare your text with Student A's and check your answers. Underline all the expressions the speaker uses to structure his presentation. Finally, go to the audio script on page 138 to check the underlined expressions.

> Did you know that back and neck problems are one of the top ten medical problems in Western countries? Twelve years ago, because of my job and my research, [1]_____ _____ _____ an average of 12 hours a day sitting at a desk. My spine was stiff. I could hardly bend any more. That's when I decided to take up Tai Chi. I'd read somewhere that it could do a lot of good to your joints, so why not give it a try?
>
> Today, I'd like to [2]_____ _____ _____ about this ancient Chinese martial art called Tai Chi.
>
> My talk is in three parts. I'll start with a little historical background. Then I'll [3]_____ _____ _____ the health benefits of Tai Chi. And finally, I'll describe what it's like to practise in a club.
>
> Let me start then with an overview of the history of Tai Chi. [4]_____, I'll take you back to the origin – 12th-century China. Then I'll say a few words about how and why Tai Chi evolved into a number of different schools. [5]_____ _____, I'd like to explain how this art reached the rest of the world. …
>
> This leads me to my next point, which is why Tai Chi can bring so many health benefits to so many people. I'd like [6]_____ _____ three areas that we can develop through Tai Chi: the muscles and the joints, the internal organs, and your powers of concentration. …
>
> Finally, what is it like to practise in a club? What do you notice when you just observe a Tai Chi session? [7]_____ _____: an instructor, demonstrating the moves and guiding the students; a group of people imitating the instructor and practising; and last but not least, an atmosphere of calm, concentration and congeniality. …
>
> At this stage, I'd like [8]_____ _____ _____ the main points of my talk. …
>
> I'd like [9]_____ _____ _____ by reminding you of something I said at the beginning. …

File 76, 1D, page 11

Student C:

Topic 1	You don't really feel like contributing anything to this discussion, so let the others argue. Don't say anything unless someone asks you.
Topic 2	You are passionately involved in this issue, so you argue strongly that private health insurance is best. Why should people who work hard pay for those who don't want to work?
Topic 3	You have no strong opinion, but you believe working from home has a lot more advantages – in fact, it's the future of work. You notice that someone is not saying much, so you try to draw them into the discussion.

File 77, 3D, page 33

Student B:

Step 1: Answer your partner's questions. Think of another way of saying *I don't know* and choose the appropriate answer from the box.

> *Your partner: What shall we get Olga for her birthday?*
>
> *You: I'm not really sure, but what about a nice engraving or something like that? I think she likes modern art.*

> _____ I always take the underground, you see.
>
> _____ I didn't watch it.
>
> _____ Losing my job, probably.
>
> _____ What about a nice engraving or something like that? I think she likes modern art.
>
> _____ Ask Suzana, she's our techie.

Step 2: Ask your partner the questions on the left. Make sure you get the correct response and a different way of saying *I don't know* each time.

You ask:	Your partner replies:
I haven't seen Simon this week. Any idea what's up?	_____ I think he's off sick.
I wonder what's wrong with the printer.	_____ Why don't you look at the instructions manual?
What do you like best about your job?	_____ Helping people and learning from them.
You could've told me about Leo.	_____ I don't even know anyone by that name.
How long will it take us to get to the centre?	_____ You know what the traffic can be like.

File 78, 8A, page 81

Student B:

People should be charged to use news websites.

Use five of the points in the box and at least one idea of your own to give a short talk on the subject. Use the active and passive form as appropriate.

> - News sites that charge risk losing visitors to their site.
> - Charges would start low but would increase each year.
> - The websites that charge are often linked to newspapers; newspaper sales have fallen and the number of online visitors will also fall.
> - Research suggests that less than 5% of visitors will pay to view news stories.
> - Advertising revenue is a better way to increase profit for news websites.
> - News sites should focus on getting more visitors in order to attract more advertisers.
> - News becomes out-of-date very quickly so websites need to offer people more interesting content rather than charge them to visit the site.

Information files

File 79, 3A, page 27

Student B:

You are the PA. Look at your to-do list on your computer. Decide which are the four most important items and tick them off because you have already dealt with them. Your office manager will phone you for a progress report, so be prepared to explain why you have done the things you have done and not the others.

To-Do List

- Email Rigley re office equipment maintenance
  - Contact maintenance company re copiers / printers
- Take inventory of office supplies
  - Place order
- Screen job applications (Customer Service Advisor)
  - Shortlist candidates
  - Arrange interviews
- Get feedback from employees about monitoring / recording long-distance phone calls (How? Questionnaire? Interviews?)
- Update health & safety regulations
  - Forward to departmental managers
- Contact various IT companies re best software solution
  - Get written quotes

File 80, 3E, page 35

Student B:

Step 1: Before you join Student A, think how you are going to give the four pieces of news below in an indirect way (see the audio script on page 142 if you need help), and be prepared to answer your partner's challenging questions!

- The lunch break will soon be ten minutes shorter.
- You cannot pay one of your suppliers on the agreed date.
- It seems that you are going to lose a contract to your main competitor.
- One of your most respected managers has decided to leave the company.

Step 2: Work in pairs. Your partner speaks first. Listen to your partner's news, react in the most appropriate way and then ask challenging questions.

Do you mean that …? / Are you saying that …?
So if I understand correctly … / You mean, …?, etc.

Step 3: Now break your bad news to your partner. Start with your first item. Listen to your partner's reaction and respond. Then move on to the second item.

File 81, 6A, page 59

Student B:

Step 1: Work on your own. Read the whole story and complete the second part with the past simple or past perfect of the verbs in brackets.

Step 2: Work in pairs. Read out the first part of the story to your partner. Then listen to your partner read out the second part and check your answers.

On 5th December 2007, someone discovered a photograph on the internet. It showed John and Anne buying some property together in Panama and it was dated 2006 – five years after John had disappeared. The police arrested John and charged him with fraud.

Newspaper reporters contacted Anne and she confirmed the photo was real. Soon after, she admitted that John had faked his death so they could claim insurance money and pay off their debts.

But Anne also claimed that when John first disappeared, she thought he was dead. 'I genuinely thought he'd had an accident,' she said.

She also said she didn't know he was alive until 11 months later. He turned up at her house unexpectedly and she almost [8]_____ (not recognize) him because he [9]_____ (grow) a beard to disguise his appearance. She begged him to go to the police, but he [10]_____ (refuse). Instead he [11]_____ (move) into the house next to hers and they lived together secretly for years.

Anne [12]_____ (insist) that their children did not know anything about it. She said, 'They thought John was dead. Now they are going to hate me.' Anne [13]_____ (return) to the UK on 9th December. She was arrested and charged with fraud and money laundering.

File 82, 8E, page 89

Interview 2

Student A: Zaheer Kumar

You only need to answer questions that you are asked.

- It was a much larger group than usual (16 people) and some members were chatting during the safety talk.
- The group doing the caving activity arrived ten minutes late. The safety talk may have been shorter than normal so that you could start caving on time.
- You told the group to check torches and other equipment before entering the cave but you didn't have time to check whether they did or not.
- When you realized that one of the group was missing, you waited for five minutes to see if they caught up. When they didn't, you took the group out of the cave and then returned to look for the missing person.
- You couldn't call for medical help because there was no mobile phone signal. You asked one of the group to run to the main building to get help.

File 83, 6D, page 65

Student B:

Read the commentary about conversations 3 and 4 in exercise 8. Jot down a few notes if you wish. Prepare to tell your partner as much as you can remember without looking back at the commentary.

> **3** A: *Your English is really good.*
>
> B: *No, it isn't. I know it's bad.*

Speaker B, probably out of modesty, disagrees directly with Speaker A, and so breaks one of the unwritten rules of responding to compliments in English-speaking countries (among others): disagreeing with the compliment may make Speaker A feel bad or stupid.

If you get a compliment that you feel is too big or that you don't deserve, what you can do is first accept it, and then make a comment to reduce the force of the compliment. Here are two examples:

- A: *Your English is really good.*
  B: *Thank you. But I need to expand my vocabulary.*
- A: *What a beautiful living-room!*
  B: *Thanks. It's a pity it doesn't have an extra window.*

- A: *That was a great performance. Well done!*
  B: *I'm now the best one in the club.*

In accepting the compliment so openly and even adding to it, Speaker B breaks the second unwritten rule of responding to compliments in English-speaking countries (among others), namely that you should avoid praising your own achievements.

File 84, 2E, page 23

1 Technology
- Unusual applications for mobile phones
- New ways to watch TV
- An instant heater/cooler that uses no electricity
- A way to destroy emails that you didn't mean to send

2 Transport
- A way to end parking problems
- Something to help people get a seat on crowded trains
- A service for people who hate checking in at the airport
- A way to help people share cars to work

3 Home and office
- The dinner that cooks itself
- A self-cleaning house
- A way to find out of your boss is nearby
- Something useful and attractive for your desk

File 85, 5A, page 49

Student A:

Step 1: First, work together with one or more A students. Evaluate the solutions below and decide which three are the best. Think about how expensive the various solutions are going to be, how long they are going to take to produce results, how popular they are going to be with staff / management, etc.

> **Possible solutions**
> - use the 'likable fools' to lead meetings where they explain the changes you want to introduce
> - pair up less experienced employees with more experienced ones who act as mentors
> - make sure project teams are made up of people who don't always agree with each other
> - identify the 'likable fools' who underperform and sack them
> - identify the 'competent idiots', give them feedback and coaching so they can change their behaviour and become better integrated
> - encourage familiarity by mixing up people's workspaces, so they can mingle more

A1: *Getting experienced staff to act as mentors will be considerably less expensive than organizing coaching for those competent idiots.*

A2: *Maybe, but it might also be less popular. I think the least expensive solution is to mix up employees' workspaces.*

Step 2: Get together with Student B, who has chosen three other solutions. Compare your six solutions. Then agree which three you want to include in your report to Avatec's management.

File 86, 7A, page 71

The bed and breakfast is great and very reasonably priced. The owner is celebrating his birthday and invites you to a party with his family and friends.

You thank him but refuse. You really need to get some sleep and ask for the quietest room in the house. Turn to File 55, page 124.

You accept the invitation and go to the party and dance until dawn. Turn to File 47, page 122.

File 87, 9E, page 101

Student B:

Read the first part of the article and prepare to answer your partner's questions. Then ask your partner questions in order to complete the rest of the article.

How can conversations employees have with co-workers be monitored?

Recent surveys have found that a majority of employers monitor their employees. Such monitoring is virtually unregulated. So, unless company policy specifically states otherwise, employers can listen to, watch and read most of your workplace communications.

Many employers track keystrokes and time spent at the keyboard. Some monitor blogs and social networking sites to see what is being written about the company.

Employers sometimes monitor phone calls with clients or customers for reasons of quality control. Besides, telephone numbers dialled from phone extensions can be recorded [5]_____ *(How?)*. It allows the employer to see a list of phone numbers dialled by any extension and the length of each call. This information may be used to evaluate the amount of time spent by employees with clients. The conversations employees have with co-workers can be monitored [6]_____ *(How?)*.

Many companies use [7]_____ *(What?)* to counter theft, violence and sabotage, and some use video surveillance [8]_____ *(Why?)*. Most employers inform employees about such practices.

File 88, 7C, page 75

Student B:

You rent an expensive villa for a short break to celebrate a special occasion with family. When you arrive, you find that the accommodation has no hot water, the kitchen is dirty and the TV doesn't work.

Do you …

a _____?

b _____?

c _____?

File 89, 9E, page 101

Student B:

You are a staff representative, while your partner represents management.

You believe the current measures are already too repressive, and there is no need to introduce any new measures. You are prepared to make concessions on the monitoring of blogs and social networking sites, but you consider the other measures off limits. Read the information below.

You believe that:
- many employees already feel over-monitored
- more monitoring will definitely have a negative effect on staff morale and motivation, and ultimately on productivity
- the monitoring policy definitely won't work unless staff are consulted
- what the company needs is to look for ways of rebuilding trust between staff and management – not ways of increasing surveillance.

When you disagree with the management representative, avoid direct confrontation but do express your opinions forcefully whenever necessary.

File 90, 9B, page 95

Student C:

Step 1: Read the story carefully.

Step 2: Students A and B will try to guess what the story is about. Answer their questions with 'yes' or 'no'. Do not answer any questions that you consider to be grammatically incorrect (ask your teacher if you are not sure).

When Students A and B have asked a maximum of five questions each, tell them the story.

Story 3

This story happened in January 2010. The Slovak authorities were trying to test airport screening procedures for checked-in luggage, so they planted, i.e. placed, illegal items on eight passengers but didn't tell them they had done this. Sniffer dogs detected seven of the illicit items, but the eighth – 90g of commercial explosives – which had been planted on a Slovak electrician living in Dublin, escaped detection. The authorities then failed to intercept the man's luggage and he was allowed to board his plane to Dublin.

Three days later, the Slovak authorities contacted the Irish police, who immediately launched a massive security operation. Blocks of flats were evacuated and the army was called in to recover the explosives. The 49-year-old electrician, who had no idea what was going on, was arrested under anti-terrorist legislation but was released a couple of hours later.

The Slovak Interior Minister apologized to the Irish authorities.

10

File 91, 6E, page 67

Student B:

Situation 1

You work as a researcher for a pharmaceutical company. You excel at your job, but after a recent performance review (PR), your manager accused you of lying on your CV.

Three discrepancies were found:

CV: No health problems
PR: had an epileptic fit three months ago

CV: 'project manager'
PR: 'assistant project manager'

CV: 1999–2004 worked for Pfizer
PR: worked for Sikra 2003–2008

Your task is to:

• prove your honesty, as in fact you did not lie: the problem is that your CV was written carelessly (e.g. problems with Select / Copy / Paste; failure to specify which jobs were full-time, part-time or occasional, etc). As regards your health, explain that when you wrote your CV, you hadn't had a fit for five years; you thought maybe you'd never have one again.

• apologize for your careless CV, emphasize your achievements as a researcher, show your genuine commitment to the company.

Situation 2

You work as a designer in the IT department of a tour operator. You attended the company's latest international sales conference, during which the CEO presented as his/her own the new logo of the company. The logo is a beautiful piece of artwork which took you weeks to produce, with a little help from a very skilful intern who has now left the company.

Your task is to:

• listen to the CEO give his/her version of the story

• react to any comment that you consider untrue, and provide arguments

• demand a public apology.

Situation 3

You are the mediator and you speak first.

Student C works as Chief Accountant for a furniture company, while Student A is a salesperson for that company. The accountant accuses the salesperson of claiming expenses he/she didn't incur.

Your task is to:

• ask the accountant to give you his/her version of the story

• ask the salesperson to give you his/her version of the story

• decide whether or not this is a case of fraud – does the company director really need to be informed?

• help both parties reach an amicable settlement.

File 92, 5E, page 57

Student D:

Your cost-saving ideas:

None. You may not have any ideas of your own, but you are very good at weighing alternatives. So, whenever you can, summarize two ideas your colleagues have put forward, and explain their advantages and disadvantages.

Be as assertive and neutral as possible at all times.

File 93, 10C, page 107

Student C:

Read about this alternative to the traditional performance review. Summarize the key points for the others in your group.

Peer review

• Two or more co-workers evaluate each other in private.

• They review a colleague on topics such as productivity, professionalism, quality of work and organizational skills.

• The review is given to the manager.

• Manager can choose to keep the results secret or share them with the employee and use them to offer constructive feedback.

File 94, 8B, page 83

Interview 2

Student A:

You are the Managing Director of a pharmaceuticals company. Your company has been in the news because of reports that a new medicine is unsafe. You are going to be interviewed for a business news website. Prepare for the questions you think the interviewer might ask. You can use the information below and also invent information where necessary. You do not respond well to very direct or aggressive questions.

• Three scientists have left the company to work on other projects (as agreed before the problem was discovered).

• Competitors have started rumours that the government has warned doctors to stop using the medicine (which is false, but your company has advised doctors to stop using the medicine until more tests have been carried out).

• The problem with the medicine is not dangerous to patients' health. There is one ingredient that has caused minor problems for some people (some have experienced temporary hair loss, but don't mention this unless asked).

• Currently 2.5 million people use the medicine worldwide.

• As soon as the problem was discovered, you stopped supplies of the medicine until the problem is resolved. (But there was a communication problem and, until this week, some doctors continued to give the medicine to patients).

• Your company is producing an alternative medicine (without the problem ingredient) and this will be available next month.

File 95, 9B, page 95

Students A and B:

Look at the words in the box. They are words from a story that you have to try and guess by asking Student C 'yes' or 'no' questions.

Student C will only answer questions that are grammatically correct.

Story 3

> airport apartment electrician explosive Irish Slovak

File 96, 7B, page 73

Student D:

You are on the emergency team.

You want the Solar event to go ahead and Carl Hamilton to be a speaker. You believe this would show that the Rockdale Centre can safely organize international events even in difficult circumstances. Think of reasons to support your argument.

File 97, 5A, page 49

Student B:

Step 1: First, work together with one or more B students. Evaluate the solutions below and decide which three are the best. Think about how expensive the various solutions are going to be, how long they are going to take to produce results, how popular they are going to be with staff / management, etc.

> **Possible solutions**
> • identify some of the most disliked 'competent idiots', and sack them
> • organize end-of-the-week get-togethers for all employees
> • make sure project teams are made up of people who know each other and always agree with each other
> • identify the 'likable fools' and give them roles where they can connect people from different departments
> • encourage familiarity by creating informal gathering areas where employees can chat
> • create inter-departmental project teams to encourage a shared identity

B1: Organizing get-togethers will be a lot more popular than sacking people.

B2: Well, of course. But I think in the long run it will be far less effective.

Step 2: Join up with a Student A, who has chosen three other solutions. Compare your six solutions. Then agree which three you want to include in your report to Avatec's management.

File 98, 10B, page 104

Student B:

Use the following information and any ideas you want to add to prepare a short anecdote. Use extreme adjectives to make it interesting.

> • Last month you went on a training course with your new boss.
> • You had to work in teams and race to locations on a map.
> • The weather was very bad.
> • After three hours you were all very tired.
> • Finally, you had to cross a river in a very small boat.
> • You started to help your boss into the boat.
> • You slipped and pushed him into the river.
> • The water was very cold.
> • Your boss was very angry.
> • You had to share a car with him on the journey home.
> • He didn't speak to you. It was very uncomfortable.

File 99, 10B, page 105

Student B:

You are at a business convention when someone that you worked with in the past (or studied with in the past) starts a conversation with you. Answer their questions about you. Find out what they are doing now. You can make up information or use the information below.

> • You left the company two years ago.
> • You went to work in another country (choose one).
> • You have been promoted and now run a department.
> • Ask about Carla. She was very, very ambitious.
> • Ask about James. He loved to cook and wanted to be a chef.
> • Remind your ex-colleague about a time when you went to visit a client and locked the keys in the car and had to get a taxi back to the office. It was very cold and it was raining. No taxis would stop and you got very, very wet.
> • You have to meet a client in five minutes. End the conversation politely and send regards to the people in your old department.

File 100, 7A, page 71

The hire car breaks down in a small town 600km from Lima.

There is a good mechanic in the village but he is away until tomorrow. You decide to wait. Turn to File 18, page 117.

You don't want to wait. Instead you get a lift to the next town, where an overnight bus will take you to Lima. Turn to File 38, page 71.

11

File 101, 6E, page 67

Student C:

Situation 1

You are the mediator and you speak first.

Student A is the manager of a pharmaceutical company who recently discovered during a performance review that Student B, a brilliant young researcher, lied on their CV.

Your task is to:

• summarize the situation in one sentence

• find out the nature of those lies, and assess their seriousness

• listen to A's and B's perspective on the issue

• discuss what measures should be taken

• get A and B to reach a compromise … but only if you are personally of the opinion that a compromise should be reached in this situation.

Situation 2

You are the CEO of an international tour operator. At the latest sales conference, you proudly presented your new company logo. It is a beautiful piece of artwork which you obtained by reformatting an image you came across in an unnamed folder on the company Intranet. The folder contained dozens of other images. One of your employees now accuses you of stealing his/her work.

Your task is to:

• present your version of the story when called upon by the mediator

• calmly counter your employee's accusations

• accept an amicable settlement, but an apology is out of the question.

Situation 3

You work as Chief Accountant for a furniture company, where Student A is a salesperson.

When you checked A's receipts last month, you noticed that a receipt to the amount of €34 was dated 21 May. The problem is that 21 May was a Sunday, and nobody works on a Sunday.

Your task is to:

• present your version of the story when called upon by the mediator

• listen to A's version of the story

• express sympathy for A, but explain why you have to inform the director.

File 102, 3B, page 29

Teacher

Pre-teach any key vocabulary that can be assumed unknown or that you feel is worth recycling (e.g. *pebble, cunning, cancel a debt*). Tell the group you are going to tell a story, but that not everyone will hear it from you. Send some students outside while you read the story (three or four students if there are 12–20 in the group). Tell the remaining Ss that the ones outside are going to retell the story one after the other, and that each time they should all make a note of the details that are changed or lost in the retelling.

Read the story. Then get one of the Ss outside (= S1) to come back inside. Ask for one volunteer who heard the story from you to do the first retelling. Everyone listens. Get another S back inside (= S2). S1 retells the story to S2, then S2 to S3, etc.

Black or White?

Many years ago, when a person who owed money could be thrown into jail, a merchant in London unfortunately owed a huge sum to a moneylender. The moneylender, who was old, ugly and evil, fancied the merchant's beautiful teenage daughter. He proposed a bargain.

He said he would cancel the merchant's debt if he could marry his young and beautiful daughter. Otherwise, he would have the merchant thrown in jail where he would spend the rest of his days. Of course, both the father and his daughter were horrified at the idea.

The cunning moneylender then offered to let fate decide the matter. He said: 'I will put two pebbles in a bag, one black and one white. Your daughter may reach into the bag and without looking choose one of the pebbles. If she chooses the black pebble, she will become my wife and your debt will be cancelled. If she chooses the white pebble, she stays with you and again your debt will be cancelled. If she refuses to choose, you will go to jail and she will surely starve.'

With a heavy heart, the merchant and his daughter agreed to the bargain.

As they talked, they were standing in the merchant's garden, on a path covered in pebbles. The moneylender bent down to pick up the two pebbles. As he was doing so, the daughter noticed he picked up two black pebbles and put them in the bag.

In that moment, with her life in the balance, she had to choose what to do. She could refuse to choose, but that would send her father to jail. She could expose the moneylender as a cheat, and risk making him furious and violent. Or she could take the pebble and sacrifice her life.

It was then that she had a brilliant idea. She reached into the bag and pulled out a pebble, and before anyone could see it, she dropped it on the ground where it became lost among all the other pebbles. 'Oh, how clumsy of me,' she said. 'But it doesn't matter. If you look in the bag, you'll be able to tell which pebble I chose by the colour of the one that is left.' The moneylender would never admit he had been dishonest, so the daughter won freedom for both herself and her father.

1A, Page 5, Exercises 5 and 6

Conversation 1

I = Interviewer, V = Vladimir

I: So, Vladimir, as you know, Professor Vera Vishneva is one of the ten most influential women in Russia today. When did you first meet her?

V: Erm … I was in my first year at Volgograd Medical University, so in 1998. She was teaching biochemistry … But the funny thing is, when I attended her first lecture, I realized I'd already met her once without being aware of it.

I: How do you mean?

V: Well, a week or so earlier, I needed to go to the admin department to hand in some documents. I didn't know my way around the university buildings, and somehow I got lost, so I had to ask for directions. Just at that moment, a woman was coming out of an office, so I asked her. … I remember she had chalk dust on her nose, and she was rather shabbily dressed …

I: What like?

V: Like she was wearing old-fashioned trousers that were too big, and a sweater that didn't match.

I: Really! … And?

V: And, well, back then I thought she must be one of the maintenance staff. But then one week later the same woman turns up again … this time to give us our first lecture in biochemistry. I couldn't believe it!

I: What was she like?

V: Well, I can't say her dress sense had improved. But that didn't matter. She caught our attention immediately. She was so brilliant! It's not just that she's an expert in her field, but she really makes it interesting for us.

I: A truly fascinating person, then.

V: Yes. She is.

Conversation 2

C = Cindy, R = Rick

C: Hi Rick! Did you watch that programme about speed-dating last night?

R: No, thank you. I have no time for rubbish like that.

C: Oh, come on! Tens of thousands of people are into it. So, how can it be rubbish, then?

R: Well … Do you know what it means to really know someone? It takes a long time, a very long time. I have always believed in that idea.

C: That sounds like romantic nonsense to me.

R: Where's the big rush, anyway? We have to learn to suspend judgement.

C: How do you mean?

R: Well, you can't read three pages of a novel and decide it's not worth reading. The same way as you can't attend the first lecture and decide the teacher's no good. And it's ludicrous to think you can find a soulmate in ten minutes. Read *The Little Prince* and you'll know exactly what I mean.

Conversation 3

S = Sharon, L = Liliana

S: You look so happy today, Liliana.

L: I've got some good news.

S: Oh, yeah? What is it? Come on, tell me!

L: I've been shortlisted for the post I was telling you about. The interview is in ten days.

S: Wow! … That's great news indeed. I'm so happy for you, Liliana.

L: Thanks. But competition will be fierce, no doubt about that …

S: … so you need to prepare as best you can.

L: I know. I'm going to do my homework, of course. Find out as much as I can about the company and about the post.

S: What are you going to wear?

L: Don't know yet. I'll decide when I find out about their dress code. But one thing is sure: I'm going to have a haircut! Oh yes, and something else: I'm reading *How To Make A Positive First Impression*.

S: Wow! I'm really impressed. You don't waste any time, do you?

L: Well, I'd certainly love to get that job. It's a unique opportunity!

1B, Page 6, Exercises 5 and 6

I = Interviewer, L = Linda

I: Good morning, Linda! A lot of our listeners have recently contacted us about speed networking, which I know is something you've had first-hand experience of. Can I ask you a couple of questions?

L: Sure! What do you want to know?

I: Erm … to start off with … how does it work?

L: Well, you bring together a number of people from related professional areas, or with similar business interests. People who know they can benefit from a larger network of contacts, and who at the same time have something to offer …

I: Do you mean job seekers and employers, for instance?

L: Exactly. But there are other categories of people as well.

I: OK. So, you bring them all together. Erm … How many people attend such events, by the way?

L: Ah. There's no rule, really. It depends on the aims of the event and on the host's resources. It could be 20, it could be 200.

I: Are people free to walk around and mingle in any way they like?

L: No, certainly not. Speed business networking events are always highly structured, even if the structures can vary a lot. Sometimes, it's like musical chairs: people sit in two concentric circles, with individuals sitting across from one another.

I: How long can they speak to one another?

L: It depends. Sometimes it's six minutes. But it can be eight, ten or more. Participants are told exactly when to start and when to stop. Then those in the outer circle stand up and move one seat to the left, and a new conversation starts.

I: What happens during those six minutes?

L: Well, typically, people exchange business cards, then they spend two minutes each talking about themselves, and during the last two minutes they decide what the next step is going to be. Um, do they want a follow-up meeting, where, when, etc.

I: Mm, sounds interesting. But … is it effective?

L: I personally enjoy those events a lot. There's so much energy flowing. But you need to have realistic expectations. If you hope to clinch a deal in a few minutes, you'll be disappointed. But if you just want to meet a lot of like-minded people in a short time, and if you are prepared to follow up those initial contacts and build on them, then I'd say yes, speed networking is very effective indeed.

1D, Page 10, Exercise 2

1
A: How are things?
B: Fine.

2
A: How about dinner together next week?
B: Great.

3
A: You know Benjamin Katz, don't you?
B: Yes.

4
A: What are your colleagues like?
B: They're nice.

5
A: Are you doing any overtime next week?
B: No.

6
A: Does your commute take long?
B: Not very.

1D, Page 10, Exercise 3

1 How are things?
2 How about dinner together next week?
3 You know Benjamin Katz, don't you?
4 What are your colleagues like?
5 Are you doing any overtime next week?
6 Does your commute take long?

1D, Page 10, Exercise 6

1
A: … and the new office manager is good, isn't he?
B: Yes, he works really hard.
C: Yes. The cleaners told me he never leaves before seven.

2
A: … you remember Ricardo, well, he's just bought one of those Volkswagen Beetles.
B: Do you know, I've never actually been in one?
C: Oh, I love them! My mother's got one, too.

3
A: … but what's she going to do now she's finished university?
B: Well, she wants to work for an aid agency.
C: Really? And where would she like to go?

1D, Page 11, Exercise 8

1
A: Ponte Vecchio is one of the best Italian restaurants in town.
B: Yeah. We had dinner there last Saturday. Fabulous!
C: Mm. I must check it out sometime. Whereabouts is it?

2
A: I thought the match was terrific.
B: Kerad's second goal was a thing of beauty.
C: Yeah. All of the second half was quite exciting.

3
A: Simon's been on sick leave for more than a month.
B: And no one knows when he'll be back.
C: Poor man. It must be something serious.

4
A: I'm a tax inspector.
B: Mm. That can't be an easy job.
C: Is there a lot of tax evasion these days?

5
A: This weather seems to be driving everyone mad.
B: It does, doesn't it. Absolutely dreadful.
C: Let's hope the rain lets up soon.

6
A: The guys in Accounts are looking exhausted.
B: They're all overworked, that's the problem.
C: You're right. You can tell we're near the end of the financial year.

1D, Page 11, Exercise 10

Conversation 1
A = Arthur, **L** = Leo, **C** = Connie

A: There's always such a queue at the cafeteria. They're clearly understaffed.
B: I'm not sure. I'd say they're just completely incompetent. … What do you think, Connie?
C: Well, I think those guys are quite good, actually. But I'm sure they need at least one extra pair of hands.

Conversation 2
V = Vince, **B** = Bill, **C** = Carol

V: If we want to cut costs, let's cancel the staff party.
B: Well, I'm not sure that's a very effective way. I doubt it will save us a lot of money. Have you got a view on that, Carol?
C: Erm … I think you're right, Bill. Besides, it will have a bad effect on morale.

Conversation 3
A = Antonella, **C** = Catriona, **S** = Stanley

A: Everyone's talking about Vietnam. It seems like the place to be.
C: Perhaps we could hold our next regional conference there. … Erm … You've been to Vietnam, haven't you, Stanley? What did you think of it?
S: Well, I was there on holiday, just for ten days, mostly in Hanoi and Ha Long Bay. It's absolutely beautiful. I'd like to go back next year.

1E, Page 13, Exercise 4

Presentation 1

A funny thing happened to me a few weeks ago. I was talking with a colleague about an issue that's very close to my heart, and after a few minutes, I had the impression that she was just hearing what I was saying, without really listening. Have you ever had that experience? … Could you just raise your hand if that has ever happened to you? … Right … Well, that's a lot of people! Now, you don't need a degree in psychology to understand the difference between active listening and mere hearing – a teenager once put it like this: 'My friends listen to what I say, but my parents only hear me talk.' Our key question today is: 'What can we do to become better listeners?'

Presentation 2

I think it was Jim Rohn, the great American entrepreneur, who said: 'Effective communication is 20 per cent what you know and 80 per cent how you feel about what you know.'

Rohn was not only a businessman, he was also an author and an acclaimed public speaker, so he was talking from experience. In this workshop, I'd like to explore with you what it really means to be talking from one's heart, and steps we can take to become better at it.

Presentation 3

Good morning, ladies and gentlemen. It's a great pleasure for me to be here with you today. As you can see on the screen, my name is Jeff Elsdale and I'm the Human Resources Manager at Bantler International. Now … the next slide … this is the title of my presentation: *Developing People Skills in the Workplace*. My presentation is divided into three parts …

Presentation 4

'We're kept in the dark.' … Did you know that one of the most frequent employee complaints in large organizations is: 'We're kept in the dark'? In other words, if you don't know what's going on, you tend to feel unhappy at work, which in turn can easily make you feel miserable outside work as well.

1E, Page 13, Exercise 6

'We're kept in the dark.' … Did you know that one of the most frequent employee complaints in large organizations is: 'We're kept in the dark'? In other words, if you don't know what's going on, you tend to feel unhappy at work, which in turn can easily make you feel miserable outside work as well.

This morning, I'd like to outline a programme which aims to improve the flow of information within an organization.

I have divided my talk into three main parts. I'll begin with a brief overview of the different types of company structures, and discuss how each one can facilitate or hinder staff communication with management. Then I'll move on to the consequences of poor information flow, drawing on the findings of some recent communication research. And after that, we'll look at ways in which any organization can ensure a better flow of information.

1E, Page 13, Exercise 7

Did you know that back and neck problems are one of the top ten medical problems in Western countries? Twelve years ago because of my job and my research, I was spending an average of 12 hours a day sitting at a desk. My spine was stiff. I could hardly bend any more. That's when I decided to take up Tai Chi. I'd read somewhere that it could do a lot of good to your joints, so why not give it a try?

Today, I'd like to talk to you about this ancient Chinese martial art called Tai Chi.

My talk is in three parts. I'll start with a little historical background. Then, I'll move on to the health benefits of Tai Chi. And finally, I'll describe what it's like to practise in a club.

Let me start then with an overview of the history of Tai Chi. First, I'll take you back to the origin – 12th-century China. Then I'll say a few words about how and why Tai Chi evolved into a number of different schools. And thirdly, I'd like to explain how this art reached the rest of the world. It is a 12th-century Taoist monk called Chang San-Feng who is generally credited with having developed the principles of an internal martial art.

This leads me to my next point, which is why Tai Chi can bring so many health benefits to so many people. I'd like to consider three areas that we can develop through Tai Chi: the muscles and the joints, the internal organs and your powers of concentration. Let's look at the muscles and the joints to begin with.

Finally, what is it like to practise in a club? What do you notice when you just observe a Tai Chi session? Three things: an instructor, demonstrating the moves and guiding the students; a group of people imitating the instructor and practising; and last but not least, an atmosphere of calm, concentration and congeniality. The instructor knows that all students are different.

At this stage, I'd like to sum up the main points of my talk. As we have seen, Tai Chi is a very ancient art, an internal martial art.

I'd like to conclude now by reminding you of something I said at the beginning. If you suffer from back or neck problems and you feel that conventional medicine isn't a great help, give Tai Chi a try. It may not work miracles, but it'll make you feel better in your body and in your mind, and besides, it's a great opportunity to meet like-minded people.

2B, Page 16, Exercises 5 and 6

D = Doug, **N** = Neil

D: Hi, Neil, thanks for seeing me.

N: So, Doug, how have you been getting on since I last saw you?

D: I'm a bit concerned, actually. I've got a really important project coming up and I can't seem to get myself motivated. The thing is, I've been working with a team updating the company website and it's been very enjoyable and creative. When I move onto this next project, I'll miss that. But my manager nominated me for the new role and it's a good opportunity – possibility of promotion and a tempting bonus when the task's complete.

N: Would you say that the bonus and promotion prospects are motivators in accepting the project?

D: If I'm honest, yes, I'd say they're definitely major factors. Is that wrong, do you think?

N: No, I'm not saying that. But it'll help you to understand the reasons you're having problems getting motivated. A lot of people take on projects because of the challenge. They get a kick out of overcoming obstacles and achieving goals. Isn't that right?

D: Yes, I'd say that's a pretty accurate assessment.

N: Well, those people usually respond to 'intrinsic motivators'. That's when the motivation comes from inside a person. They like the challenge or the feeling they get when they succeed. But I think you're taking on this new project because of 'extrinsic motivators'. That means a reward or punishment as an incentive to do something. In this case, the extrinsic motivator is your bonus and the possibility of promotion. Most people respond to one type of motivation more than the other. So it's natural that you feel a little uncertain about this.

D: So, what should I do? Turn down the new project?

N: I didn't say that – I'm your mentor, not your boss. Do you remember some of the motivation techniques we discussed in our last session?

D: Yeah, erm, the first one was have clear objectives, and the second one was visualize outcomes – is that right?

N: Yeah, that's right. In your case, I think it'll help if you start by identifying the objective of the project. Visualize how interesting it'll be to learn new skills and how proud you'll be when you successfully complete it. It'll help you to think positively and kick-start your motivation. Can you remember the other two techniques?

D: One of them was set yourself rewards or penalties, wasn't it? The reward here is the bonus and chance of promotion, I guess.

N: Well, yes. But you could also think of a personal reward at the start and end of the project. Something that you would enjoy doing.

D: OK.

N: And the last technique?

D: Wait … it'll come to me in a second. Oh, yeah, stay focused.

N: Uh-huh. If our attention is on too many things at the same time, it's easy to lose motivation. In your case, you could lose focus by thinking about what's happening on the website project.

D: Yeah, it'll be difficult to cut ties with the team, and I still have lots of ideas for it.

N: Well, my suggestion would be, don't cut ties with it. Ask the team to send you a weekly update on what's happening and offer to contribute your ideas. If you stay involved from a distance, then you can still have the satisfaction of completing the task and that's important to you. But work out exactly how much time you can spend on it. It mustn't interfere with the new project.

D: I'm not sure my manager will agree.

N: Have you asked her? You might be imagining obstacles where they don't exist, and that can have a negative effect on motivation.

D: You're right. Nothing ventured, nothing gained. Thanks for your help, you've given me a lot to think about.

N: When are we next meeting?

D: In a couple of weeks, I think. Same time?

N: Yep, that's fine for me. Well, good luck with it, Doug. We can talk about it again next session.

2B, Page 17, Exercises 8 and 9

Speaker 1

… I'm in training to run a marathon and I wear a T-shirt saying 'Honk if you see me walking'. If I stop running, cars honk their horns at me and I get embarrassed and start running again. The race takes place this weekend, so wish me luck! … Sorry, got to go.

Speaker 2

My mate wants to lose weight but he likes his food. Every time he loses a kilo, he puts money in an envelope and he's going to use it to go for a huge meal when he reaches his target weight. He reckons he'll lose more than ten kilos. … But he'll probably put about five kilos back on when he goes for his celebration meal.

Speaker 3

My parents are going to travel around China when they retire next year. They have very different ideas about the places they want to visit. So, every week after their Mandarin lesson, they test each other on new vocabulary. The winner gets to choose a place they'll visit on their trip.

Speaker 4

My friends decided to go on a sailing holiday. It's not my cup of tea, but I said I'd go, too. They didn't think I was serious at first. I often agree to things and then drop out at the last minute, you see. So I said that if I changed my mind about this trip, I'd clean their house every Saturday for a month. I guess it's worked because we're sailing to Stavanger in Norway in ten days' time.

Speaker 5

I'm building a swimming pool in my garden. It's really hard work. I have a recorded message on my alarm clock that shouts 'get up and start digging!' It helps get me out of bed. When I look at the big hole in the garden, I imagine me and my family swimming in the pool over the summer, nice and cool. Hopefully, I'll have finished it by July.

2C, Page 19, Exercises 4 and 5

It may surprise some of you to hear this, but how we sit and stand has a direct effect on how we feel. In tests, people who use power poses report feeling more confident. So, what is a power pose? Well, for instance, sitting with your hands behind your head and your feet on the table, that's a power pose. Another example is standing upright with your hands resting on a table or desk. Remarkably, people who sit, or stand, in these poses for just a few minutes report feeling more powerful than they felt before adopting that position. They not only think they look more impressive, they actually feel more impressive, too.

2C, Page 19, Exercise 6

In contrast, low power poses made people feel less confident. One example includes sitting with your arms close to your sides and hands folded. Another example is standing with your arms or legs crossed. People who hold these poses for a few minutes report feeling less powerful. This might be because when we feel threatened or under attack, we adopt a defensive pose to become less visible and to protect our body. However, when we take up more space, our body sends the brain signals that help it to reduce stress and increase confidence.

So, how can we put this information to use? Well, the main message we can take away from this research is that if we sit or stand in a power pose, even for a short time, it could give us a vital confidence boost when we most need it. Try it next time you're preparing for an interview, before you give a talk or before an important meeting. You might be surprised at the difference it makes!

Audio scripts

2D, Page 21, Exercises 5 and 6

TA = Travel agent, **C** = Customer

TA: So, you're looking for a short break somewhere romantic.

C: That's right. But I have a very tight budget. You see, it's a surprise for my wife for her birthday.

TA: Oh, really? Ah, well, what about Venice? I'm sure your wife would love it there.

C: But isn't it very expensive?

TA: Oh, no, and it's one of our most popular short break destinations at the moment. And everyone knows that it's the most romantic city in the world. So many of our clients come in to tell me what a wonderful time they had there. In fact, the head of our company went there only last weekend. He said it was amazing.

C: Really? So, how much will it cost?

TA: Well, it's your lucky day because we have a very special offer on at the moment. Book today and you can get four days for the price of three.

C: Well, I only really wanted to go for three days. I have to work, you see.

TA: It's up to you, sir, but I'd advise you to think about this deal. It's in a beautiful hotel in an excellent location. Not only that, you also get breakfast and dinner included in the price. Actually, you'll save a considerable amount on restaurants.

C: You haven't said how much this will cost yet.

TA: I can tell you right now. Er, … Two people, flights and accommodation, gold class.

C: Gold class?

TA: Well, after all, it is a special occasion, isn't it, sir? Let me see, um, … that'll be £350 per person.

C: Well, er, it's quite a bit more than I wanted to pay …

TA: Look, I tell you what, I'll give you an additional five per cent discount. I shouldn't really, but it's such a romantic present.

C: Well, that's very kind of you.

TA: And I'm sure you don't mind getting up at 4 a.m. for the early flight.

C: Oh, 4 a.m. – that's a bit early, isn't it?

TA: Ah, but the good thing about that is you'll have more time to enjoy the city. I'll go ahead and book that then, shall I?

C: Erm, maybe I should think about it.

TA: Well, I don't want to put pressure on you, but the offer does end at midnight tonight. Oh, and I can see on my computer that the flights are booking up very quickly. As I said, it's a very popular destination.

C: Oh. Um, … Right, you'd better book it then.

TA: Wonderful. Your wife will have such a lovely surprise. Now, as I'm sure you're aware, there are transfer fees on top of that price. That's £20 extra per person.

C: No, erm … I wasn't aware of that.

TA: And you'll also need to add baggage allowance and airport tax. … that'll be £58 … And insurance, of course.

C: I think I have insurance at home. I can check.

TA: Well, of course you may already have travel insurance. However, it's still worth bearing in mind that our insurance covers you for water accidents.

C: Water accidents?

TA: Well, there's quite a lot of water in Venice, isn't there, sir? I mean, you could fall out of a gondola or off a bridge. Take out our insurance and you'll have peace of mind knowing that no little problems will spoil your holiday.

C: … Oh, OK then, go ahead.

TA: Marvellous. Now, let's look at any excursions you might like to take your wife on, after all it is her birthday.

2D, Page 21, Exercise 9

H = Hanesh, **D** = Dev

H: Hi Dev, I haven't seen you for ages. Actually, I'm really pleased that I ran into you. I wonder, could you do me a favour?

D: Well, it depends what it is.

H: You see, my cousin's in town this weekend but I'm working. Could you show him around on Saturday evening? Maybe take him to dinner?

D: I can't, actually – I'm busy Saturday evening.

H: Oh, really? That's such a shame. You'd really like my cousin. Well, what about Sunday?

D: I'd like to help but I'm going out on Sunday, too.

H: Really? Well, maybe he could come with you, er?

D: No, that's not possible, I'm afraid.

H: Look, I'd really appreciate it if you could help me out with this. I'm worried he'll be lonely. You must have some free time over the weekend.

D: No, I'm busy all weekend. Maybe your cousin could come another time when you're not working.

2E, Page 23, Exercises 5 and 6

Hi, I'd like to introduce myself. I'm Caitlin Sweeney and I'm a research scientist. Now, what is the most annoying thing about picnics in the summer? Yes, it's insects. Ants get in your sandwiches, flies get in your drink and wasps make you run indoors. The Bugzap is for people who want to enjoy life outdoors but who don't like bugs. You wear it around your neck and it sends out a safe electrical signal that insects don't like. Unlike other products on the market, it doesn't use harmful chemicals or leave a nasty smell. The Bugzap is small, attractive and is completely safe for adults and children to use.

3B, Page 28, Exercises 3 and 4

D = Dan, **S** = Sandra

D: Hi, Sandra!

S: Hello, Dan.

D: What's up?

S: Oh, nothing much. How about you?

D: Er, same as usual. Just another frantic day at work.

S: Looks like it!

D: So, anything new about the merger? I saw you coming out of Vic's office earlier this morning.

S: Oh, did you? … Well, the merger's still only a possibility, you know. … I mean, nothing's been decided … erm … the negotiations have hardly started.

D: Ah, so they have started, then. But why is it all so hush-hush?

S: Well, in fact we aren't supposed to know. I mean, not all of us. Not at this early stage. … Erm … Look, this is just between you and me, right? Don't let on to anyone, OK?

D: You have my word. Come on, Sandra, out with it!

S: Well, I think Vic is, like … disappointed. He feels let down by the other directors. They say he worries without reason.

D: What's he worried about, d'you think?

S: The costs involved, I guess. And … erm … how … how savings can be made.

D: Savings, eh? Well, I don't like the sound of that. It usually means redundancies …

S: That's exactly what Vic's worried about. Production may have to relocate to India …

D: To India? I can't believe it …

S: Oh, sorry Dan, I've really got to rush … My in-tray's full … See you! …

B: … Hi, Dan! What's new?

D: Hi, Bob. Guess what I've just heard from Sandra. Lots of us are going to be made redundant …

3B, Page 29, Exercise 10

A = Alison, **B** = Bernard

A: So, what was Isabel rattling on about at lunchtime?

B: Well, she just feels she's been passed over for the marketing job. And of course she isn't happy about it. I mean, she's quite upset.

A: Shame. But frankly I think Nick is the right person for the job. He's got a wealth of experience, you know.

B: Yeah, that's right. He's been in the department for, like, six years, hasn't he? And he's been playing golf with the boss for just as long. Well, according to Isabel, that is.

3C, Page 30, Exercises 3 and 4

Podcast 1
Passengers at Wilston Airport suffered severe disruption yesterday after it was hit by a computer glitch which left them unable to check in. The problem caused a baggage backlog but was fixed shortly after 6 p.m.

Podcast 2
Germany's economic recovery prospects have suffered an unexpected setback, with industrial orders dropping by four per cent in September compared with the previous month.

The fall, reported by the economics ministry on Friday, suggested that growth could slow markedly in the final months of the year.

Podcast 3
Olive Mitchell, an 85-year-old grandmother from Preston, has just started taking driving lessons. Asked what prompted her decision, she replied: 'I don't want to be a nuisance, asking people to drive me around all the time.'

Podcast 4
An operation to transfer 800 government staff to private companies went off without a hitch yesterday. Union leaders have expressed concern about the deal, but the government has stressed that pay and conditions will be protected.

Podcast 5
According to recent research, teenagers have difficulty concentrating on lessons and homework because their brains are less developed than was previously thought. The new study claims that the brain does not become fully developed until the late twenties or early thirties, so teenagers have brains more similar to those of younger children.

3C, Page 31, Exercises 10 and 11

R = Rose, **L** = Lina

R: Hi, Lina. How are you getting on with all the organizing?

L: Well, I've suffered an unexpected setback, unfortunately.

R: Sorry to hear that. What happened?

L: Well, it's been one thing after another since I started planning this event five months ago. Do you remember Sven Karlsten?

R: Of course! He's our keynote speaker, isn't he?

L: Well, he was. The thing is, he's just cancelled.

R: Oh dear! Just one month before the event. Any particular reason why he withdrew?

L: He wasn't very specific, but I've just found out his company has run into serious financial difficulties. I mean, it's looking as if they might go bankrupt.

R: Really? It seemed such a successful company. What a shame! Erm … And what about participant numbers, by the way?

L: That's another thing I'm getting concerned about.

R: Why? How many have registered so far?

L: About 40. This time last year, we had, like, 150.

R: Mm, right, but then this year we didn't start promoting the event till March, did we? Let's be patient, I'm sure numbers will grow.

3D, Page 32, Exercises 2 and 3

1
A: Dave seems pretty low these days, don't you find? What's going on?

B: I'm not really sure, but I think he's been downgraded.

2
C: Um. This is a rather heavy-going talk, isn't it?

D: It sure is. I'm afraid I don't have a clue what he's on about. I wish my daughter was here.

C: Why's that?

D: She's an economics graduate.

3
E: What's so good about being a freelancer, then?

F: It's hard to say, but I guess it's the feeling of independence it gives you. Mind you, I still have to meet deadlines!

4
G: Who's that guy talking to Karlo?

H: I haven't the faintest idea. But whoever it is, he seems to be winding Karlo up.

G: Yes, and Karlo's usually so calm.

5
I: How long do you think it'll take?

J: Your guess is as good as mine. It all depends on the kind of virus that's infected it.

I: Fingers crossed it's not a really awful one.

3D, Page 32, Exercise 5

S = Shirin, **R** = Rachel

S: Hi, Rachel. I've just had Phil on the phone.

R: Oh, yes? Everything OK with him?

S: You'll never guess … He got the job. He's now regional director!

R: Are you serious?

S: Yeah. He's off to Berlin.

R: Wonderful! He's always wanted to go there. But … erm … how about you?

S: Well, it's not easy, I mean, not for either of us, but I simply can't go now.

R: You poor thing! What about later? Is there a possibility …?

S: Sure. When my research project comes to an end, things will be simpler.

3D, Page 32, Exercise 6

R = Rachel, **E** = Elio

R: D'you know what? My brother is moving to Berlin soon.

E: Philip? I can't believe it!

R: It's true, I'm telling you. He's been promoted to regional director.

E: Wow! That's fantastic news. And what does his wife say?

R: Well, she's happy for him, of course. But unfortunately she won't be able to go right away.

E: That's a shame. Is it because of the research she's doing?

R: That's right, yes. She's got another six months to do. So I guess she'll be in Berlin in December.

E: Great. Just in time for the festive season, then.

3E, Page 34, Exercise 4

1 I'm afraid there are questions about the CEO's credibility.

2 We can't say that the project was a complete success.

3 They don't exclude the possibility of industrial action.

4 We're going to streamline our production process.

5 We're experiencing a slight delay.

6 More than half of our admin staff will keep their jobs.

3E, Page 34, Exercise 5

1

A: I'm afraid there are questions about the CEO's credibility.

B: Er, does that mean some people think he's a liar?

2

A: We can't say that the project was a complete success.

B: Are you saying that you've failed?

3

A: They don't exclude the possibility of industrial action.

B: If I understand correctly, they threaten to go on strike?

4

A: We're going to streamline our production process.

B: Does that mean a lot of production workers are going to be made redundant?

5

A: We're experiencing a slight delay.

B: You mean, you won't be able to meet the deadline?

6

A: More than half of our admin staff will keep their jobs.

B: Are you saying that almost half will lose their jobs?

4B, Page 38, Exercises 4 and 5

A = Albin; **B** = Belinda

A: I don't regret buying it.

B: Don't you?

A: No, after all, it gave me the two happiest days of my life.

B: Two?

A: Yes, the first one was the day we splashed out and bought it.

B: I wasn't keen on the idea right from the start. We couldn't really afford it.

A: But remember when we first stepped on it and knew it was ours. You've got to admit that was a great day – sailing up the river with the wind in our hair. I was on top of the world.

B: Yeah, I remember. Mind you, that feeling didn't last long.

A: No. Well, it needed a bit of work.

B: A bit of work? We had to spend every weekend working on it, and evenings, too.

A: OK then, a *lot* of work. I have to admit it got quite stressful. We were always tired.

B: And the repairs cost a fortune. We were spending money like water. It began to get us down.

A: Yeah. Something was always going wrong with it.

B: Do you remember that night we sat down and looked at all the bills?

A: Yep, that's when we realized it had to go.

B: So, what was the other happiest day?

A: Pardon?

B: You mentioned the two happiest days of your life.

A: Oh, yeah. The second happiest day was the day we sold it.

B: I was a bit surprised that you weren't more upset to see it go.

A: Nah, when I saw our bank balance, it soon cheered me up.

B: Yeah, well, I reckon our bank manager was probably over the moon, too.

4D, Pages 42 and 43, Exercises 4 and 5

D = David (the chairperson), **L** = Luke, **J** = Janine, **M** = Mila

D: … OK, then, everyone, let's get started. We're here, as you know, to review the staff reward scheme, and I'm looking forward to hearing your ideas. Shall we start by looking at the first item on the agenda?

L: Before we do that, David, I'd like to clarify what the budget is for bonuses this year.

D: We'll be covering that later in the meeting, Luke. We don't have a lot of time, so it would be helpful if we could stick to the agenda.

J: Good idea, I have to be at a presentation by 10:30.

D: OK, let's look at the first point, which is how to make staff feel valued. Any ideas how we can make our staff feel appreciated? Mila, would you like to share your thoughts on this? You mentioned that you've been looking into it.

M: Certainly, erm, well, research suggests that practical changes such as flexible working hours or the opportunity to develop professionally are highly valued. So I asked my staff to take part in a quick survey.

L: I wouldn't need to do a survey with my team. I already know they'd prefer cash.

D: Just to remind you, we're looking at non-monetary rewards. Mila, would you like to finish your point?

M: Well, as I was saying, I did a survey with my staff, and the idea of flexible working proved the most popular.

J: Now you mention it, a few people in my department have enquired about changing their working hours.

D: Right, well, it sounds as though it'd be useful to do more research on this. Would you be willing to look into the practicalities of flexible working hours, Mila?

M: Sure.

J: Ooh, I've just thought of a great idea for an end-of-year gift for staff.

D: We'll get on to that in a moment, Janine. Getting back to flexible working, perhaps the rest of us could liaise with our teams and get their opinions? Let's arrange another meeting for next Thursday to firm up ideas. Is that OK with everyone?

[General murmurs of agreement]

D: Now, moving on to the next point: last year's staff gift. As you know, we traditionally give all staff a small end-of-year reward. Luke, any feedback on what your team thought of last year's gift?

L: That was the voucher for an experience day, wasn't it? Yeah, well, they, erm, they seemed to quite like it, actually.

J: Yeah, I had pretty good feedback, too. They liked the fact that it could be personalized to their own interests. A couple of people used it to go to a spa. Others used it to do more adventurous stuff, spending a day driving sports cars and that sort of thing.

M: One of my team used it to go on a balloon ride.

D: Well, that's very positive. I think that just about covers everything on that item. OK, let's move forward.

M: David, I'm afraid I'm running out of time. I've got to go to another meeting shortly.

D: Fine. Let's try to get through the next point quickly. Any thoughts on what we could give staff as a gift this year? Janine, what was the idea you mentioned? …

4E, Page 45, Exercises 5 and 6

Part 1

Well, it's someone who wants to make more than profit. It's someone who runs a social business, where all or a large percentage of the profits are returned into the community that it serves. So, a social entrepreneur has got the ability to run a normal business. You know, they can pitch for start-up money, develop a business plan, sell a business idea or a service that customers really want, attract talent and all the things a good company needs to do. But they do all that in a way that is helping to solve a real social problem. If you're talking about becoming a social entrepreneur, it's the same skill set as any entrepreneur – but we use it to change society.

Part 2

Amongst others, we've won the *Guardian* Charity of the Year and the Social Enterprise of the Year Caroline Walker Trust. And we've also won the government's No. 10 Big Society award. Yes, it has been useful. It shows we have credibility and it can help with corporate sponsorship. It attracts media attention, and that's important because it gives us a chance to tell our story and make a case for change. And to be honest, winning also boosts morale.

Part 3

Well, the first point is that it's genuinely solving an important social problem. You have to be absolutely clear about what the goal is and have a really clear social purpose. You know, you have to be very specific. For us, it's that no kids go to school without breakfast. The second thing is that the enterprise has to have a robust trading model. It needs to actually sell a product or service to finance the project. The amount of times that I've been invited to give a speech at a social entrepreneur gathering and I say, 'OK, tell me about your products; tell me about your service,' and they say, 'Well, we haven't really thought about that,' and I say, 'Well you're not a social entrepreneur then, you're a charity.' You know, that's fine, but you can't talk about being an entrepreneur if you're not selling something. And finally, the third thing is it needs a sustainable plan; an ability to trade through the first five years so it doesn't run out of cash. It's got to have, you know, enough of a network for it to be sustainable.

5C, Page 52, Exercise 3

Interview A
Usually yes. That's what a diary is for, isn't it? I tend to write everything down, otherwise I forget. And if I pencil things in, I can put my memory to better use.

Interview B
On the whole, I think it's all right. But there's certainly room for improvement. For example, I know I don't always get my priorities right.

Interview C
Hardly ever. Missing a deadline is probably one of the worst things that could happen to me at work – that's why I always try hard to be on schedule. In fact, I'm happiest when I can be ahead of schedule.

Interview D
Well, I spend about an hour every Monday morning planning the week ahead. I think it's time well spent. Planning gives me a sense of direction.

Interview E
Well, I try to! At the start of the week I usually have three or four clearly defined and achievable goals, but then come Wednesday I often have to set myself new ones because I have to deal with unexpected tasks.

Interview F
As a rule, I try to deal first with the tasks which are both urgent and important. But that's not always possible. My manager's priorities may change from one day to the next, which of course affects my own priorities.

5C, Page 52, Exercise 4

1
I tend to write everything down, otherwise I forget. And if I pencil things in, I can put my memory to better use.

2
I know I don't always get my priorities right.

3
Missing a deadline is probably one of the worst things that could happen to me at work – that's why I always try hard to be on schedule. In fact, I'm happiest when I can be ahead of schedule.

4

I spend about an hour every Monday morning planning the week ahead. I think it's time well spent. Planning gives me a sense of direction.

5

At the start of the week I usually have three or four clearly defined and achievable goals.

6

As a rule, I try to deal first with the tasks which are both urgent and important.

5C, Page 53, Exercise 7

Conversation 1

A = Angus (the Manager), **S** = Suzi

A: Erm … Suzi, have you found us a new maintenance company, by the way?

S: Well, I'm working on it. I've been looking into a number of companies. I haven't got all the information I need to make an informed choice. It may take a while.

A: Why's that?

S: I don't want to rely on quotes only. We can't afford to take risks. So what I've been doing is finding out who those companies' major customers are, and then getting feedback from three different customers for each company. I've also been trawling through a number of consumer protection blogs for extra information about them. We don't want to go for second best, do we?

Conversation 2

R = Ramesh, **J** = Julie (the Manager)

J: Hi Ramesh. How are things?

R: Fine, thanks.

J: Erm … I was just wondering… You know, that translation … How's it coming along?

R: Fine. I'm working on it.

J: How soon can you do it? Erm … I mean, you know it was due in the day before yesterday?

R: Sorry, Julie. I'm not sure I know which translation you're talking about.

J: What do you mean? Our spring catalogue, of course!

R: Well, I'm afraid we're talking at cross-purposes here. I sent you the translation of the spring issue quite a while ago … Hold on a sec … Let me check my email … Ah, here it is … the 25th of February … You acknowledged receipt the same day …

J: Hang on … February … 25th of February … Ramesh … Oh dear, you're absolutely right! I'm so sorry, Ramesh. It was such a long time ago, I completely forgot.

R: No worries, Julie. These things happen.

J: I suppose I should have downloaded it immediately. Anyway. What are you working on these days?

R: Well, as a matter of fact I've been putting together some material for the summer catalogue … First I thought that's what you were phoning me about.

Conversation 3

K = Keith (the Manager), **F** = Fadila

K: Hi Fadila. How's work?

F: As hectic as ever. I've been running around all week. I meant to finish your report a couple of days ago, but then my computer let me down …

K: Computers can be a nuisance, can't they? Erm … When can I expect it?

F: I'll see what I can do. I'd say by the end of the week, definitely.

K: Good. Oh yes, just one more thing. Have you talked to Dario? You know, about the graphs and illustrations?

F: Oh, erm … Not yet. I tried to see him yesterday afternoon, but then it turned out he'd already left. But I'll do it first thing tomorrow morning.

Conversation 4

L = Lynne (the Manager), **S** = Stefan

L: Stefan, hi! Just wanted to ask about the sales forecast we need for next month's meeting.

S: Oh! Yes … um, … Lynne … I'm afraid I haven't got around to it yet. Sorry.

L: Mm. I know it's been rather hectic lately, but … what's taking so long?

S: The thing is, I'm doing some background research for Laura Henkel's project. And HR has asked me to screen applications for the post of administrative assistant. And …

L: OK, Stefan. I see, I see. But I need you here with me. I'll find someone else to do the screening. We need you in the team. You're too valuable to work as a freelancer for the rest of the company.

5C, Page 53, Exercise 8

1

Suzi: I haven't got all the information I need to make an informed choice. It may take a while.

2

Julie: I was just wondering ... You know, that translation ... How's it coming along?

Ramish: Fine. I'm working on it.

Julie: How soon can you do it? Erm … I mean, you know it was due in the day before yesterday?

3

Keith: When can I expect it?

Fadila: I'll see what I can do. I'd say by the end of the week, definitely.

4

Stefan: Oh! Yes ... um, Lynne ... I'm afraid I haven't got around to it yet. Sorry.

Lynne: Mm. I know it's been rather hectic lately, but ... what's taking so long?

5D, Page 54, Exercises 2 and 3

Suggestion A

Well, these people need help to become more assertive. Somehow you need to get the message across that you don't expect them to agree with whatever you say or do. Tell them how much you value their work, but then point out the problems they'll cause if they aren't realistic about schedules and become overloaded.

Suggestion B

As we all know, it's virtually impossible to communicate with someone who's yelling, so what do we do? Keep calm and do not sink to their level. State your point of view assertively but don't shout back or be drawn into an argument. The main thing is to maintain a professional, neutral tone at all times.

Suggestion C
Begin by listening to what they have to say. You can sympathize a little, but then try to move the discussion forward. Shift the conversation to problem solving, but don't suggest what to do yourself. The key is to try to get them to decide what to do.

5E, Page 56, Exercise 4

B = Brigitte, **S** = Selim, **V** = Victor, **A** = Alena

B: As you know, our department needs to cut costs, and the purpose of this meeting is precisely to discuss some cost-saving measures that we could implement. So, what are our options? Who'd like to start the ball rolling? Selim?

S: Sure. One of my concerns is the amount of paper we waste. At the moment most if not all our copies are single-sided. The best way to reduce our paper consumption is to switch to double-sided printing.

V: That's an excellent idea. On the other hand, it's clear that not all our documents can be double-sided. Another thing we could do is invoice by email. And whenever possible, I think we should allow our customers the option to pay online.

B: Yeah, I agree. The advantage of online transactions is that both sides benefit. But we've been doing that for a couple of years already. Yes, Alena?

A: Let's look at it from a different angle. Let's look at our own printing behaviour. I think that's what we need to change first. Clicking 'Print' on the screen has become like a reflex. We don't ask ourselves if we really need a printout.

V: That's only too true … So … What would happen if we introduced password- or card-controlled printing? At least we'd be able to track paper and printer use on an individual basis.

S: Yes, but who decides how many copies each individual employee is allowed to make?

6B, Page 60, Exercises 3 and 4

I = Interviewer, **J** = Jim Kulver

I: Several psychological experiments have shown that visual clues can't really help us decide whether someone is lying or telling the truth. … Telling a liar from a truthful person is a rather difficult task, isn't it, Jim?

J: Yes, that's right. Recently, there was an experiment in which psychologists filmed a TV journalist answering the same questions twice. The first time the journalist answered, he lied, and the second time, he told the truth. They showed the two films to thousands of people and asked them which was which.

I: And … what happened?

J: It may seem hard to believe, but the audiences got the answer wrong as often as they got it right.

I: Really? But … why is that, Jim?

J: Well, first of all, there's the fact that a lot of honest people find formal interviews stressful. … I mean, people who have no intention of misleading or deceiving anyone. And when people are under stress, they often fidget in their seat, or they blink more often than usual, or they avoid eye contact and things like that. …

I: But, as you say, these are signs of stress, aren't they? They're not reliable signs that someone is lying …

J: Absolutely. So that's one problem. And the other thing of course is that experienced criminals know about those psychological tricks and so they can avoid giving any of those visual clues.

I: You mean, instead of fidgeting, for example, they'd sit still, or cut down on the number of gestures they use, … things like that?

J: Yeah, exactly. That's why verbal clues seem to be more reliable. For example, liars sometimes try to distance themselves from the lie, so they avoid saying words like 'I', 'me' and 'mine', and say 'he' or 'she' instead.

I: What other examples of verbal clues are there?

J: Well, fairly recently scientists have started experimenting with a technique called reverse story-telling …

I: Reverse story-telling … Mm, that sounds intriguing. What does it consist of?

J: Once the suspect has told his story, he is asked to retell it, but this time from the most recent event backwards. Fabricating a story is hard enough, but telling it backwards is extremely demanding, especially if you've just made it up.

I: Are the results convincing?

J: Yes, it's a very promising technique. The research clearly shows that liars hesitate quite often and make a lot of mistakes when telling their story backwards.

6C, Page 62, Exercises 3 and 4

I = Interviewer, **W** = Professor Roy Wilkinson

I: Professor Wilkinson, thank you for being with us this afternoon to talk about the connection between words and emotions. You hear a lot of people say 'If I want to know the meaning of a word, I look up its definition in the dictionary.' Does that work?

W: Well, yes, it does, but only up to a point. Dictionaries give us the literal meaning of words, but they don't often tell us about the connotations words have.

I: Could you explain what you mean by connotation?

W: Let's take an example. Imagine two people describing the same person, say Jane. One could say Jane is slim, and the other might well say she's skinny. The words *slim* and *skinny* have different connotations, they evoke different feelings and associations, they reveal your evaluation of what you're talking about. As you know, *slim* has positive connotations, while *skinny* has negative connotations. If you describe someone as skinny, you mean that you find them too thin. Language is full of pairs like *slim* and *skinny*. Consider for instance *bureaucrat* and *public servant*, *rebel* and *freedom fighter*, *mean* and *thrifty* – the first word in each pair being the one with negative connotations.

I: Do all words have connotations, then?

W: Oh no. Most words are probably neutral, in fact. And many words simply acquire particular connotations in context. Take *laid-back*, for instance. You could say, 'Peter's quite laid-back as a manager. His style encourages people to be careless and miss deadlines.' But you could also say, 'Rosa's quite laid-back as a manager. That's why her employees are so happy and productive.'

I: So … a lot of words, like, for example, *laid-back*, are neutral, but can be positive or negative depending on the context.

W: That's right. And …

6C, Page 62, Exercise 5

I = Interviewer, **W** = Professor Roy Wilkinson

I: So … a lot of words, like for example *laid-back*, are neutral, but can be positive or negative depending on the context.

W: That's right. And besides context, I'd say culture. Words can have different connotations in different cultures. In some business cultures, a laid-back management style is seen as positive, but not so in other cultures. Another example is *old*. In the West, nobody wants to be old, at least to be told that they're old. In China, by contrast, *lǎo*, the Chinese word for *old*, has very positive connotations and is associated with wisdom – traditionally, at least.

I: So I suppose translators and all of us who want to speak another language need to be familiar with the connotations of words.

W: You're absolutely right. But I'd go further than that. Knowledge of connotations is equally important in our mother tongue. Language can influence the way we see things, and a lot of people use language to influence us.

I: You mean, like politicians, for example?

W: Yes, but also the media more generally. The same event can be described as a war in some media, and as an invasion in others; the same people can be called terrorists on Channel 1 and insurgents or rebels on Channel 2. I mean, we get so much information … Being aware of the connotations words have, and how they are used to influence us, is a crucial first step if we want to form our own unbiased opinion.

6D, Page 64, Exercises 3 and 4

1

L = Lucas, **G** = Gina

L: Hey, Gina! Is that your new smartphone?

G: Yeah. I bought it last week.

L: It looks fantastic!

G: I really needed something different. I'd had the previous one for almost a decade!

L: Can I have a look?

G: Yeah, sure.

L: Wow! Much more sophisticated than mine. It's even got GPS!

2

A = Anna, **B** = Bob

A: I've got to say it, Bob, I really love the way you've decorated your office. It looks gorgeous!

B: Oh, thank you, Anna. I'm so glad you like it. As you can see, I got some of my inspiration from seeing yours.

A: I was going to say that – in spite of all the obvious differences.

3

H = Helen, **S** = Svetlana

H: Hi, Svetlana. How's things?

S: Fine, thanks. Wow! That's a really nice coat.

H: I like yours, too. Very attractive design.

S: Er, that's not what my husband says.

H: Oh well. At least yours notices when you wear something new.

4

J = Joy, **A** = Albert

J: What a great presentation! I enjoyed every minute of it.

A: Very kind of you to say so. But I can't take full credit for it. It's my daughter who designed the slides.

J: She seems very talented.

A: Yeah. In fact we'd very much like her to go to art school next year, but she has other plans.

5

R = Ron, **M** = Maria

R: Nice car!

M: It's all right, but it really guzzles petrol. It consumes over 20 litres per 100 kilometres.

R: Good thing then you don't have to drive to work, unlike me.

6D, Page 65, Exercise 5

1 Well done! You made the deadline.

2 Fantastic report – really clear!

3 Wow! That's a really nice laptop.

4 I love your new briefcase.

5 I thought you handled that customer really well.

6 What a brilliant idea!

6E, Page 67, Exercises 5 and 6

When Joe first told me the truth, I was furious. Our whole life together had been a web of lies. I thought he was a struggling divorcee who could only afford to take me to cheap noodle bars. Suddenly, he was telling me he had enough money to buy anything he wanted. I felt betrayed. It was only when he explained how badly he'd been hurt before, by women who just wanted him for his money, that I started to realize why he'd gone to such lengths to hide his fortune from me.

Now we're married, I'm glad he lied. Because there's a 23-year age gap between us, people sometimes look at me and think I'm after his money. But it's not like that. I can say with complete honesty that I fell in love with a man who I believed had nothing. Our married life together has been the happiest seven years of my life. For about six months after he told me about his money, it felt as though I was living in a dream, – a very nice dream, but it didn't feel real. I kept having to stop myself from offering to split the bill like I'd always done. But there is just so much more to Joe than his money, so it didn't change our relationship.

6

7A, Page 70, Exercises 2 and 3

I = interviewer, **L** = Lin

I: I think most people would agree that there were severe problems with this project. So what do you think went wrong?

L: Well, let me start by saying that it's always much easier to analyze these factors after the crisis. If I'd identified the problems before they happened, I'd be very popular now …. But seriously, in this case, the situation was complicated – a number of things went wrong at the same time. And, yes, mistakes were made.

I: If they'd been small mistakes, it wouldn't have been a problem. But that wasn't the case, was it? Losses in the first five days of opening came to $16 million.

L: Well, as I see it, there were three main problem areas. For a start, the project didn't finish to deadline. If they'd finished the building on time, there wouldn't have been so many difficulties. The unfinished work caused trouble in other areas.

I: From the passengers' viewpoint, that was less serious than the chaos and disruption to their journeys. During the week after it opened, more than 23,000 bags were lost.

L: Oh, yes, some passengers had a very difficult time. There were a lot of delays and disruption – about 500 flights were cancelled.

I: You can understand why people were angry. This was meant to be one of the most technologically advanced terminals in the world. Yet one report said there were 275 lifts, but 28 of them weren't working.

L: Which brings me to the second factor: technological problems. As you say, it was one of the most technologically advanced airports in the world, but it was actually technology that caused many of the problems during the opening week. There were major IT problems. Areas such as baggage handling rely on computer data to move luggage onto the plane and from aircraft to aircraft when people are changing flights. There was a massive breakdown in that computer communication.

I: Surely they should have tested these things before the opening?

L: Well, yes, if they had carried out enough checks, they might have discovered the problem earlier. But this is where the problems are linked. Apparently, they were unable to run adequate system checks that could have identified the IT problems because the construction work didn't finish on time.

I: But it wasn't just IT and construction delays. There were difficulties with personnel, too: staff shortages and inadequate training. If I listed all the problems, we'd be here all day.

L: Well, quite. For me, the most bizarre problem was that many airport workers couldn't get to their job because the staff car park was full. A simple error caused staff shortage problems. So the third issue was organizational problems. There was a lot of pressure to open on time and when you are dealing with huge amounts of people, things can go wrong.

I: Would you have been as understanding about the problems if you were a busy traveller?

L: … No, probably not. But you have to bear in mind that about 67 million people use Heathrow airport every year. When Terminal 5 opened, it was incredibly busy right from the start. Workers were dealing with problems beyond their control. To be honest, it doesn't shock me when things go wrong on large projects like this. It's more of a surprise when everything goes to plan.

7A, Page 71, Exercise 8

Welcome to business travel update. Air traffic controllers in Colombia, Ecuador, Peru and Bolivia have made an unexpected announcement that they are taking strike action over pay and conditions with immediate effect. All flights across the region have therefore been cancelled until further notice. Travellers are advised to make alternative transport arrangements as the disruption is expected to continue for several days.

7B, Page 72, Exercises 2 and 3

I was delighted to be offered the position. I knew I had a chance provided that I prepared well for interview and demonstrated that I had relevant experience. Now I work with the emergency planning team. Our main role is to anticipate anything that could go wrong and to make sure that there are procedures in place in case there's an emergency. This could include anything – um, fire, natural disasters, acts of terrorism or any threats to health for visitors to the facility. Although I'm quite a positive person, I always need to imagine the worst case scenario. Unless I do, I won't be able to work out the best way to deal with problems when they occur. For example, what if there's an outbreak of food poisoning or a virus? What would we need to do? Good analytical skills and quick decision-making are vital in this role. Supposing that there's a conference or some other big event taking place in the centre, the first step would be to carry out a risk assessment. My team would have a meeting to identify anything that could go wrong. When we're confident that we've thought of all the potential problems, we then check that there are appropriate procedures in place to deal with them. We make sure that this is a very safe environment for our guests. Unfortunately, an emergency will sometimes occur, in which case I'll work with my team and the emergency services to take appropriate action as quickly and effectively as possible.

7B, Page 73, Exercise 9

Carl Hamilton, the troubled CEO of Lerwood Chemicals has today refused to comment on claims that his company has been involved in illegally dumping toxic waste in the Black Sea. The price of shares in the company has fallen to a three year low and environmental groups are demanding an enquiry. This is the latest problem in a series of problems for the company. Only last month, employees staged a series of strikes when it was revealed that their pensions were in danger due to failed financial investments. Mr Hamilton is a key speaker at the Solar conference which is taking place next weekend. Organizers of the event have confirmed that he will still be taking part despite the latest revelations.

7D, Page 76, Exercises 4 and 5

K = Katalin, **L** = Louise

K: Louise, you wanted to see me. Why don't you tell me what this is all about?

L: Well, I wanted to ask about the training course that you've put me on next month.

K: Ah, yes, is there a problem?

L: No, not really. But as you know, the training takes place at the weekend.

K: Yes, it's an excellent course and I'm sure you'll find it very helpful. It also means that you can take more responsibility in the department. We really need someone to be trained up in this area.

L: Yes, it looks great. But I think I should get paid for my time at the weekend.

K: It's a very expensive course, Louise. We were very lucky to get you a place on it. There is normally a waiting list of a year.

L: Yes, I realize that, but …

K: And not only that, they normally only take candidates who have taken the initial management training. You were very lucky to have been put forward for this at all.

L: Yes, I'm aware of that. But that doesn't mean that I shouldn't get paid. It's three hours away, so I'll have to stay in a hotel. That's another expense, and I have to pay that myself. I'm not asking for overtime, just my normal hourly rate.

K: As you know, we don't pay staff to work at the weekend. Anyway, you can hardly call a training course 'work', can you? To be honest, I really can't see what you are complaining about.

L: I'm not complaining. But it's only fair that participants should get paid. I might not be working in the office, but I'm still learning skills that will be useful to the team, and that's sort of like working. After all, this isn't a course that I asked to go on, and it benefits the department, too.

K: OK, don't go then.

L: Pardon?

K: Don't go. It's taken a long time to get allocated a place on this course. I'm sure we can wait another year.

L: Th … that isn't what I meant. This isn't the best thing for the department.

K: I'll be the judge of that. Now, if you will excuse me, I'm very busy.

7D, Page 77, Exercises 8, 9 and 10

S = Supplier, **C** = Client

S: Thanks for coming in today. How was your journey?

C: Good thanks. Your directions were very helpful.

S: Glad to hear that. Can I get you a tea or coffee?

C: I'm fine, thanks. I'm afraid I don't have much time, I have to leave for the airport at four.

S: No problem. Shall we get straight down to business? Erm, perhaps you could outline the main areas you'd like to discuss?

C: Well, the way I see it is we have similar ideas on price and quantity. But I still have some reservations about your delivery times. These are fresh products, so we want them to arrive in our restaurants as quickly as possible. We have a policy that there should be no more than three days between the items being picked and when they're on the table.

S: I understand where you're coming from. However, we use state-of-the-art refrigeration systems to keep the products fresh for longer. For the size of order that you want, five days is our normal delivery time. But we want to do business with you so if you were able to increase your order by five per cent, we might be able to deliver a day earlier.

C: Well, we're certainly moving in the right direction. Say we increased our order by seven per cent, could you cut your delivery time by two days?

S: I'll need to agree that with our logistics manager, but I don't see a problem there.

C: So, we'll increase our order by seven per cent and you'll guarantee three-day delivery for all orders.

S: That's correct. I'm happy with those terms. Well, it looks like we have a deal. Would you like me to draw up a contract?

C: I need to leave to catch my plane. We're opening the latest branch of our chain in Poland tomorrow. Let's arrange another meeting when we've had time to think things over. I'll give you a call when I get back from Krakow.

8A, Page 80, Exercise 3

Part 1

Hi, my name is Hazel Rawlings and I'm here to talk about the way that news consumption has been affected by new technology. Firstly, let me ask you a question. Has everyone in this room at least glanced at the news headlines today? *[yes, uh-uh]* Yep, I thought so. Recent research confirms that our interest in news stories remains strong. However, advances in technology mean that there are now a variety of ways to read, watch or listen to the news. So, I'll start by looking at the changes in the way that we access the news. Then we'll see what effect this has had on our habits and the way that we interact with the news. Finally, we'll consider whether these changes mean that we spend more or less time reading or watching the news every day.

8A, Page 80, Exercise 4

Part 2

Let's start by looking at the way that we access news stories. Traditional news platforms such as newspapers, radio and TV are still popular. But increasingly, news stories can be accessed with digital devices such as smartphones. Friends and colleagues send interesting stories to each other by email or on social networking sites. The proportion of people who get their news online continues to grow. Recent research in the USA shows that 44 per cent of people now use the internet, mobile phones or other digital devices to follow the news. While local and national TV news remain the most popular way to view news stories, the internet is now used more than newspapers and radio broadcasts. In the USA, 92 per cent of Americans get their daily news from multiple sources rather than simply from newspapers or TV. Interestingly, while men and women are equally likely to get news from one or more traditional sources such as TV or a newspaper, far more men than women get news digitally. Online or digital platforms are used by 50 per cent of men to get their news compared with 39 per cent of women. And men are twice as likely as women to look at news stories on their mobile phones. Digital technology isn't used by a particular age group. You may be surprised to hear that online news is more likely to be read by those in their thirties and forties than by younger people. And, in the near future, it is thought that the internet will be used as a key news source for those in the 50–65 age group.

7

8A, Page 80, Exercise 5

Part 3

Now we'll move on to look at the way that this technology is used in our everyday lives. Have our news habits been changed by the internet? Well, recent research indicates that technology allows us to interact with the news in a different way. In the past, the news was accessed at particular times in most households. People read the newspaper over breakfast or watched or listened to the news at a certain time in the evening. However, digital technology means that news updates are now available wherever and whenever we want. We can check news stories while commuting to work or college. Now we have 24-hour news channels and websites that break news stories and constantly update and analyze them as they develop. In the past, many households had the newspaper delivered to their door, and it was often read from beginning to end. Today, people are more likely to scan the headlines online and click on those stories that attract their attention. In the past, it was the producer of a news programme or the editor of a newspaper who decided which stories were most important. Now we decide that information for ourselves and follow the stories that we are most interested in, whether they are sports results, international incidents or local news. As a result, individuals are much more involved in managing their own news content.

8A, Page 80, Exercise 6

Part 4

To sum up, we are now more interested than ever in following the news. Traditional news media and digital technology are used for different purposes by consumers. For example, individuals might use their mobile phone to read news headlines on the move, a news website to follow breaking news stories and newspapers, or TV broadcasts for news analysis and in-depth reports. So, what should we conclude from this? Well, the next few years will be interesting times for news media. The challenge in the future will be to create news content that responds to new technology and to offer more opportunities for users to customize their news to reflect their own interests.

8B, Page 82, Exercise 2

I = interviewer, **P** = Paul Valera

I: Welcome to our Media Today podcast, and we have an interview with Paul Valera, the founder of P Valera Productions. Mr Valera, there are reports that you have been in talks with cable TV channels – is that correct?

PV: Well, it's true that I've had interesting discussions about the media industry with some of the leaders in the field.

I: The timing is interesting, isn't it? These meetings have occurred on the same day that senior staff from your own company publicly accuse you of entering negotiations to sell P Valera Productions without consulting the shareholders. Are these accusations true?

PV: What statements from senior staff? These accusations are completely unfounded.

I: So you didn't meet with representatives from international media organizations?

PV: I've already stated that I've been in discussions and I have nothing more to add to that statement at this point.

I: Your company has a reputation for making documentaries and drama series that deal with serious issues, hasn't it? Whereas the companies that you are in talks with make game shows and sitcoms. If you sell, that would mean a change of direction for the type of programmes you make, wouldn't it?

PV: As I have said, I have no comment to make on …

I: And it could also mean that jobs would be lost at P Valera Productions, isn't that right?

PV: Don't be ridiculous. Where did you get this information?

I: Are you refusing to answer the question?

PV: I don't see any point in discussing this further. I have nothing else to say to you.

8B, Page 82, Exercises 3 and 4

I = interviewer, **PV** = Paul Valera

I: Welcome to Business Tonight, and we have an interview with Paul Valera, the founder of P Valera Productions. Paul, there are reports that you've been involved in talks with some of the giants of the media industry – is that correct?

PV: Well, yes, it's true that I've had the opportunity to get together with some of the leaders in the field.

I: Could you tell me whether it's true that an offer has been made to buy your company?

PV: There has been interest in the company, but no decision would be made until I've consulted with the shareholders.

I: That must be very exciting for you. After all, P Valera Productions was only founded four years ago when you were still at university.

PV: Yeah, there's no doubt that this is a very great time for the company. We have a brilliant team and we're very proud of what we've achieved so far.

I: That brings me to my next question. P Valera Productions has a reputation for making documentaries and drama series that deal with serious issues, hasn't it? Can you say whether this would mean a change of direction for your company?

PV: I'm glad that you asked that question. I'd like to take this opportunity to state that we would continue to make challenging and interesting programmes that we believe in. P Valera Productions will continue to make the same high quality television that we always have.

I: That's good to hear. There have also been rumours that there might be job losses if you sell. Do you know if there might be changes to your production team?

PV: There won't be any changes to the production or management teams in the company. These are the teams that have made the company the success it is today. Without their creativity and expertise, we wouldn't be able to make award-winning programmes. I guarantee that there will be no redundancies, you have my word on that. Why would I change a winning team?

I: Do you think you could tell us about your latest project? Er … haven't you been working on a secret programme in the Amazon rainforest?

PV: Well, this is a world exclusive: it will feature animals and plants which have never been filmed before. It's taken us three years to make and I can honestly say that it will be the most amazing wildlife documentary that has ever been seen on television.

I: Well, we certainly look forward to seeing it. Thanks for coming in today, Paul and we'll follow your company's plans with interest.

PV: It's been a pleasure.

Audio scripts

8B, Page 83, Exercise 5

1 The timing is interesting, isn't it?

2 Are these accusations true?

3 Could you tell me whether it's true that an offer has been made to buy your company?

4 Why would I change a winning team?

5 Haven't you been working on a secret programme in the Amazon rainforest?

8C, Page 84, Exercise 2

1

P = Presenter

P: Well, Magda, so far you've won 35,000 euros. Now you have the chance to double your money. All you have to do is give me the correct answer to this question. Fraser Island is the largest sand island in the world. Can you tell me what country it belongs to?

2

E = Eleanor, **LA** = Lord Ashgrove

E: … Lord Ashgrove, what are you doing here? …

LA: I had to see you, Eleanor.

E: You must leave immediately – the king is on his way.

LA: Too late, my dear.

3

P = Presenter

P: This week on Lifeswap, the Lucas family are getting ready to leave their home in Glasgow to spend a month with the Cheng family in Hong Kong. They are already late for their flight, and 15-year-old Zoe Lucas has decided that she doesn't want to leave her friends and is refusing to get into the taxi to the airport.

4

A = Amelia, **C** = Charles

A: Charles, you haven't forgotten what day it is today, have you?

C: Of course not … it's Tuesday, isn't it? …

A: … No. Listen, I'll give you a clue. [Hums.]

C: Ah, is it the day you start singing lessons?

5

J = James, **M** = Mei-ling

J: … The door's locked. I'll have to break in. …

M: Look, over there, under the desk. It's a body.

J: It's Giles Carfax, the CEO. But there's no gun. The doors and windows are locked. No one has come in or gone out – so who shot him?

8D, Page 86, Exercises 2 and 3

Speaker 1
I'll see you on Thursday around lunchtime outside that place that Kate mentioned serves good coffee.

Speaker 2
Flights to Oman leave at eight o'clock, and business class passengers are reminded that they can check in before arriving at the airport. Leave time to clear security and please remember that only one bag per person is allowed on the plane.

Speaker 3
If you take 15 milligrams a day for five days, you'll start to feel better. Though it's not a good idea to take it all at once as you might feel sleepy. Food helps, so it's probably better to take it at meal times.

Speaker 4
I made a few contacts at the trade fair – they don't work in the same sector as we do, but I thought it might be a useful networking opportunity, so I invited them to lunch. We planned to go to a local café, but two had special dietary requirements, so it … it wasn't suitable. In the end, we jumped into a taxi and found another place, which is why it came to just over three hundred.

8D, Page 87, Exercise 7

S = Sara, **T** = Tony

S: Hi, Sara Campbell here.

T: Hi, Sara, it's Tony. I'm phoning about the email that you sent this morning. Why did you say that the project has been postponed until November?

S: I didn't say that.

T: Well, that's what you meant. You say the start date has been changed.

S: The start date has been changed. What's the problem?

T: The problem is that you're sending out an inaccurate communication and it's making my department look bad. The start date hasn't been postponed or changed, it's just been rescheduled.

S: Tony, they all mean pretty much the same thing.

T: Not to me, Sara. And while we're on the subject of your email, I found some of the information ambiguous.

S: Ambiguous? What do you mean?

T: I mean, it isn't clear. For example, you say that training will be offered to the teams in the autumn. What do you mean there – September, October, November?

S: I think it's in September, but I'd need to check the exact dates. They're just details, though.

T: Hardly! My team have to plan their workload around the training courses, so the exact dates are very important to them.

S: … Anything else? …

T: Are you typing an email?

S: Sorry, Tony. Just replying to an urgent message. Now, where were we?

T: You were about to explain to me why we should be interested in the fact that Peter De Marco is planning a visit to our branch. In your email you just say 'We're welcoming Peter De Marco next month'. Why is he coming to the branch?

S: As you know, he's the new Finance Director at head office. We're not sure yet, but we think he might be coming to discuss spending cuts. Could be important for next year's budget.

T: And you didn't think it was worth including that information?

S: Sorry, Tony, I have a call coming in on the other line. I'll have to call you back later.

8D, Page 87, Exercise 8

S = Sara, T = Tony

S: Hi, Sara Campbell here.

T: Hi, Sara, it's Tony. I'm phoning about the email that you sent this morning. Could I just clarify a few things?

S: Sure, fire away.

T: You mention changes to the start date of our project. If I understand correctly, you're saying that it's been postponed. The thing is, it makes it sound as though my department has failed to start the project on time. D'you see what I mean?

S: Oh, yes, I see. Sorry, there's been a misunderstanding, Tony. That wasn't what I meant. What I was trying to say was that the board of directors has decided to change the start date. I'll clarify that to the management team.

T: Great. The other thing I wanted to check was the dates of the training. The email says that it will be offered to teams in the autumn. We have the conference in November, so I presume you mean early autumn – is that right?

S: Yep, exactly.

T: Do you have any more information on this? You see, my team will need to plan their schedules, so it'd be useful to have an exact date.

S: Ah, got you, you need the exact dates, don't you? Yeah, I think it's planned for September. Tell you what, I'll check the dates and email them to you today.

T: Thanks, Sara. There was one last thing. Your email says that Peter De Marco is visiting the branch at the end of the month. Can you tell me a little more about why he's coming?

S: He's the new Finance Director at head office, as you know, and there's a possibility that he might want to discuss spending cuts in next year's budget. I'll send a memo with more details later this week, but I'd appreciate it if you didn't discuss it with your team until then. Do you follow?

T: OK, of course.

S: Thanks, Tony, and sorry for any misunderstandings in the email.

T: No problem. That's all clear now.

8E, Page 89, Exercises 5 and 6

TC = training coordinator, HSO = health & safety office

TC: Dave Rowson.

HSO: Hello, it's Kelly Robinson here, Health and Safety Officer at Waterside. I'm returning your call about the caving accident.

TC: Hi, Kelly, thanks for getting back to me.

HSO: I wanted to extend the company's apologies once again. This was a very unfortunate incident. How is Sam doing?

TC: Out of hospital and recovering at home, thankfully. It could have been much more serious.

HSO: Well, yes, exactly. That's why I'm calling. I've interviewed Zaheer Kumar, our instructor, and filed an incident report. Now, according to Zaheer's statement, the group was given a fifteen-minute training talk before they went caving and they were told what to do in case of emergencies. In addition, they all had safety equipment and were told to stay together during the activity. We're confident that Zaheer followed company safety guidelines.

TC: But there was still an accident. I've interviewed Sam Hughes and he suggests that the training talk lasted less than five minutes. Sam's torch wasn't working. While trying to get it to work in the cave, Sam got lost because the rest of the group went on ahead.

HSO: Well, that's a little different from what I've heard. Zaheer says that the group was told to check their equipment before entering the cave. And apparently, Sam was chatting all through the safety talk.

TC: Well, Sam says they weren't advised to check the equipment at all. Well, we seem to have different versions of what went on, don't we? We still need to find out why it took the instructor ten minutes to realize that one of the party was missing. And when Zaheer discovered Sam was missing, why did it take so long to start a search? It seems that there was some delay in getting medical help, too.

HSO: We also need to check why Sam didn't simply follow the signs back to the entrance of the cave. The accident happened in an area of the cave which is closed to the public. It's clearly marked with a sign saying, 'Danger, do not enter.' If he hadn't gone in there, he wouldn't have ended up with a broken leg.

TC: It sounds like we need to interview Sam and Zaheer again to clarify what happened, doesn't it?

HSO: Yes, I'll speak to Zaheer today. Can you speak to Sam?

TC: Yes, will do. We might get a clearer picture of what happened if we ask for more details, and for confirmation of what they've already told us.

9A, Page 92, Exercises 2 and 3

Interview A

Well, in my country I know that credit card payments have become extremely popular over the last decade. I think it's unlikely that credit card payments will decrease in popularity in the years ahead – in my country, at least. But a number of people today seem to prefer mobile payments, so it's quite probable that more and more consumers will turn to mobile banking. After all, mobile payments are safer than credit card payments, aren't they?

Interview B

I wish I knew the answer to that one! I don't want to sound too pessimistic, but, you know, it's taking a long time to get out of this recession. So, really, I doubt whether access to credit will be easier. And I'd go further than that: for those who have credit cards, it will definitely be more difficult to spend.

Interview C

Well, plastic cards probably won't become any safer to use – they'll continue to get stolen or lost. But the other day I was reading about recent developments in biometric technology. Fascinating, really. Hitachi, for example, has come up with the idea of letting customers make payments simply by scanning their hand instead of using a credit card. So there's sure to be a great improvement in security in the next few years.

Interview D

Well, for one thing it's clear that credit card companies can't continue to offer valuable rewards to entice customers to use credit cards as a primary payment tool. For that and several other reasons, the number of credit card customers is bound to decline sharply over the next few years, I think. It's highly likely that debit cards will become everybody's preferred plastic. Their use is already accelerating as more people want to pay with money they know they have.

9B, Page 94, Exercises 3 and 4

I = interviewer, R = Renata

I: So, Renata, what went wrong, in your opinion?

R: I suppose you mean at the UN?

I: Yeah, that's right!

R: Well, I certainly agree with the UN spokeswoman: this security breach should not have happened. The guards should have checked the actor's identity.

I: Now, considering that this was a promotional stunt, how do you think the KFC people felt about this incident?

R: The whole idea could have been a terrible failure, of course, but then even traditional advertising stunts often fail. I think the guys behind the stunt must have planned everything very carefully.

I: And what about the actor they'd hired?

R: Well, first of all, it can't have been easy to find an actor willing to take the risk. From the company's point of view, he did a great job. Let's not forget that the story went round the world. They must all have been very pleased.

9C, Page 96, Exercises 2 and 3

The parents of a high-school student from Philadelphia have filed a lawsuit against the school district after it appeared that the laptop issued freely by the school was equipped with security software that allowed the school district to activate the computer's webcam and view the students at any time.

According to the lawsuit, 15-year-old Blake Robbins and his parents only became aware of the secret webcam after he was accused of bad behaviour in his home. The only evidence the school was able to present to support the accusation was a photograph taken from the webcam embedded in the laptop. It later turned out that the student had simply been pictured holding some candies which one of the teachers had mistaken for something else.

The Robbins are complaining that the school's actions amount to spying, and Blake's lawyers have also expressed serious concern over the officials' actions and said they could face criminal charges.

The school authorities maintain that the secret webcam has only been used for the limited purpose of locating a lost, stolen or missing laptop.

Apparently, other schools have similar technology. A middle school in the South Bronx of New York City has installed software in the laptops issued to its students that allows officials to view whatever is displayed on the screen.

9D, Page 98, Exercise 2

1

M = Marianne, G = Geoff

M: Sorry, Geoff. My computer's frozen again. Do you think you could help?

G: No. I can't. Sorry.

2

R = Rick, B = Boris

B: IT support, Boris speaking.

R: Hi, Boris. Rick here. Erm ... Sorry to bother you, but I seem to have a bit of a problem.

B: Yeah? What is it?

R: I've been trying to change my password, but somehow the system doesn't accept it. I was wondering if you could possibly help me, please.

B: Sorry, Rick, are you saying you just need a new password?

3

A = Anya, S = shop assistant

A: Hello. Good afternoon. I want the Vectra anti-virus software package.

S: Sorry?

9D, Page 98, Exercises 3 and 4

People all over the world have to make requests at one time or another. Requesting is a universal phenomenon, but the ways in which we can make our requests appropriate are not universal – they are culture specific. For example, if you translated a Japanese request into Arabic or English, it might sound very strange, perhaps even rude.

In most English-speaking countries, the way in which we express requests is influenced by at least three factors. Firstly, there's the relationship between the interlocutors. For example, two complete strangers have a high degree of social distance, so language tends to be more formal, and more words are used, except in so-called service encounters, like shopping, checking in or out at a hotel and things like that. Secondly, we need to consider power relationships: do the interlocutors have equal status and power, or is one inferior and the other superior? Thirdly, consider the size of the request: are you asking for a big or a small favour?

So the most appropriate requests are the ones which take into account all three dimensions. And of course there's something else we should never forget: it's not just what we say, it's how we say it. At the end of the day, the words we use don't really matter if our body language and intonation send a negative message.

All in all, I don't think I've said anything revolutionary. Most people will accept that there's a huge difference between asking a close friend if they can lend you a pen, and asking a visiting overseas director if they can send you a copy of the PowerPoint slides they used for their presentation at your annual sales conference.

Let's now turn to our three situations. The way Marianne words her request is fine. The problem is with Geoff's response. To begin with, we generally avoid starting a negative response with 'no'. And then if we can't give a positive response, we usually give a reason. So Geoff could've said something like: 'Sorry, I can't just now. There's this huge backlog of work I have to go through. Try Linda.'

Now, turning to Rick's request, the problem is that it's far too indirect, it's too formal. Rick and Boris obviously know each other, and the request seems to be a very small one, so Boris probably expected something more direct like: 'Could you help me change my password?'

Finally, the problem with Anya's request is the use of 'want', which is almost a taboo word in requests, at least in service encounters. So the shop assistant must've been shocked. In this situation, you'd expect something like: 'I'm looking for the Vectra anti-virus package' or 'I'd like the Vectra anti-virus package.'

9D, Page 98, Exercises 5 and 6

Conversation 1

S = Seb, **J** = James

S: Hi, James. Sorry to bother you, but could you do something for me?

J: Yes, of course.

S: I've been trying to install some new software, but it doesn't work. Would you mind having a look at it when you have a minute?

J: Not at all. Can we do that in the coffee break?

S: Sure.

Conversation 2

C = Claire, **L** = Lev

C: Erm ... Excuse me, Lev. I know you're very busy, but do you think you could go through this translation for me? It's a short letter to a potential customer in St Petersburg.

L: No problem. Just take a seat and we'll have a look at it together.

C: Fantastic. Thanks.

Conversation 3

Z = Zoe, **R** = Raimundo

Z: Hi, Raimundo. There's something I need to ask you. You know it's very hectic for all of us here because of our annual conference next month.

R: Yes, I know. I ... I sent out the last invitations yesterday, but there's still quite a bit of work to do on the programme.

Z: Yes, that's what I had in mind. I wonder if you could possibly do some overtime on Thursday and Friday, please?

R: The thing is, I've got to be home by six Thursday evening. We've got a family reunion. But I'd be happy to do a couple of extra hours on Friday, if that's any help.

Z: Great!

Conversation 4

R = Ray, **F** = Felipa

R: Hi, Felipa. Could I ask you something?

F: Go ahead.

R: You know that photo editing program you showed me last month?

F: Yeah?

R: Well, I could really use it these days. Would it be all right if I copied it onto my laptop?

F: I'd love to help you, but I'm afraid it was only a trial version. As a matter of fact, it expired last week.

9D, Page 99, Exercise 13

L = Lea, **N** = Nathan

L: Hi, Nathan. Could I have a word with you about our project?

N: Sure. What's up?

L: Well, it seems that we're running behind schedule. So could you and the rest of the team possibly work on Saturday morning?

N: I'm afraid I can't on Saturday. I've planned something with the family.

L: I know it's not easy, Nathan. But we really need an extra project meeting, and we need you. We're only talking about three or four hours.

N: I see. Well, couldn't you plan it for Thursday instead?

L: I'm afraid not. Most of the team members are doing fieldwork on Thursday.

N: I understand. Well ... all right, then. If it's only for a couple of hours, I suppose I could be there Saturday.

L: Excellent! And I thought it would be great if you could coordinate the work of the team as I'll be away in Vancouver.

N: Oh, I don't think I have enough experience for that. Um, how about a teleconference instead? I'm sure all the coordinating could be done from Vancouver.

N: Thanks, Nathan, I'll just have to make sure I get up in the middle of the night then ...

9E, Page 101, Exercise 6

According to a US survey:

more than 75 per cent of employers monitor their workers' website connections

60 per cent of firms use software to monitor external (incoming and outgoing) email

only 27 per cent take advantage of technology tools to monitor internal email conversations that take place between employees

79 per cent of employers have implemented a written email policy

almost 20 per cent of employees report sending and receiving inappropriate and potentially damaging content (for example, jokes, gossip, confidential information about the company, etc.).

10A, Page 103, Exercise 9

I've been in my present job at a pharmaceutical company for three years now. I work in sales and have had a lot of praise from my manager about my performance. The problem is that recently I've started to feel as though I'm not developing my skills. Sometimes I think that I should try to move departments as this is a big company and it usually looks after its employees. Or perhaps I should change career completely. You see, I've always wanted to get into acting. I haven't joined any amateur theatre groups, but I really enjoyed acting in productions at college and everyone said that I was really good. Maybe I should retrain as a drama teacher or even do a course in acting. What do you think?

10B, Page 104, Exercise 2

Did I tell you that I met an old colleague of mine, Karl last week at a trade fair in Moscow? I hadn't seen him for more than two years. It was very cold in the city and I almost didn't recognize him because we were all wearing very large coats and hats to keep warm. Anyway, we went to a very good restaurant and talked about old times.

Karl reminded me of an incident that happened when we worked together. We used to share an office with our manager, who liked everything to be very clean. One day, the boss was out of the office and apart from Karl and myself, the whole department was deserted. Anyway, Karl had a problem with his motorbike, but because it was raining he couldn't work on it outside. He persuaded me to help him bring it into the office and he took it apart to try to fix it. Soon the whole place was very dirty. You can guess what happened next. Our boss came back early and walked into the office. The first thing he saw was part of a motorbike engine on his desk. As you can imagine, he was very angry with us, his face went really red, and for some reason, Karl and I found this very funny and started to giggle. Soon we were laughing so much that we could hardly breathe.

Needless to say, our relationship with our manager was never the same again. Not long after, Karl left to work for another organization and a little while later, I left, too. That's when I came to work here and it was definitely the best career move I've ever made. I suppose you could say that it's all thanks to Karl and his motorbike.

10B, Page 104, Exercise 5

Did I tell you that I met an old colleague of mine, Karl last week at a trade fair in Moscow? I hadn't seen him for more than two years. It was freezing in the city and I almost didn't recognize him because we were all wearing huge coats and hats to keep warm. Anyway, we went to an excellent restaurant and talked about old times.

Karl reminded me of an incident that happened when we worked together. We used to share an office with our manager, who liked everything to be kept spotless. One day, the boss was out of the office and apart from Karl and myself, the whole department was deserted. Anyway, Karl had a problem with his motorbike, but because it was raining he couldn't work on it outside. He persuaded me to help him bring it into the office and he took it apart to try to fix it. Soon the whole place was filthy. You can guess what happened next. Our boss came back early and walked into the office. The first thing he saw was part of a motorbike engine on his desk. As you can imagine, he was furious with us, his face went really red, and for some reason, Karl and I found this hilarious and started to giggle. Soon we were laughing so much that we could hardly breathe.

Needless to say, our relationship with our manager was never the same again. Not long after, Karl left to work for another organization and our boss retired. After he left, I finally got promoted to assistant manager and soon became manager. It might never have happened without Karl and his motorbike.

10B, Page 105, Exercise 7

M = Martine; **L** = Lars

M: Excuse me, could you tell me what time the next seminar starts?

L: Oh, Martine, is that you? It's me, Lars.

M: Oh, Lars, hello. How are you? I haven't seen you in ages. What have you been up to?

L: I've been incredibly busy, actually. I set up my own business and it's going really well. It's hard work but I enjoy it very much. How's everyone in the department?

M: Same as ever. Donald from Accounts has been promoted.

L: You're joking! He was completely useless at his job.

M: I know, but amazingly, he's now on the board of directors.

L: You can't be serious! Mind you, he always was rather good at office politics.

M: They quickly realized their mistake. But it's too late now.

L: What about Jasmine? If I remember rightly, she wanted to leave to become a professional musician. She plays the violin absolutely brilliantly, doesn't she?

M: That's right. She's doing well, too. There's talk of her moving to Sydney to work in the Australian branch.

L: That's hardly surprising. She's extremely intelligent, isn't she?

M: Look, the talk's about to start. Hopefully, we'll get a chance to talk later.

L: Unfortunately, I have to drive to the airport straight after the seminar. You'll give my regards to everyone at the office, won't you?

M: Of course. It was great to catch up.

10C, Page 106, Exercises 4 and 5

T = Tom; **M** = Marta

T: Listen, I'm a bit concerned about Jozef. Have you noticed any changes in his behaviour recently?

M: Funny you should say that. You know how conscientious he is. Well, since he started this latest project, I've noticed that he's making a lot of mistakes. His work's started to become quite slapdash and that's not like him.

T: No, it's not, is it? And whereas I'd normally describe him as calm and easy-going, I've had reports that he's permanently grumpy with everyone in the team lately. They avoid approaching him in case he bites their head off.

M: Have you mentioned any of this to him?

T: It's difficult because he's quite reserved. I'm not sure if he'd be comfortable discussing private matters.

M: But it might not be private. Perhaps he's stressed about the new project he's working on. You won't know until you ask.

T: OK, I'll think about it.

10D, Page 108, Exercises 3 and 4

R = Robert (the team leader), A, B and C = (members of the team)

R: … Hello, everyone, could I have your attention for a moment? I've just come from a meeting with Mayhew Telecoms, to talk about our bid for the contract to build their new workspaces.

A: Have they given you any feedback on our designs yet? Do they like them?

R: That's what I want to talk to you all about. Let me start by saying that they were very impressed by your work, and they thought the designs were bright and modern. Exactly what was asked for in their brief, in fact. Unfortunately, due to factors which are beyond our control, they've had to turn the designs down. … I realize that this must be disappointing for you all. And I'm aware how much hard work went into this. The reason that Mayhew Telecoms turned them down is because they're having some problems and they now have less money to spend on this project. But the good news is that we're still their first choice to design the new workspaces – we just need to amend our designs a little.

B: But we worked really hard on this.

R: I know, and you all did an excellent job. … Come on, we can do this. We need to pull together to get this done.

A: But Robert, it's not our fault that the client has financial problems.

R: No, but what we need to focus on is the next stage of this project. This client still thinks you're the best team to design these workspaces. They have faith in you. Let's concentrate on resolving this and getting the job done. They now want new designs with a more traditional feel, using less expensive materials. So I'd like you to come up with some fresh ideas.

C: Look, couldn't we just revise the designs that we've already done? We all believe these are the best designs for these workspaces. Why don't we just use less expensive material but try to keep to the original ideas?

R: That's certainly worth considering, but I think the first thing we need to do is arrange a meeting and look at the designs again. For the moment, I think you should all go home early. You've been working late nights and weekends and you all need a break. Go and get some rest. We'll have a team meeting first thing tomorrow and talk about how to proceed. … Oh, and before you go, I'd like to thank you for your understanding. I really appreciate all your efforts on this project. And I have every confidence that the new designs will be even better. OK, off you go, see you tomorrow.

[Bye, thanks …]

10E, Page 111, Exercise 5

Hello. It's good to be working with you all. As you know, this is a multi-million pound project and we at Landwing Holdings are very excited to hear your ideas. The target market for membership of Holden Lodge will be people aged 30 to 55. In general, the members will be successful business people who lead busy and sometimes stressful lives, and they will come to Holden Lodge to relax and keep fit. As a first step, I would like you to brainstorm ideas for the activities and facilities that we could offer customers. You can use the plans to decide where some of these facilities could be placed. Although we will be employing a professional advertising company, it would also be very useful for you to provide ideas for a logo for Holden Lodge, and a slogan that we could use to encourage prospective customers to become members of the leisure complex. As you can see, we included a draft logo and slogan on the plans, but we want to work on them and improve them.

10E, Page 111, Exercise 7

Hi, team. Sorry to call you without warning but we've had some new information. I'll keep this brief. Our market research company has advised us that our target market should now be families with young children. And they also recommend that we include some activities that will appeal to teenagers. Forget the 30- to 55-year-olds target market. Can you now make any necessary changes to the activities and facilities that we offer to attract the new target customers? Oh, and that means you might also need to change the logo or slogan, too, I guess. Sorry about this – you're doing a great job. I'd really appreciate your ideas as soon as possible – this really is extremely urgent.

10E, Page 111, Exercise 8

Hi again – I have a couple of final tasks for you. Firstly, we'd like you to think of a special promotion to get people to sign up for membership. You know, like a month's free membership or something, but I'm sure you'll think of a more interesting idea than that. Secondly, it's important that we maximize profits, so can you identify any interior or exterior spaces that you haven't already used for your planned leisure activities and facilities? What could these spaces be used for? It doesn't necessarily have to be anything to do with health or fitness. For example, they could be used for concerts, parties, shops … let your imaginations run wild. Thanks again for all your hard work on this project. You're a great team.

Present tenses

Present simple

Use

We use the present simple to talk about regular activities, long-term situations and things that are always true.

> I **watch** TV every evening.
> Leila and Selim **live** in Tunis.
> Winter **begins** on 21 December.

We also use the present simple for timetabled events.

> My plane **leaves** at 12.50.
> The conference **starts** next Tuesday.

We use the present simple instead of *will* in subordinate clauses that refer to the future.

> I'll phone you as soon as I **arrive**. (~~as soon as I will arrive~~)
> You won't laugh when you **read** his report. (~~when you will read~~)

However, note that *when* can be followed by *will* (or *would*) in reported and embedded questions (see **Asking questions**, page 163).

> I wonder when Julie will be back.

We also use the present simple for giving and asking for directions and instructions.

> How **do I get** to your office?
> You **go** down the high street and **turn** right after the park.

Form

(+)
I/You/We/They **work** full time.
He/She/It **works** day and night.

(–)
You **don't work** at weekends.
He **doesn't** usually **work** late.

(?)
Where **do** you **work**?
Do I/you/we/they **work**?
Does he/she/it **work**?

Do you often **play** tennis?	Yes, I **do**.
Does she **travel** a lot?	No, she **doesn't**.

Verbs not used in the continuous

Some verbs are never or hardly ever used in the continuous form of any tense.

These verbs are sometimes called 'state', or 'stative', verbs'. They include:

- verbs referring to the senses, e.g. *feel, hear, see, smell, sound, taste*:
  > I **see** what you mean. (~~am seeing~~)

- verbs referring to mental and emotional states, e.g. *believe, doubt, imagine, know, realize, recognize, suppose, understand, like, dislike, hate, prefer, want, wish*:
  > They **understand** our point of view. (~~are understanding~~)

- other verbs, e.g. *agree, disagree, mean, promise, depend on, belong, need, owe, own, possess*:
  > The group **owns** a supermarket chain in Spain. (~~is owning~~)

> ⚠ Note that some state verbs can also be 'action', or 'dynamic', verbs. Action verbs can be used in the continuous.
>
> Compare: *I **see** what you mean.* (state; meaning = understand)
>
> *I'm **seeing** the boss tomorrow.* (action; meaning = have an appointment with)
>
> *I **think** you're right.* (state; meaning = this is my opinion)
>
> *I'm **thinking** about what he said.* (action; meaning = reflecting)

Present continuous

Use

We use the present continuous to talk about actions happening now or around now.

> *I'm **waiting** for my flight.*
>
> *We're **working** here in Denver for a week.*

We also use it to talk about present trends.

> *The number of passengers **is rising**.*

We can use the present continuous for repeated actions and events if they are happening around now.

> *The new manager **is travelling** a lot these days.*

We also use the present continuous to refer to future arrangements and plans. We often use a future time expression in this case.

> *Our company **is relocating** to India next year.*

Form

(+)	
I **am** (I**'m**) **working** full time this week.	
He / She / It **is** (He**'s** / She**'s** / It**'s**) **working**.	
We / You / They **are** (We**'re** / You**'re** / They**'re**) **working**.	
(–)	
I **am not** (I**'m not**) studying any more today.	
You **are not** (You**'re not** / You **aren't**) working hard enough these days.	
It **is not** (It **isn't**) working properly.	
(?)	
What **is** Jim **doing** right now?	
What **is** Jim **doing** right now? **Is** he **looking** for a new job?	Yes, he **is**. / No, he **isn't**.

Present perfect simple

Use

We use the present perfect simple to talk about a present situation which is connected to the past. The main uses can be grouped under three headings:

1 **Recent news / New information** – we are focusing on the current importance of the past event, i.e. on the present result of the past event. *When* it happened is not important and is not mentioned.

> *I'**ve finished** the report.* (You can have it now.)

We often use the present perfect to give news.

> *Guess what. My computer **has crashed**!*

2 **Experience** – finished actions that happened in our life up to now.

> *I love that film. I'**ve seen** it three times.* (three times in my life so far)
>
> *Alex **has won** several business awards.* (up to now)
>
> **Have** you ever **been** to Singapore? (at any time in your life)
>
> *I'**ve** never **given** a business presentation.* (never in my life so far)

3 **Duration from the past until now** – unfinished actions, i.e. actions or states that began in the past and are still continuing now.

> *Barbara **has worked** as an accountant for a long time.*
>
> *Rick **has worked** for Breitner & Schultz since 1995.*

The time expressions *for* and *since* are often used to connect the past and present. We use *for* with a period of time and *since* with a point of time.

When we speak about 'unfinished time' we often use the adverbs *already* and *yet* to describe things which are happening or expected to happen around the present. The adverb *already* may express some surprise, e.g. because something has happened sooner than expected.

> *She's only 28 but she's **already** written three novels.*

We use *not yet* to describe something that hasn't happened so far but is expected to happen in the future.

> *He **hasn't** found the right business partner **yet**.*

Form

We form the present perfect with the auxiliary *have/has* + past participle.

(+)	
I / You / We / They **have** (I'**ve** / You'**ve** / We'**ve** / They'**ve**) **worked** hard.	
He / She / It **has** (He'**s** / She'**s** / It'**s**) **worked** effectively.	
(–)	
I/You/We/They **have not** (I/You/We/They **haven't**) **worked** hard enough.	
It **has not** (It **hasn't**) **worked** properly.	
(?)	
What **has** Linda **written***?	
Has she **finished** her training?	Yes, she **has**. / No, she **hasn't**.

See page 176 for a list of common irregular verbs.

Present perfect continuous

Use

We use the present perfect continuous to talk about actions and situations which started in the past and are still going on or have just stopped.

Food prices **have been going up** steadily all this year. (still going on)

Sorry I'm out of breath. I**'ve been running**. (just stopped)

When we use it together with another verb in the present, there is often a relation of cause and effect between the two verbs.

He has a nice tan. He**'s been sunbathing**.

My hands are dirty. I**'ve been painting** the shed.

We also use the present perfect continuous for repeated actions.

Customers **have been phoning** me all day.

How long **have** you **been taking** those tablets?

The present perfect continuous is also often used with words and expressions that refer to a period of time up to now (e.g. today, this week, recently, lately, for, since, how long, etc.).

The kids **have been playing** computer games since 4 o'clock.

It**'s been raining** for the last two weeks.

> ⚠ We do not use the present perfect continuous with words and expressions that refer to a finished period of time.
> I was in Montenegro last November. It rained for two weeks.

Form

We form the present perfect continuous with the auxiliary have/has + been + present participle.

(+)
They **have been studying** English for two years.

(–)
She **hasn't been feeling** very well lately.

(?)	
What **have** you **been doing**?	
Your eyes are red. **Have** you **been crying**?	Yes, I **have**. / No, I **haven't**.

Present perfect simple vs present perfect continuous

We can often use either the present perfect simple or continuous, and there is only a small change of emphasis.

Danilo has worked / has been working as a firefighter for twelve years.

It has snowed / has been snowing non-stop since Monday.

We tend to prefer the present perfect simple for permanent or long-term situations, and the present perfect continuous for temporary or shorter actions and situations. Compare:

These giant rocks have lain here for centuries.

Sven has been lying on the beach since breakfast.

My aunt has always worked really hard.

My aunt has been working really hard lately.

When we use the present perfect simple, we are interested in the result of the action, not so much in the action itself.

Giancarlo has fixed the engine. (= so now it's working normally)

But when we use the present perfect continuous, we are more interested in the action itself.

'Why are your hands dirty?'

'Well, I've been fixing the engine.' (I may or may not have finished)

We use the present perfect simple to say how many things we've done, or how much we've done, or how many times we've done something. But we use the present perfect continuous to say how long we've been doing something. Compare:

I've written 25 emails.

I've been writing emails all day.

I've visited my main customers five times this month.

I've been visiting a lot of my customers over the last three days.

> ⚠ Remember that certain verbs are not normally used in the continuous (see **Present simple**, page 156).
> Have you known Mr Deng for a long time?
> (Have you been knowing)

Past tenses

Past simple

Use

The past simple is often considered the default tense to talk about past actions and situations, i.e. we use it unless we have a particular reason for using another past tense. We often use it when we tell stories or when we describe past events, and we also often use it together with words or phrases referring to the past (e.g. two hours ago, yesterday afternoon, last week, in 2009, when I was a child, etc).

However, past time expressions (e.g. last year, two years ago, etc.) are not always in the sentence, e.g. To everyone's surprise, Jill left the company. This is the case when it is clear that the speaker is talking about the past.

Form

(+)	
The manager **invited** us to her party. We all **went*** to her party.	

(–)	
She **didn't invite** Sam. Sam **didn't go** to her party.	

(?)	
What time **did** you **arrive**?	
Who **took** you **there**?	
Did she **invite** Raoul?	Yes, she **did**. / No, she **didn't**.
Did Raoul **go** to her party?	Yes, he **did**. / No, he **didn't**.

* See page 176 for a list of common irregular verbs.

Past simple vs present perfect simple

We use both these tenses to talk about actions that started or finished in the past. The main difference is that we use the past simple to describe actions that happened in a completed time period, whereas we use the present perfect when there is a connection with the present.

When we use the past simple, our focus is on 'When?', while we use the present perfect to say something about 'now' in one way or another. Compare:

How many symphonies did Beethoven compose?

Have you heard Hefner's latest recording of Beethoven's symphonies?

Expressions like *last year, in 1989, when I was a child, three months ago*, etc. are about a finished time and are therefore always used with the past simple.

By contrast, expressions such as *since, already, this week, never, ever, today*, etc. connect the past to the present and are therefore used with the present perfect.

Compare:

Past simple	Present perfect
She went to Vietnam **last year**.	Have you **ever** been to Vietnam? (= Do you know Vietnam? / Can you tell me something about Vietnam now?)
The museum opened **in 1977**.	Tim has **already** visited that museum three times. (= So now he really knows it well.)

Note that the time expression *for* can mean

1 from a point in the past till another point in the past:
   He worked in Barcelona for six years. (e.g. from 1995 till 2001)

2 from a point in the past till now:
   He has worked in Barcelona for six years. (he still works there)

However, time expressions are not always to be found in the sentence itself. That is because when we communicate, we often assume that the context makes it clear to our interlocutor whether we are focusing on the past or making a link with the present. We also often assume that our interlocutor has some knowledge of what we are talking about, and so will understand what our focus is.

Hey, Jim, did you see Kerad's goal? (= both speaker and listener know that the question is about yesterday's football match, in which Kerad scored a spectacular goal)

So the choice between past simple and present perfect often depends on where your attention is. Compare:

I've passed my driving test.

I passed my driving test.

Both these sentences are 'correct' but they mean different things. The first one is news; you are giving new information; your attention is on now. In the second sentence, by contrast, you are telling a story; you are probably talking about a series of past events.

When we give new information or break a piece of news, we use the present perfect to present our 'topic'. But if we go on to give details, we normally use the past simple.

You know what? I've lost my passport. I think I lost it at the airport. It was in my handbag.

 British speakers use the present perfect simple slightly more in conversation than American speakers. American speakers sometimes use a past tense where only the present perfect simple is possible in British English.

British and American speakers both use *yet, already* and *just* with the present perfect simple.

***Have** you **done** it yet?*

*I've **already done** it.*

*I've **just finished**.* (BrE and AmE)

American speakers might also use a past tense with *yet* and *already*.

***Did** you do it **yet**?*

*I **already** did it.* (AmE)

British and American speakers both use *just* with the past tense to describe something that happened a moment ago.

***Did** you **just** call me?*

British speakers generally use *just* with the present perfect simple to give news.

*I've **just passed** my driving test!*

American speakers might say this, too, but they also use the past tense to give news.

*I **just passed** my driving test!*

Past continuous

Use

We use the past continuous to say that something was going on around a particular time in the past.

*What **was** the manager **doing** when you went into his office?*

We often use the past continuous and the past simple together; the continuous form describes the background action or situation, while the simple form describes a shorter action or event that happened in the middle of it.

*We first **met** while we **were travelling** around the world.*

We can also use the past continuous to show that two or more actions were in progress at the same time.

*While she **was studying** for her M.A., she **was** also **working** part-time.*

In narratives, we often use the past continuous for descriptions, and the past simple for events and actions.

*The rain **was falling** in torrents. The trees **were swaying** like windscreen wipers. Suddenly a figure **appeared** from behind the hedge.*

We sometimes use the past continuous in phrases like *I was thinking / wondering / hoping* to make a request or a suggestion sound less direct.

*I **was thinking** that it might be a good idea to leave earlier.*

*I **was wondering** if you'd like to join me for lunch.*

We do not normally use the past continuous to talk about repeated or habitual actions.

I sent them three emails but never got an answer. (was sending)

We went out every weekend when we were younger. (were going out)

Remember that certain verbs are not normally used in the continuous (see **Present simple**, page 156).

I knew a couple of people in Moscow. (was knowing)

Form

We form the past continuous with the auxiliary *was/were* + present participle.

(+)
She **was checking** her email.
They **were** all **wearing** safety helmets.
(–)
I **was not** (I **wasn't**) **doing** anything special.
They **were not** (They **weren't**) **wearing** security badges.
(?)
What **were** they **wearing**?

Was Linda **making** progress?	Yes, she **was**. / No, she **wasn't**.
Were they **working**?	Yes, they **were**. / No, they **weren't**.

Past perfect simple

Use

We use the past perfect simple when we are already talking about the past and we want to refer back to an earlier point in time or period of time.

> We arrived at the conference venue late. The first workshop **had** already **started**.

> The boss wasn't in when I arrived. He **had** just **gone** out.

Compare past simple and past perfect simple:

> When I arrived, Diego left. (first I arrived, then he left, i.e. these two events are in chronological order)

> When I arrived, Diego had left. (he had left before I arrived, i.e. the sequence of events is not chronological)

We often use the past perfect simple in reported speech, and with verbs like *said, thought, informed, realized*, etc.

> They informed us they **had found** another supplier.

> I realized I **had left** my wallet at home.

We also use the past perfect simple after words like *if, wish*, etc. to talk about hypothetical actions and situations, i.e. to talk about things that did not happen.

> If you **had seen** me last week, you wouldn't have recognized me. (= you didn't see me)

> I wish you'**d told** me the truth. (= but you didn't tell me)

Form

We form the past perfect simple with *had* + past participle.

(+)
When I went back after 12 years, the town **had changed** a lot.
(–)
I was late, but fortunately the meeting **hadn't started** yet.
(?)
What **had** they **told*** you earlier?

Had they already **left*** when you phoned?	Yes, they **had**. / No, they **hadn't**.

*See page 176 for a list of common irregular verbs.

Past perfect continuous

Use

We use the past perfect continuous to talk about actions and situations that started in the past and continued up until another time in the past.

When we use it together with another verb in the past simple, there is often a relation of cause and effect between the two verbs.

> Jane wasn't doing anything special when I went round to her place but she was exhausted. She **had been digging** her garden.

Compare past continuous and past perfect continuous:

> I went out. It was snowing. (= snow was falling)

> I went out. It had been snowing. (= the snow had stopped falling, but there was snow on the ground)

Compare past perfect simple and past perfect continuous:

> Emma **had been reading** reports all day, so she was in a bad mood.

> Emma **had read** all the reports, so she knew the facts.

The continuous form stresses the continuation of an activity, whereas the simple form stresses the idea of completion.

> ⚠ Remember that certain verbs are not normally used in the continuous (see **Present simple**, page 156).
> *He had known Mr Klein for a few years before he started working for him. (had been knowing)*

Form

We form the past perfect continuous with *had* + *been* + present participle.

(+)
Rosa **had been learning** Russian for three years before she decided to settle down in St Petersburg.
(–)
Stefan and Julie **hadn't been going out** for very long when they decided to get married.
(?)
What **had** they **been** doing?

Had they **been talking**?	Yes, they **had**. / No, they **hadn't**.

Past simple and past perfect

We often use the past simple to describe past events or to tell a story in chronological order.

> *I slipped, tripped, stumbled and fell.*
>
> *Sheila worked for Singapore Airlines for fifteen years. She retired three years ago.*

But when we talk about a past event, and then want to mention an event that happened before that event, we need to make the sequence of events clear. We can do this in different ways, e.g. we can use words like *earlier, later, before, after,* etc.

> *She retired before she wrote her bestseller.*

We can also use the past perfect to talk about the earlier event.

> *She **had** already **retired** when she wrote her bestseller.*

Note that if we use *before* or *after* to make the time sequence clear, we can use either the past simple or the past perfect for the earlier action.

> *A lot of people **left / had left** the room **before** we got there.*
>
> *We got there **after** they **left / had left**.*

Time expressions like *since, for, already, yet, just, meanwhile, once, by,* etc. are often used with the past perfect.

> *She **had worked** in Singapore **for** fifteen years when she retired.*
>
> ***By** the time she retired, she **had worked** in Singapore for fifteen years.*

We often use the past perfect with verbs like *remember, realize, know, think,* etc. (when these are in the past simple).

> *I **thought** you **had forgotten** me.*
>
> *We **were sure** we **had followed** the instructions carefully.*

Future forms

There are many different ways to talk about the future in English. The form we choose depends on the situation and how certain we feel.

Present simple

Use

We can use the present simple to talk about events that are scheduled in the future or that are in a timetable.

> *My flight **gets in** at 12:15.*
>
> *Our sale **doesn't start** until next Wednesday.*
>
> *What time **does** the train to Tallinn **leave**?*

We can also use the present simple to refer to the future, after *as soon as, by the time, when* and *until*.

> *We'll inform you of the outcome **as soon as** we **make** a decision.* (at some point in the future)
>
> *The painting will be finished **by the time** the furniture **arrives**.*
>
> *He's going to call **when** he **leaves** Mexico City.*
>
> *They won't send the goods **until** we **pay** the deposit.*

Form

See **Present simple**, page 156.

The modal verb *will*

Use

We often use *will*

1 when we're making predictions:
> *In ten years' time, he**'ll be** CEO of this company.*
>
> *Oil prices **will rise** steadily in the next quarter.*

2 when we're deciding something at the moment of speaking:
> *There isn't any printer paper so we**'ll buy** some later.*
>
> *It's a lovely day so I**'ll walk** to work.*

3 to make offers and promises:
> *I**'ll open** the door for you.*
>
> *We**'ll meet** your train and give you a lift to the office.*

4 in sentences with *if* (see **Conditional sentences**, page 168).

Form

(+)
*She**'ll call** you back after her meeting.*
*Your shares **will increase** in value by next year.*

(–)
*They **won't finish** the building work on time.*
*He **won't arrive** until after lunch.*

(?)
*When **will** the sales manager **be** back?*
*How long **will** it **take** to finish the project?*

Will that solve the problem?	*Yes it **will**. / No, it **won't**.*

> ⚠ We often use *shall* instead of *will*
> **1** in formal written English:
> *We **shall** inform customers of any further changes to interest rates.*
> **2** with *I* or *we* in offers and suggestions:
> ***Shall I** ask him to call you back after his meeting?*
> ***Shall we** finish this tomorrow?*

going to

Use

1 We often use the expression *going to* when we talk about intentions and future plans when we have already decided to do something.

> I'm **going to** buy a new car tomorrow. (I intend to purchase a car)

> Are you **going to** work late this evening? (Do you intend to work late?)

2 We can also use *going to* when present evidence or trends suggest that something will happen in the future.

> That pile of wood doesn't look safe. It's **going to** fall.

> This traffic is really bad. We're **going to** miss our flight.

Compare these sentences using *going to* and *will*:

> Property prices in the city centre **are going to** rise in the next six months. (based on present evidence or trends)

> Property prices in the city centre **will** rise in the next six months. (in the speaker's opinion)

Form

(+)
He's **going to** finish the report tomorrow.
I'm definitely **going to** learn Polish next year.

(–)
They **aren't going to** send the parcel until Thursday.
She never studies so she **isn't going to** pass her exams.

(?)	
When **are you going to** finish the decorating?	
Are they **going to** hire a car when they get there?	
Is she **going to** book the tickets later?	Yes, she **is**. / No, she **isn't**.

> ⚠ It isn't necessary to use *going to* with the verbs *go* and *come*. We usually use other future forms such as the present continuous or *will*.
>
> We're going to Dubai. / We'll go to Dubai.
>
> They're coming to the restaurant after the theatre. / They'll come to the restaurant after the theatre.

Present continuous

Use

We often use the present continuous to talk about future plans and firm arrangements.

> He's **flying to** Japan tomorrow morning.

> We **aren't meeting** the board of directors until Friday.

> When **are** you **leaving** for the airport?

Compare these sentences using the present continuous and *going to*.

> I'm **taking** our new clients to lunch. (This is arranged and is in my diary.)

> I'm **going** to take our new clients to lunch. (This is my intention but it isn't arranged yet.)

Form

See **Present continuous**, page 157.

Future perfect

Use

We can use the future perfect to say that something will have been done or completed by a point in the future.

> By June, I'll **have finished** my training course.

> They'll **have made** a decision by the end of the week.

We often use *by* with the future perfect. We can use *by* to talk about a future event that will occur at or before a future moment.

> Will the money have been paid into my account **by** the end of the month?

> The contract won't have arrived **by** the deadline.

Form

(+)
We'll **have completed** the task by lunchtime.
Carly **will have briefed** the candidates before we meet them.

(–)
They **won't have designed** the logo by the launch date.
The director **won't have read** the report before the next meeting.

(?)	
What **will** you **have achieved** by the end of the year?	
Will Zara **have sent** out a schedule prior to the visit?	Yes, she **will**. / No, she **won't**.

Question forms

yes/no questions

In *yes/no* questions, the word order is: auxiliary + subject + main verb.

> A: Do you work full-time?   B: Yes, I do. / No, I don't.

> A: Are you working on a new project?   B: Yes, I am. / No, I'm not.

> A: Did you see Jim yesterday?   B: Yes, I did. / No, I didn't.

> A: Were you working when he called?   B: Yes, I was. / No, I wasn't.

> A: Has the manager told you?   B: Yes, she has. / No, she hasn't.

> A: Had the meeting already started?   B: Yes, it had. / No, it hadn't.

> A: Will they arrive in time?   B: Yes, they will. / No, they won't.

The auxiliary can be *do/does*, *did*, *was/were*, *has/have*, *had* or a modal (*will*, *can*, *should*, etc.).

When we use *be* as a main verb, we use it before the subject.

> Are you late?   Was she efficient?

wh- questions

In *wh-* questions, the word order is: question word/phrase + auxiliary + subject + main verb.

Why do you want a bigger office?

When are they leaving?

Where did you see that advertisement?

Whose translation were you correcting?

Which candidates have they selected?

Where had you worked before then?

How much will the new equipment cost?

Subject questions

We do not use *do / does / did* when the question word is the subject of the question. Compare:

Who did you call? (*you* is the subject; *Who* is the object)

Who called you? (*Who* is the subject; *you* is the object)

What did they do? (*they* is the subject; *What* is the object)

What happened? (*What* is the subject)

How many copies do they need? (*they* is the subject; *How many copies* is the object)

How many people know about it? (*How many people* is the subject)

Asking questions

Embedded questions

When we ask for information, we often begin our question with a phrase like *Could you tell me ...?, Do you know ...?, Do you think ...?, I wonder ..., I'd like to know ...,* etc. Such forms are called 'embedded' or 'indirect' questions, and we often use them to sound less direct or more polite.

The word order in an embedded question is the same as in a statement. Compare:

*Where **is the warehouse**?*	*Could you tell me where **the warehouse is**?*
*When **can you do it**?*	*Do you know when **you can do it**?*
*Who **are those people**?*	*I wonder who **those people are**?*

If the direct question is a *wh-* question and therefore has the auxiliary *do/does/did*, we do not use the auxiliary in the embedded question:

*What time **does the meeting start**?*	*I'd like to know what time **the meeting starts**.*
*What **do you think**?*	*I don't know what **you think**?*
*Why **did you agree** to do it?*	*I don't understand why **you agreed** to do it.*

If the direct question is a *yes/no* question, where there is no question word or modal, we use *if* or *whether* in the embedded question:

***Does** Tom **like** working shifts?*	*I wonder **if** Tom **likes** working shifts?*
***Did** they **sign** the contract?*	*Can you tell me **whether** they **signed** the contract?*

The rules regarding word order in embedded questions also apply to reported questions:

*'What **has Jo** done?' asked Bill.*	*Bill asked me what **Jo had** done.*
'Why do you need a holiday?' the boss asked me.	*The boss asked me **why I needed** a holiday.*

Negative questions

Use

We can use negative questions for confirmation of a positive belief when we expect the answer to be 'yes' and for confirmation of a negative belief where we expect the answer to be 'no'. They can also be used to express surprise or disapproval:

Weren't you in Madrid last week? (I believe you were)

Haven't you finished that report yet? (I believe you are too busy)

Didn't you get my email yesterday? (I don't think you have)

Doesn't he ever stop talking? (disapproval)

Negative questions can also be used to make polite invitations:

Won't you take a seat?

Wouldn't you like something to drink?

Negative *yes/no* questions can suggest a positive meaning:

Didn't I say that we'd win the contract? (I said that we'd win the contract)

Haven't we spent enough time on this agenda point? (= we have spent enough time on the point)

We can also use *wh-* question words with negative questions to get information and make suggestions:

Who hasn't had time to read the report?

Why don't they buy an apartment in Berlin?

When we respond to negative questions, we use *yes* to suggest a positive verb and *no* to suggest a negative verb:

Haven't you sent the email?   *No (I haven't sent it).*

Yes (I have sent it).

Form

We make questions negative by adding *not* to the auxiliary or modal verb.

Doesn't he work in Sales?

Weren't the team supposed to complete the task yesterday?

Haven't you seen my new car yet?

Tag questions

Use

We usually use question tags at the end of a sentence when we speak or write informally.

We can use the question tag as a real question, e.g. to find out if something is true. In this type of question, our intonation rises on the question tag.

*You've haven't used this software before, **have you**?* (I'm not sure whether you have used it or not)

We can also use question tags to check something we believe to be true. In this case, our intonation falls on the question tag.

*He doesn't like jazz, **does he**?* (I don't think he likes jazz)

Form

After a positive statement, we use a negative question tag and after a negative statement we use a positive question tag. If the main sentence has an auxiliary verb, it is repeated in the question tag.

*It **was** a great speech, **wasn't** it?*

*You **weren't** at the seminar yesterday, **were** you?*

*You**'re** with the Lisbon branch, **aren't** you?*

*The meeting **isn't** over yet, is **it**?*

If the sentence has no auxiliary, then the auxiliary of the verb in the main clause is used in the question tag.

*You eat fish, **don't** you?*

*I gave you directions, **didn't** I?*

Question tags come after positive or negative statements, but not after questions.

*He's the new manager, **isn't** he?*

*He isn't the new manager, **is** he? (Is he the new manager, ~~isn't he~~?)*

We usually use contractions with negative question tags. The contracted form for *I am* is *aren't I*.

*I'm always the last person to hear the news, **aren't** I?*

We use *will you* after imperatives. After *Let's*, we use *shall we*.

*Don't forget the car keys, **will** you?*

*Let's start the presentation, **shall** we?*

We use *it* in question tags after *nothing, everything* and *something*. We use *they* in question tags after *someone/somebody, everyone/everybody, no one/nobody*.

*Everything went well, **didn't** it?*

*Nothing's wrong, **is** it?*

*Something's happened, **hasn't** it?*

*Someone spoke to the client, **didn't** they?*

*Everybody's used a computer before, **haven't** they?*

*No one's attending the trade fair tomorrow, **are** they?*

We usually use positive question tags after *no, never* and *no one / nobody*.

*There's no point in arguing, **is** there?*

*They never phoned back, **did** they?*

Rhetorical questions

We can use rhetorical questions

1 when we already know the answer or where the answer is obvious to the speaker and the listener:

Do you think that's wise? (it obviously isn't wise)

What's the point of complaining? (we know it won't do any good)

What do you expect me to do about it? (you know I won't do anything about it)

Do they think the shareholders are fools? (they're obviously not fools)

2 to draw attention to something negative:

What time do you call this? (you're late)

Are you really wearing that to the meeting? (it isn't appropriate for a meeting)

When we use a rhetorical question, we don't necessarily expect an answer.

Modality

Modal overview

Introduction

Compare the sentences in column A with those in column B.

A	B
1 Temperatures reached 35°C yesterday.	**1** It must be hot in the south.
2 This vase is 700 years old.	**2** This vase might be 700 years old.
3 We never eat meat.	**3** We could have fish tomorrow.
4 Luke drives fast.	**4** Luke shouldn't drive so fast.
5 They worked quietly.	**5** Be quiet!

The sentences in A are all objective statements of fact, whereas those in B tell us something about the speaker's attitude towards, or perception of, the events talked about. In B1, we learn that the speaker is almost certain of the accuracy of what is stated; B2, by contrast, is a pure speculation; in B3, the speaker is making a suggestion; B4 expresses disapproval, while B5 expresses a command.

Sentences B1–5 all demonstrate modality.

These sentences also illustrate the two main types of modality. In B1 and 2, the speaker expresses *degrees of knowledge*. B4 and 5, on the other hand, express the speaker's attitude to social factors such as *responsibility*, *obligation*, *permission* and *prohibition*.

Modality is expressed by the main modal verbs (*can, could, shall, should, will, would, may, might*) and a number of other verbs which express similar kinds of meaning (*ought to, have (got) to, need, dare*).

But there are many other ways of expressing modality, as the following examples illustrate.

> *It is likely that there'll be a long queue.*
> *It is probable that they'll be late.*
> *I believe that she is unhappy here.*
> *Maybe she's just overworked.*
> *You aren't allowed to take photos.*
> *We'd better take a break.*

The main modal verbs are always used with a verb in the infinitive.

> *You should **tell** the boss.* (infinitive)
> *He might **be watching** TV.* (continuous infinitive)
> *You could **have phoned** earlier.* (perfect infinitive)

The modal perfect uses the perfect infinitive, formed with *have* + past participle. Forms such as *may have told, could have fallen,* etc.) are not 'tenses', – they are just modal forms with a multiplicity of meanings and functions.

So, apart from paying attention to form and meaning, we also need to be aware of the multiplicity of functional uses of modals (e.g. making suggestions, asking for and giving permission, speculating, giving orders, etc.). The sections that follow describe a number of such functional uses.

Grammar reference

Obligation

1 We use *should* and *ought to* for moderate obligation or to say that something is a good idea. The meaning of *should* and *ought to* is similar and they can often be used interchangeably.

> They **should / ought to** put the new recycling facilities near the centre of town.

> I really **should / ought to** go to the gym after work but I'm feeling quite tired.

We can use *shouldn't* and *oughtn't* to give advice not to do something or to say that something isn't a good idea.

> You **shouldn't** go to work, you don't look well.

> She **oughtn't** leave her computer plugged in when she leaves the office

We can use *should* and *ought to in* questions when considering what to do. In questions, *should* is used more frequently than *ought to*.

> **Should / Shouldn't** they lock the office when they leave?

> **Ought / Oughtn't** we leave a message to say where we're going?

We can use *should* (rather than *ought to*) to make instructions and orders more polite.

> Invoices **should** be paid within thirty days.

> Guests **should** vacate their room by 10 a.m.

2 We use *must* and *have to* to say that something is a strong obligation or is necessary. They are stronger than *should* or *ought to*.

We use *must* in the following situations:	
When we think something is necessary	I **must** get a haircut – my hair's too long.
When someone in authority is speaking	Students **must** complete the assignment by Friday.
In written rules and instructions	Visitors **must** wear identity badges on the premises.

We use *have to* in the following situations:	
When an action is necessary because someone else requires it	We **have to** finish the catalogue design tonight, as the client wants it by tomorrow.
Because something is a rule or law	She **has to** get a visa for her trip to India.
To talk about habits or routines	They **have to** take the train every day.

We usually use *have to* in questions, not *must*.

> What time do you have to leave for work?
> When do we have to pay the invoice?

But we can use *must* as well as *have to* to question a command or order (formal).

> Command: *Put on your safety helmets as soon as you enter the plant.*

> Question: **Must** *we wear them all day? / Do* **we have** *to wear them all day?*

3 We use *don't have to* to say that there is no obligation do something and *don't need to* to say that there is no necessity. They can often be used interchangeably.

> You **don't have to / don't need to** pay for the goods in advance; the company will send an invoice.

> You **don't need to / don't have to** drive me to the airport, I can take a taxi.

Permission and prohibition

We use *can* and *may* to ask for and give permission. In questions, we use *May I* but not *May you*.

> He **can** use my laptop to check his emails.

> You **may** enter through the green door but not through the red door.

> **Can I / May I** have your business card, please?

We use *can't*, *may not* and *mustn't* to say that something is not permitted.

> I'm afraid you **can't** smoke in here, it's prohibited.

> Visitors **may not** park at the front of the building.

> You **mustn't** talk on your mobile phone while you're driving.

We can also use verbs such as *be allowed to* to talk about permission and prohibition.

> She's **allowed to** work from home on Fridays.

> Students aren't **allowed to** enter the lecture theatre before 9 a.m.

> Are you **allowed to** leave early tonight?

Speculating

We use *may / might / could* to say that something is possible now or in the future.

> Ask Lucy, she **may / might** know. (perhaps she knows)

> I **may / might / could** be wrong, so don't quote me! (perhaps I'm wrong)

> Let's get ready. Our guests **may / might / could** arrive at any time.

> Don't call him this evening. He **may / might / could** be watching the match. (perhaps he'll be watching the match)

We use *must* to say that we feel sure about something, because it is a logical deduction or a logical necessity, rather than a possibility.

> You **must** be exhausted after such a long journey.

> One hundred euros for that? You **must** be joking!

But we sometimes use *must* to make an approximate estimate.

> Olga **must** be 15 centimetres taller than I.

> Bogdan **must** be well over seventy.

In these senses, the opposite of *must* is *can't*.

> One hundred euros for that? You **can't** be serious!

> Vedrana **can't** be more than forty.

6

Making predictions

may (not) / might (not) / could

We use these modals to say that we think something is possible (or not) in the future.

> Online shopping **may / might / could** become more secure sooner than you imagine.

We can add *well* if we are more sure.

> Passwords **may well / might well / could well** be replaced by scanners.

> ⚠ We cannot use *could not* to make predictions.
> Lisa **may not / might not** attend the conference next summer.
> (~~Lisa could not attend the conference next summer.~~)

will / won't

We often use *will / won't* together with certain adverbs to show how certain we are.

> China **will almost certainly** become the first economic power.
> Scientists **will probably find** a solution to global warming.
> The global population **definitely won't stop** increasing.

(not) likely to

We use *likely to / not likely to* when we think something will probably / probably won't happen.

> Governments **are likely to** impose restrictions on internet use.
> Europe **isn't likely to** become the greatest economic power.

Patterns

Many of the words and phrases presented in Unit 9 can occur in a variety of patterns. For example:

1 doubt : You *can complain, but I* **doubt if / whether** *it'll make any difference.*

  I **doubt (that)** *we'll ever see him again.*

2 likely: *Experts say this trend* **is likely to** *continue throughout the decade.*

  *It is likely **that** their railways will be privatized.*

3 unlikely: *The new relationship between government and the unions* **is unlikely to** *last.*

  *It is unlikely **that** the new relationship between government and the unions will last.*

4 sure/certain: **There's certain to be** *a rise in unemployment.*

  Dan **is sure to** *get nervous and say something stupid during the interview.*

5 chance: *I think Jim has* **a chance of** *being elected again.*

  The new country **has every chance of** *economic success.*

  There **is little chance** *that economic sanctions will solve the problem.*

Modal perfect

Commenting on / Criticizing past actions

We generally use *could* + perfect infinitive to talk about things which were possible but did <u>not</u> happen.

> Why didn't you tell us you were coming to London? You **could have stayed** with us. (it would have been possible for you to stay with us – but you didn't)

We often use this structure to express criticism.

> You **could have told** me your friends were coming. I'd have bought some nibbles.
> (you <u>didn't</u> tell me, so I didn't buy anything)
> It was stupid to jump off the balcony into the pool. You **could have killed** yourself.
> (you <u>didn't</u> kill yourself, but what you did was stupid)

Note that in this sense, we sometimes use *might* instead of *could*.

> It wasn't a good idea to light a fire there. You **might have set** the whole forest ablaze.

We use *you (he/we, etc) should* + perfect infinitive to talk about things *you (he/we, etc)* didn't do although we think it would have been the right thing to do.

> I'm so sleepy. I **should have gone** to bed early. (I went to bed late)
> You **shouldn't have pressed** those two keys together. You could have erased your hard disk. (you pressed them together, which was a dangerous thing to do)

Note that in this sense, we sometimes use *ought to* instead of *should*.

> It was a fabulous concert. You **ought to have come** with us.

Speculating about past actions

We use *may / might* + perfect infinitive to speculate about past events.

> Nobody picked up the phone. They **may have been** in the garden.
> A: I can't find my mobile phone.
> B: You **might have left** it at the office.

We generally use *could* + perfect infinitive to talk about events which were possible but did not happen.

> Why didn't you go to Malibu? You **could have gone** to the beach every day.

We use *must* + perfect infinitive for deductions about the past.

> Tim almost fell asleep at his desk. He **must have been** dead tired.
> I haven't seen the neighbours for ages. They **must have gone** away.

In this sense, the opposite of *must* is *can't* or *couldn't*.

> The talk **can't / couldn't have been** very interesting. A lot of people just walked out.
> He never found the place. He **can't / couldn't have been listening** to my directions.

Conditional sentences

Conditional sentences have two or more clauses joined by *if*. There are four main types of conditional sentence: zero conditional, first conditional, second conditional and third conditional.

We can use conditional sentences to talk about situations or events that are generally true or possible (zero or first conditional).

Zero conditional	**If** I cycle to work, it **takes** half an hour.
First conditional	The shop **will give** me a refund if the clothes **don't fit**.

We can also use conditional sentences to describe imaginary or unreal situations, or to express regret.

Second conditional	They **would finish** the project sooner **if** they **had** better equipment.
	(they don't have better equipment so they won't finish sooner)
Third conditional	**If** she**'d explained** the problem, I **would have changed** the design.
	(she didn't explain the problem so I didn't change the design)

We can use modal verbs to replace *would*. For example, we can use *might / could* to show possibility, or *should have* to give advice about or criticize a past condition.

*If you hadn't lost the plans, I **might have** realized that the parts were in the wrong place.*

*Someone **should talk** to the project leader if we suspect the team are unhappy.*

The *if*-clause can be used in the first or second part of the sentence. When it comes at the beginning, we usually put a comma between the two clauses.

If the building work is finished on time, our staff will move into the new offices in March.

Our staff will move into the new offices in March if the building work is finished.

Mixed conditionals

Use

In addition to the four types of conditional described in the introduction, we can also use other verb forms in conditional sentences. We can use mixed conditionals to refer, for example, to the past and present at the same time. The main clause and the *if*-clause refer to different time periods. Both types of mixed conditional below refer to unreal or imaginary situations.

1 We can use mixed conditional 1 to describe the past result of a present or continuing condition:

*Our sales **would have been** higher last month **if** our suppliers **delivered** on schedule.* (the supplier doesn't deliver on schedule and as a result our sales weren't higher in the past)

2 We can use mixed conditional 2 to describe the present result of a past condition:

***If** the management team **had agreed** to our terms, the unions **wouldn't be** on strike at the moment.* (the management team did not agree to our terms in the past and the present result is that the unions are on strike)

Form

Mixed conditional 1	
(+) if + past simple, *would have* + past participle	**If** they **came** to the meetings, they **would have heard** about the change of plan.
(–) One, or both clauses, can be in the negative form.	**If** they **didn't come** to the meetings, they **wouldn't have heard** about the change of plan.
(?) Change the word order.	**Would** they **have heard** about the change of plan **if** they came to the meetings?

Mixed conditional 2	
(+) if + past perfect, *would* + base form of the verb	**If** the system **had been tested** at the beginning, it **would work** effectively now.
(–) One, or both clauses, can be in the negative form.	**If** the system **hadn't been tested** at the beginning, it **wouldn't work** effectively now.
(?) Change the word order.	**Would** the system **work** effectively **if** it **had been tested** at the beginning?

7

Passives overview

Use

1 We use the passive when we are interested in the action more than who does it.

*The documents **were destroyed** by someone in the department.*

2 We use the passive when we don't know who did the action or when we want to avoid saying who is responsible for something.

*An enquiry **has been launched** into the matter.*

*The luggage **was lost** during transit.*

*Unfortunately, the document **has been misplaced**.*

3 We can use the passive to emphasize important information.

*The news channel **has been taken over** by a large media corporation.*

*Thousands of passwords **were stolen** by cybercriminals.*

4 When we want to say who or what did the action, we use the preposition *by*. When we want to say what was used to perform the action, we use the preposition *with*.

*The speech was made **by** the president.*

*The front of the building was completely covered **with** paint.*

5 We can use modal verbs in the passive form.

*The safety equipment **must be worn** at all times.*

*Appraisals **should be carried out** every six months.*

*The CCTV camera **could have filmed** the theft.*

6 In formal contexts, we can use *it* to introduce passive phrases. This suggests a distance between the speaker and the opinion.

***It is thought / believed / said** that the construction work has cost taxpayers millions of pounds.*

***It is expected / understood / reported** that the seminar will be introduced by the managing director.*

Passives are more common in written than in spoken English. We often use them when we are writing or speaking in a formal style.

We can use passives in all tenses, but for reasons of style we don't use them in the present perfect continuous, the past perfect continuous or the future continuous.

Form

(+)
*Candidates **were interviewed** by the HR manager.*
(–)
*The identity badges **weren't given** to the visitors.*
(?)
*How **is** news **being consumed** by older people?*

(?)	
***Are** people **influenced** too much by the media?*	*Yes, they **are**. / No, they **aren't**.*

Present simple	*The technology **is used** by a variety of age groups.*
Present continuous	*The information **is being sent** by email.*
Past simple	*The incident **was reported** by a member of the public.*
Past continuous	*The devices **are being bought** by teenagers.*
Present perfect	*Our viewing habits **have been changed** by mobile technology.*
Future	*The survey **will be published** / **is going to be published** in June.*
Modals	*Pictures **can be taken** with smartphones.*

> ⚠ When verbs are followed by a preposition in an active sentence, the preposition is also included in the passive sentence.
> *They broke into the warehouse last night.*
> *The warehouse was broken into last night.*
> *They turned the lights off in the laboratory.*
> *The laboratory lights were turned off.*

Verb patterns

Certain verbs, prepositions, adjectives and expressions are followed by an *-ing* form and others are followed by the *infinitive + to*.

Some verbs can be followed by either an *-ing* form or *to + infinitive* with little difference in meaning:

It **started to rain** soon after we arrived.

It **started raining** soon after we arrived.

Will the marketing department **continue analyzing** the data?

Will the marketing department **continue to analyze** the data?

But sometimes there is a difference in meaning:

She **stopped taking** phone calls. (ceased the activity)

She **stopped to take** phone calls. (interrupted a previous action in order to take the calls)

You must **remember locking** the door. (surely you remember that you locked the door)

You must **remember to lock** the door. (don't forget to lock the door)

-ing

In the following situations, we use the *-ing* form of the verb.

1 After certain verbs:

A member of staff **proposed taking** a sabbatical.

The board **recommends accepting** the changes.

We **discussed having** a holiday in September.

He **avoided talking** to his manager about the problem.

Other verbs that are followed by *-ing* include: *admit, consider, delay, dislike, finish, keep, mention, report, risk, suggest.*

2 After prepositions:

He became CEO at twenty-five **by listening** to the advice of his mentor.

I usually check my emails **before having** a coffee.

After finishing the seminar, he bumped into an old colleague.

3 After idiomatic expressions:

You can't make an omelette **without breaking** eggs.

I look forward to hearing from you in the near future.

There's no point getting upset about minor mistakes.

It's no use telling me, it's not my problem.

I could **get used to having** my own private pool.

It's not worth working late on the project tonight.

I'm **having difficulty making** a decision.

Infinitive + to

In the following situations, we use the infinitive + to.

1 After certain verbs:

I **attempted to** explain the problem.

We **forgot to lock** the front door.

He **needs to speak** to a supervisor immediately.

They **volunteered to work** at the weekend.

Other verbs that are followed by the infinitive + *to* include: *agree, arrange, decide, demand, expect, hope, offer, plan, refuse, want.*

2 After adjectives:

It was **easy to find** a solution.

He was **unable to make** an appointment.

We were **amazed to discover** the results of the survey.

The team would be **happy to discuss** this further.

3 After *would like, would prefer, would love*:

Would you **like to see** the price list?

I'd prefer to have a table by the window, please.

We'd love to hear your ideas.

> ⚠ We use the infinitive without *to* after
> *would rather*: **I'd rather walk** to the office than get the bus.
> modal verbs: We **mustn't be** late. / You **can leave** your bag at reception.
> *Let's* and *Why not?*: **Let's have** a coffee. / **Why not give** me a call?

8

Countable and uncountable nouns

We use nouns to name objects, places, ideas or things.

Countable nouns

Countable nouns have a singular and plural form. We use *a/an* or *the* with singular nouns and *the*, no article, numbers or *some* with plural nouns.

a computer	five computer**s**
an example	some example**s**

Some nouns have irregular forms.

a shelf	three shelves
a child	four children
a foot	two feet
a person	six people
a tomato	three tomatoes

Some countable nouns have the same singular and plural form.

There was **a deer** in the forest.	There were **several deer** in the forest.
He saw **a sheep** crossing the road.	He saw **eight sheep** crossing the road.
We bought **a fish** for my son's birthday.	**Thousands of fish** are caught every day.

Uncountable nouns

Uncountable nouns do not have a plural form. We don't use *a/an* with uncountable nouns.

Here's some water.

He wants advice.

They have some news.

I don't need money.

Some nouns end in -s but they are uncountable and do not have a singular form. These include nouns that have more than one part (jeans, glasses, pyjamas, etc.) They are followed by a plural verb.

*The **binoculars come** with a leather case.*

***Are** the **scissors** on your desk?*

*The **goods have** arrived in the warehouse.*

*These **trousers are** too small. (These trousers is too small.)*

But we can say: *This **pair of trousers** is too small.*

Other nouns end in -s but are uncountable and are followed by a singular verb. e.g. *gymnastics, maths, athletics, news, politics, physics, economics.*

*Economics **is** an interesting subject. (Economics are an interesting subject.)*

Some determiners can be used with countable nouns and others can only be used with uncountable nouns.

*How **many** computers are there? (How **much** computers are there?)*

*Here are a **few / some / several** examples.*

*How **much** money is there in the account? (How many money is there in the account?)*

*Would you like **a little** cake with your coffee?*

Nouns that are both countable and uncountable

Some nouns can be both countable and uncountable, often with some change in meaning.

There were six different types of exercise in the test.

He was told to take exercise to improve his health.

The price of paper is increasing.

She always buys a daily paper.

Can I have a glass for my drink?

Glass is one of the most fragile materials.

We don't have enough time to finish the task.

How many times do I need to ask you to be quiet?

Uncountable nouns can sometimes be used in a countable way when we are talking about kinds, classes or varieties.

The waters of Budapest are very good for your health.

The wines of Italy are famous throughout the world.

Pineapples and bananas are both tropical fruits.

Collective nouns refer to groups of people or things. Whether they are followed by a singular or plural verb depends on the meaning the speaker wishes to convey.

The team is very competitive. (the group as a whole)

All the team are working late again. (each individual)

Collective nouns include: *audience, committee, army, community, police, staff, company, government.*

Concrete and abstract nouns

Countable and uncountable nouns can be categorized as concrete or abstract.

Concrete nouns describe things that we can we can see, touch, hear, taste or smell.

Examples: tree, snow, guitar, food, flower

Abstract nouns describe things that are concepts, ideas, emotions, states or qualities.

Examples: success, knowledge, pride, peace, beauty

Articles overview

a/an

We use *a/an* with singular countable nouns

1 to talk about a person or thing for the first time:
   *I have **an** idea to help cut costs in the department.*
   *We carried out **a** survey.*

2 when we refer to something in general and it isn't important which one:
   *Is there **a** bank near here?   Can I borrow **a** pen?*

3 with expressions of frequency or quantity:
   *We visit the Turin branch three times **a** year.*
   *Our supplier usually makes four deliveries **a** week.*
   *I have **a** couple of questions about your data.*
   *The price of petrol will increase by 30p **a** litre.*

the

We use *the* with countable, uncountable and plural nouns

1 to refer to a person or thing after the first time *it/he/she* is mentioned:
   *I have **an** idea to help save money. **The** idea is to reduce heating costs.*
   *We carried out **a** survey. **The** survey looked at three main areas.*

2 when we refer to a thing in particular or when there is only one of something:
   *I'd like **the** table by **the** window, please.*
   ***The** person that I'm looking for is wearing a green coat.*

3 with geographic areas where countries are connected or with countries that consist of a group of states or islands, and also with rivers, seas and mountain ranges:
   The Middle East   The United States   The Netherlands   The West Indies   (The Europe)
   The Pacific   The Atlantic Ocean   The Nile   The Amazon
   The Alps   The Himalayas   The Andes

4 to talk about inventions:
   *Art changed forever after **the** camera was invented.*

No article

We don't use an article

1 for continents, countries, cities, individual mountains and lakes:
   Africa   Belgium   Barcelona   Mount Everest   Lake Tahoe

2 when we talk about public buildings referring to their general function rather than as a specific place:
   *You should go to **hospital**.*
   *The thieves were sent to **prison**.*
   *When I went to **school**, exams were easier.*
   *Which **college** did you go to?*
   When we talk about a specific building we use *the*:
   *I work at **the** hospital.*
   ***The** college was closed this evening.*

3 to talk about meals, sports, games and academic subjects.
   *What time would you like **dinner**?*
   *He plays **backgammon** very well.*
   *Are you taking **Geography** next term?*

4 to talk about people or things in general when they are uncountable or in the plural:
   ***Staff** use **computer software** to create **documents** and **presentations**.*

9

Comparison and contrast

Comparative and superlative adjectives

	São Paulo	Shanghai	Mumbai
Population	11.2 million	19.2 million	13.8 million
Cost of living	$$$	$$	$

Use

1 We use the comparative form of an adjective to compare two things.

*Mumbai is **larger than** São Paulo.*

*Shanghai is **more expensive than** Mumbai but it is **less expensive than** São Paulo.*

2 We use the superlative form to compare three or more things.

*Shanghai is **the largest** of the three cities in the survey.*

*São Paulo is **the most expensive** of the three cities.*

Form

One-syllable adjectives Add *-er* / *-est*. (NB: add only *-r* / *-st* if the adjective ends in *-e*: *nicer* / *the nicest*.)	*Shanghai is **cheaper than** São Paulo, but Mumbai is **the cheapest**.*
One-syllable adjectives ending in vowel + consonant Double the final consonant and add *-er* / *-est*.	*In Mumbai, June is hot**ter** than July, but May is the hot**test** month of the year.*
One- or two-syllable adjectives ending in consonant + -y Change *-y* to *-i* and add *-er* / *-est*.	*December in São Paulo is rainy, but January is rain**ier**. The rain**iest** month of the year is February.*
Two or more syllables Use *more* / *the most* or *less* / *the least*.	*Brasilia is **more modern than** São Paulo. It is also **less expensive**.*

⚠ With some two-syllable adjectives, we use either *-er* / *-est* or *more* / *the most*:
clever, simple, quiet, polite, tired, narrow, stupid, common
cleverer or *more clever*; *the cleverest* or *the most clever* / *simpler* or *more simple*; *the simplest* or *the most simple*, etc.

Irregular adjectives			
good	better	the best	*Some people say that the climate in Mumbai is **better than** in Shanghai, and some say São Paulo has **the best** climate.*
bad	worse	the worst	
much/many	more	the most	
far	farther/further	the farthest / the furthest	

Comparing equivalent or similar things

1 We use *the same as* to talk about two things that are equivalent.

*Is the weather in São Paulo **the same as** in Rio de Janeiro?*

2 We use *as* + adjective (or adverb) + *as* to say that things are similar in some way.

*London is **as expensive as** Paris.*

We often use *almost* / *nearly* / *not quite* with *as ... as*.

*Istanbul is **almost** as populated as Mumbai.*

*Seoul is **not quite** as populated as Moscow.*

We simply add *not* for the negative.

*Vienna **is not as expensive as** Rome.*

(NB: *not so* is sometimes used instead of *not as*.)

Large and small differences

We use adverbs like *a lot / much / far / considerably* to indicate a big difference in a comparison.

> *São Paulo is **a lot older than** Brasilia.*
>
> *The cost of living in New York is **considerably higher than** in Dublin.*

We also use the phrase *not nearly as ... as* for large differences.

> *Tokyo is **not nearly as big as** Shanghai. (Shanghai is much bigger than Tokyo.)*

We use adverbs like *a bit / a little / slightly* to indicate a small difference in a comparison.

> *April is **slightly colder than** March.*
>
> *Vancouver is **slightly more expensive** than Toronto.*

Other types of comparative sentences

1 We use *the* + comparative followed by *the* and another comparative to talk about changes that happen together.

> ***The bigger** the team, **the more difficult** it is to manage.*
>
> ***The more cohesive** the team, **the easier** it is to manage.*

2 Other phrases with *as ... as*.

City	Population	
Mexico City	8.8m	Mexico City is twice as big as Sydney.
Sydney	4.4m	
Jakarta	10.1m	Jakarta is almost three times as big as Berlin.*
Berlin	3.4m	

> * With *three / four / five*, etc. *times*, the comparative form is also possible.
>
> *Jakarta is almost three times bigger than Berlin.*

> ⚠ The comparative form is never used with *twice*.

3 We can use a double comparative to indicate that something is changing.

> *A lot of cities are getting **bigger and bigger**.*
>
> *Basic commodities seem to be getting **more and more expensive**.*

4 We often use phrases like *different from / similar to / like / compared to / in comparison with* when we compare things.

> *How much cheaper is Podgorica **compared to** Paris?*
>
> *Leeds is a nice city but very small **in comparison with** London.*
>
> *Some people say Thessaloniki is very **similar to** Izmir.*

Other types of superlative sentences

> ***Some of the** tallest people in Europe can be found in Croatia.*
>
> *Buenos Aires is **one of the** largest cities in the world.*
>
> *Moscow is **by far** the largest city in Russia.*
>
> *New York is **easily** the most expensive city in the US.*
>
> *What's **the second largest** city in Japan?*
>
> *Is Tianjin **the third largest** city in China?*
>
> *Susan says Copenhagen is **the fourth most expensive** city in the world.*

Comparative and superlative adverbs

1 We use *more / the most* for the majority of adverbs.

slowly	more slowly	the most slowly
carefully	more carefully	the most carefully

2 We use *-er / -est* with some adverbs, e.g. adverbs that have the same form as adjectives.

hard	harder	the hardest
fast	faster	the fastest
early	earlier	the earliest
late	later	the latest

3 The adverbs *well* and *badly* change their form completely.

well	better	the best
badly	worse	the worst

Use

We can use adverbs

1 to modify verbs:

> *He was speaking **quickly** and I could **hardly** understand a word.*

2 to make adjectives stronger or weaker:

> *It's **totally pointless**.*
>
> *The concert was **completely amazing**.*
>
> *He was driving **extremely fast**.*
>
> *The results were **slightly worse** than expected.*

3 before the past participle of adjectives:

> *It's a **well-designed** device.*

4 to make other adverbs stronger or weaker:

> *The plan worked **really well**.*
>
> *He plays the piano **absolutely wonderfully**.*
>
> *They finished the task **extremely quickly**.*
>
> *The negotiation went **fairly well**, I suppose.*

5 to describe whole sentences:

> ***Unfortunately,** we can't accept the invitation.*
>
> ***Hopefully,** this will solve the problem.*

Form

1 We usually make adverbs by adding letters to an adjective. Most adverbs are made by:

adding *-ly* to the adjective.	quick – quickly amazing – amazingly bad – badly
Adjectives that end in *-y* add *-ily*	funny – funnily steady – steadily
Adjectives that end in *-ic* add *-ally*	dramatic – dramatically frantic – frantically
Adjectives that end in *-able* change to *-ably*	capable – capably reasonable – reasonably

10

2 Some adverbs have the same form as adjectives e.g. *early, late, fast, hard, free, high*

3 Some adverbs have two forms and two different meanings.

*You always arrive **late**.* (not on time)

*Have you used the printer **lately**.* (recently)

*The ball hit the player **hard**.* (not soft)

*I've **hardly** seen her this week.* (a minimal amount)

*The exam was **fine**.* (went well)

*You should chop the onions **finely**.* (into small pieces)

*During the sales promotion, they gave away **free** bottles of shampoo.* (not necessary to pay)

*We were given keys to all the rooms and were allowed to move around **freely**.* (without restrictions)

4 We don't usually use an adverb after certain verbs such as: *sound, taste, smell, seem*.

*That sounds / tastes / smells / seems **good**.* (*That sounds / tastes / smells / seems well.*)

Position of adverbs

We do not usually put adverbs between the verb and its object:

*Carlos demonstrated the product **well**.* (*Carlos demonstrated **well** the product.*)

The position in the sentence depends on the type of adverb.

1 Adverbs that describe **how** something is done follow the verb or the object. They often go at the end of a sentence:

*The time went **slowly**.*

*She carried out all the tasks **capably**.*

*He handled the meeting **badly**.*

*You reacted **angrily**.*

2 To add emphasis, they can sometimes go at the beginning of a sentence or between the subject and the main verb.

***Quickly**, she phoned the fire brigade.*

***Silently**, the door opened.*

*He **reluctantly** admitted that it was his fault.*

*We **suddenly** decided to travel the world.*

3 Adverbs that describe **how often** something happens or **how certain** something is can go in front of the main verb:

*He **regularly** works from home.*

*They **probably** went to the wrong address.*

4 after the verb *be*:

*He's **usually** the first to arrive.*

*We're **definitely** going to win the competition.*

5 at the beginning or end of the sentence:

***Sometimes** we finish early. / We finish early **sometimes**.*

***Obviously**, you've heard the news. / You've heard the news, **obviously**.*

6 in the middle of the sentence between verbs:

*The marketing campaign has **certainly** been a success.*

*I didn't **always** want to work in finance.*

If there is more than one type of adverb in a sentence, the order is usually: *how, where, when*:

*The students worked **quietly outside yesterday**.*

how · where · when

how	where	when
badly	in (Paris)	every day
well	upstairs	today
noisily	around	tomorrow
angrily	at the end of the street	afterwards
happily	here	in August
suddenly	downstairs	weekly
hard	out of the window	last year
slowly	to the kitchen	for months

Extreme adjectives

Extreme adjectives and adverbs such as *excellent, useless* and *brilliantly* cannot be qualified by *very*.

*Our old printer was **very** useless.*   *Our old printer was **really** useless.*

You can use *really*, which can be used to modify both extreme and ordinary adjectives and adverbs.

*Jane's new office is **really huge**.*

*The exam was **really difficult**.*

*The team finished the task **really quickly**.*

Words that can be used instead of *really* to modify extreme adjectives and adverbs include *quite, completely, absolutely, totally*.

*The meal was **quite excellent**.*

*Their proposal was **completely ridiculous**.*

*Our client was **absolutely delighted**.*

*The results of the survey were **totally remarkable**.*

Irregular verb list

Verb	Past simple	Past participle
arise	arose	arisen
awake	awoke	awoken
be	was/were	been
bear	born	born
beat	beat	beaten
become	became	become
begin	began	begun
bend	bent	bent
bet	bet	bet
bind	bound	bound
bite	bit	bitten
bleed	bled	bled
blow	blew	blown
break	broke	broken
breed	bred	bred
bring	brought	brought
broadcast	broadcast	broadcast
build	built	built
burn	burnt/ burned	burnt/ burned
burst	burst	burst
buy	bought	bought
catch	caught	caught
choose	chose	chosen
come	came	come
cost	cost	cost
creep	crept	crept
cut	cut	cut
deal	dealt	dealt
dig	dug	dug
do	did	done
draw	drew	drawn
dream	dreamt/ dreamed	dreamt/ dreamed
drink	drank	drunk
drive	drove	driven
eat	ate	eaten
fall	fell	fallen
feed	fed	fed
feel	felt	felt
fight	fought	fought
find	found	found
flee	fled	fled
fly	flew	flown
forbid	forbade	forbidden
forget	forgot	forgotten
freeze	froze	frozen

Verb	Past simple	Past participle
get	got (BrE) gotten (AmE)	got (BrE)/ gotten (AmE)
give	gave	given
go	went	gone
grind	ground	ground
grow	grew	grown
hang	hung	hung
have	had	had
hear	heard	heard
hide	hid	hidden
hit	hit	hit
hold	held	held
hurt	hurt	hurt
keep	kept	kept
know	knew	known
lay	laid	laid
lead	led	led
lean	leant/ leaned	leant/ leaned
learn	learnt/ learned	learnt/ learned
leave	left	left
lend	lent	lent
let	let	let
lie	lied	lied
light	lit/lighted	lit/lighted
lose	lost	lost
make	made	made
mean	meant	meant
meet	met	met
pay	paid	paid
put	put	put
quit	quit	quit
read	read	read
ride	rode	ridden
ring	rang	rung
rise	rose	risen
run	ran	run
say	said	said
see	saw	seen
seek	sought	sought
sell	sold	sold
send	sent	sent
set	set	set
sew	sow	sewn/ sewed
shake	shook	shaken
shine	shone	shone

Verb	Past simple	Past participle
shoot	shot	shot
show	showed	shown
shrink	shrank	shrunk
shut	shut	shut
sing	sang	sung
sink	sank	sunk
sit	sat	sat
sleep	slept	slept
slide	slid	slid
smell	smelt/ smelled	smelt/ smelled
speak	spoke	spoken
spell	spelt/ spelled	spelt/ spelled
spend	spent	spent
spill	spilt/ spilled	spilt/ spilled
spit	spat	spat
split	split	split
spoil	spoilt/ spoiled	spoilt/ spoiled
spread	spread	spread
spring	sprang	sprung
stand	stood	stood
steal	stole	stolen
stick	stuck	stuck
sting	stung	stung
strike	struck	struck
swear	swore	sworn
sweep	swept	swept
swim	swam	swum
swing	swung	swung
take	took	taken
teach	taught	taught
tear	tore	torn
tell	told	told
think	thought	thought
throw	threw	thrown
understand	understood	understood
wake	woke	woken
wear	wore	worn
weave	wove	woven/ weaved
weep	wept	wept
win	won	won
wind	wound	wound
write	wrote	written